ROBERT HENRI
AND HIS CIRCLE

Figure 1. Robert Henri, 1906. Photograph.

ROBERT HENRI
AND HIS CIRCLE

By William Innes Homer

with the assistance of Violet Organ

Cornell University Press » « Ithaca and London

First published 1969

Standard Book Number 8014-0498-3

Library of Congress Catalog Card Number 75-81594

*Printed in the United States of America by
Vail-Ballou Press, Inc.*

To My Parents

Preface

ROBERT HENRI was regarded by many of his contemporaries as the most influential single force affecting the development of American art in the generation preceding the Armory Show of 1913. He was a prolific painter, teacher, and author; he organized exhibitions of progressive art; and he was the leader of the group of painters known as "the Eight." But a mere listing of his activities cannot convey the extent of his influence upon the young avant-garde artists of his time. Perhaps the best way to describe his influence is to say that he was a living embodiment of the message he preached in his book *The Art Spirit*. And this message, as we shall see, reached an exceptionally large number of American artists in the late nineteenth and early twentieth centuries. Many of them responded to his personal encouragement inside and outside the classroom; others benefited from his letters of advice; and still others followed his example. Because Henri gave himself so completely to the advancement of the arts in America, his self-appointed mission as crusader was brilliantly successful.

I was in my teens when I first discovered Robert Henri's teachings. His insights into the creative process, as revealed in *The Art Spirit*, impressed me as much as his sound technical advice. At the time, I was interested in how that book related to my own intellectual and artistic development; the author's biography and historical position seemed irrelevant.

I was exposed to Henri's influence again while I was working toward a Ph.D. degree in the history of art at Harvard in 1953–1955. Henri's relation to the Eakins tradition, as carried on by Thomas Anshutz, struck me as a challenging theme for a research paper for a graduate seminar in American art. This time, appropriately, my approach to the subject was historical. As is often the case with research papers, the topic demanded more study than a harassed graduate student could give it. So a fuller exploration of Henri and his influence had to wait until the spring of 1964, when a postdoctoral fellowship from the American Council of Learned Societies enabled me to devote an uninterrupted period to the project.

During Henri's lifetime, there appeared several brief biographies and volumes illustrating his work. Informative books have been written about his friends and associates, as well as about the Eight, and these have necessarily touched upon the subject of the present volume. But until now, no single full-length study has been devoted to Robert Henri, his art, and his influence.

The need for such a book was recognized in 1965 by Norman Geske, who wrote in the catalogue of the Henri Memorial Exhibition held at the University of Nebraska that "Robert Henri as an important figure in American painting is badly in need of a biographer and, more particularly, an historian who will clarify in a way that none of his eulogists and critics have done, the exact character of his work and personality. One would like to see a detailed consideration of his sources, both at home, in the tradition of Eakins and Anshutz, and abroad in his predilection for the Dutch and Spanish masters with Manet as an extension of them." While these remarks were published after my research and writing were well under way (and without Geske's having any knowledge of my work), they aptly summarize the need this book seeks to fill.

I also agree with Mr. Geske's observation that Henri's image has been badly distorted in many previous writings and exhibitions. These distortions add up to the myth that Henri merely painted on the side and was primarily a gifted and persuasive teacher, producing students whose artistic achievement surpassed his own and who turned out to be much more sympathetic to avant-garde movements than he was. As a painter, the myth continues, he excelled at portraits and figure studies of picturesque characters—Irishmen, gypsies, Indians, and so on—executed in a superficial, dashing style that paid little attention to the inner man. While there is some truth to the last accusation, the structural and coloristic properties of his work have been largely overlooked. Furthermore, few scholars or critics have come to grips with his early work, which includes stunning, little-known landscapes, seascapes, and cityscapes of remarkably high quality. All in all, the myth gives an inaccurate and not entirely fair picture of Henri—an image that I hope this book will change.

Fortunately, Henri was an indefatigable collector of letters, documents, and memorabilia pertaining to himself and his friends. He also compiled a detailed catalogue of his own paintings and kept extensive diaries during long periods of his life. In addition to studying such documentary sources in private and public collections, I interviewed and corresponded with the artist's friends, former pupils, and associates. Those whom I interviewed were uniformly cooperative and generous in sharing their reminiscences, a testimony, I believe, to their affection for Henri. To those who answered my letters of inquiry I am also most grateful; their replies constitute an invaluable archive of primary source material.

My research for the book was facilitated by many museum and library officials, art historians, archivists, and art dealers. Special thanks go to William C. Agee, Whitney Museum of American Art; Donald W. Buchanan; John Clancy, Rehn Galleries; Professor Gibson A. Danes, Yale University; Professor Donald Drew Egbert, Princeton University; Norman A. Geske, Sheldon Memorial Art Gallery, University of Nebraska; Lloyd Goodrich, Whitney Museum of American Art; Mrs. Edith G. Halpert, Downtown Gallery; Stewart Klonis, Art Students League; Antoinette Kraushaar; Guy Luster, Graham Galleries; Garnett McCoy, Archives of American Art; Professor Charles Hill Morgan, Amherst College; Daniel Robbins, Museum of Art, Rhode Island School of Design; Professor Hedley H. Rhys, Swarthmore College; Joseph S. Trovato, Munson-Williams-Proctor Institute; Evan H. Turner, Philadelphia Museum of Art; Alfredo Valente; Maynard Walker; Louise Wallman, Pennsylvania Academy of the Fine Arts; and Virginia Zabriskie.

In the course of my researches, I interviewed the following individuals, whose kind cooperation and hospitality I gratefully acknowledge: Edward R. Anshutz, Edith C. Barry, Frank Bechtel, Jr., Samuel L. Borton, Louis Bouché, Robert Brackman, Christian Buchheit, Mrs. Livingston Corson, Kent Crane, Stuart Davis, Rudolph Dirks, Mrs. Rudolph Dirks, Virginia Myers Downes, Marcel Duchamp, Mrs. Lucius Fairchild, Ira Glackens, Dorothy Grafly, Edward Hopper, Mrs. Edward Hopper, Joseph Kling, Leon Kroll, Brenda Kuhn, Richard Lahey, John C. Le Clair, Mrs. A. F. Levinson, Robert G. McIntyre, Jr., Amédée Ozenfant, Nikifora L. Pach, Man Ray, Edward Redfield, Margery Ryerson, Mari Sandoz, Davidson Shinn, Mrs. John Sloan, Carl Sprinchorn, Henry Strater, and William Zorach.

The following persons supplied essential data in the form of letters to me or reminiscences written specifically for my information in preparing the book: H. B. Allen, Edward R. Anshutz, Maurice Becker, Mrs. Homer Boss, Maria-Theresa Bourgeois, Mrs. Alphaeus P. Cole, John Cournos, Andrew Dasburg, Mrs. Helen S. Davis, Major Dermot Freyer, Grattan Freyer,

Dr. Robert H. Gatewood, Mrs. Jay Hambidge, Emil Holzhauer, Morris Kantor, Mrs. William Sergeant Kendall, Brenda Kuhn, Mrs. Alfred Walster Lawson, Stanton Macdonald-Wright, William Pène du Bois, Arthur Pope, Nathaniel Pousette-Dart, Mrs. Ernest Thompson Seton, Carl Sprinchorn, Mrs. Allen Tucker, and Harry Wickey.

My greatest debt is to John C. Le Clair of Glen Gardner, New Jersey, and New York City, for his generous cooperation in making available all of the materials in the Henri estate. In addition to placing invaluable records, diaries, letters, and photographs, and other source material at my disposal, he opened his home and Henri's former studio and apartment to me so that I could study the artist's paintings and documents on the site. The catalogue Henri kept of his own work, which is in Mr. Le Clair's hands, was available to me whenever I asked for it. From his knowledge of Henri's life and work, Mr. Le Clair was able to provide many leads to important research sources that have enriched the content of this book. I could not have asked for greater cooperation.

After Henri's wife, Marjorie, died in 1930, her sister, Miss Violet Organ, undertook the writing of a biography of the artist on which she was still working at the time of her death in 1959. The manuscript, placed at my disposal by her nephew, John C. Le Clair, was of real value, particularly as a primary source relating to the artist's later years. Miss Organ is responsible for most of Chapters 2 and 11, the latter a chronicle based on firsthand knowledge of the activities of Robert and Marjorie Henri and their friends.

Mrs. John Sloan's assistance has also been of inestimable value. She placed the entire John Sloan Collection at my disposal, without restrictions, and spent many hours helping me locate material pertaining to Henri and the Eight. This collection of paintings, documents, books, and photographs, housed in the Delaware Art Center, Wilmington, proved to be one of the outstanding resources for the study of American art in the 1851–1951 period. I wish to thank Mrs. Sloan for her kindness in giving me permission to quote from unpublished material in the Sloan Collection.

Bruce St. John, Director of the Delaware Art Center, was most cooperative in facilitating my study of the Sloan archives, the Jerome Myers papers, and the unpublished material relating to the 1910 Exhibition of Independent Artists that he and his staff reconstructed in 1960.

George and Robert Chapellier, of the Chapellier Galleries, New York, which has exclusively handled the Henri estate since 1964, helped me at every turn. I am grateful for their continuing assistance in keeping my records of the location of Henri's works up to date and for directing me to several of the artist's friends whose reminiscences were of considerable value. The Chapellier Galleries supplied many of the photographs that appear in the book, along with color slides for my study files. The gallery has been, since 1964, the foremost collecting point and clearinghouse for information about Henri's works in museums, exhibitions, and private collections; the Chapelliers' gracious cooperation made my task much easier.

Norman Hirschl and A. M. Adler, of the Hirschl & Adler Galleries, New York, generously opened their photographic files to me and cooperated in helping me trace the owners of paintings by Henri sold by their gallery.

Donald C. Gallup of the Yale University Library also deserves special mention for his kind assistance and counsel in facilitating my use of the collections at Yale that pertain to Henri and his associates.

Thanks to Grattan Freyer, a previously unknown group of papers which Henri left behind in Ireland was brought to my attention in 1965. This small but important collection, purchased by Cornell University Library in that year, enabled me to fill in many previously unknown details about the period in Henri's later life spent at his estate on Achill Island, Ireland.

Special thanks go to my wife, who followed the progress of the book with continued interest, made valuable editorial suggestions, and edited the final draft of the manuscript; to Clara Bailey, a dedicated Henri enthusiast, who handled a large measure of the correspondence and typing in the later phases of preparing the manuscript; and to Judith Yellin for her skilled assistance in checking the notes and bibliography and preparing the illustrations.

I am indebted also to the following individuals who read parts of the manuscript and made helpful suggestions: Robert Chapellier, Donald Drew Egbert, Lloyd Goodrich, Sidney Hill, John C. Le Clair, Margery Ryerson, Meyer Schapiro, and Mrs. John Sloan.

Finally, I wish to acknowledge the tangible assistance provided by a post-doctoral fellowship from the American Council of Learned Societies (1964–1965), Cornell University Faculty Research Grants (1965–1966 and summer 1966), and a special Grant-in-Aid from the University of Delaware (1966–1967), which helped to cover costs of travel, photographs, and typing. The Winterthur Program in Early American Culture also contributed to the costs of typing.

WILLIAM INNES HOMER

Department of Art History
University of Delaware
January 1969

Contents

Preface   vii

1. *The Man and the Milieu*   1
2. *The Early Years, 1865–1886*   7
3. *An Art Student in Philadelphia, 1886–1888*   21
4. *Study in Paris, 1888–1891*   38
5. *Life and Work in Philadelphia, 1891–1895*   68
6. *Paris and Philadelphia, 1895–1900*   85
7. *Maturity and Public Recognition, 1900–1906*   99
8. *Henri and the Independent Movement, 1906–1910*   126
9. *Teachings and Philosophy of Art*   157
10. *Aspects of Henri's Career, 1910–1929*   165
11. *Recollections of the Later Years*   195
12. *The Art of Robert Henri, 1892–1928*   211
13. *Epilogue*   268

Notes   271
Bibliography   291
Index   301

Illustrations

Color

I. Robert Henri, *Girl Seated by the Sea*, 1893   *facing page* 214

II. Henri, *The Rain Storm—Wyoming Valley*, 1902   232

III. Henri, *Blonde Bridget Lavelle*, 1928   252

IV. Henri, *Color Notes*, July 3, 1916   260

Black and White

1. Robert Henri, 1906   *frontispiece*

2. Henri, *John Jackson Cozad*, 1903   *page* 9

3. Theresa Gatewood Cozad   11

4. Robert Henry Cozad (Robert Henri)   14

5. Thomas P. Anshutz, *Iron Workers' Noon-Day Rest (Steelworkers—Noontime)*, c. 1880   26

6. The dissecting room, Pennsylvania Academy of the Fine Arts, c. 1886–1888   29

7. Thomas Eakins, *The Gross Clinic*, 1875   33

8. Studio at the Académie Julian, Paris, 1889   41

9. Henri and his friends in the studio at 1717 Chestnut Street, Philadelphia, c. 1893–1894   77

10. Henri, *Lady in Black*, 1904   91

11. Henri, *Woman in Manteau*, 1898   93

12. Henri, *La Neige*, 1899   95

13. Arthur B. Davies, *Unicorns*, 1906   101

14. Maurice Prendergast, *The Flying Horses*, c. 1908–1909   103

15. Ernest Lawson, *Harbor in Winter*   104

16. Henri, *Portrait of George Luks*, 1904   114
17. Henri, *Portrait of Bishop Henry C. Potter*, 1904   117
18. Henri, *Gypsy Mother*, 1906   124
19. Henri and the night class, New York School of Art, 1907   132
20. Henri, *Cori Looking over Back of Chair*, 1907   134
21. Henri, *Martsche in White Apron*, 1907   135
22. Henri, *Eva Green*, 1907   137
23. William Glackens, *The Shoppers*, 1908   140
24. John Sloan, *Election Night*, 1907   142
25. George Luks, *East Side Docks*, 1905   143
26. Everett Shinn, *Sixth Avenue Elevated after Midnight*, 1899   144
27. Henri, *The Ancient Dress (The Masquerade Dress)*, 1911   147
28. Thomas Eakins, *Portrait of Professor Leslie W. Miller*, 1901   178
29. Henri, *Color Chart*, 1915   188
30. *Triangle Palette (Charles Winter "Universal" Palette)*, 1919   190
31. Henri, *Diagram of Color Notations for Portrait of Helen Geary*, 1919   191
32. John Sloan, *Studio of Robert Henri, A.D. 1950*, 1904   198
33. George Bellows, *Kids*, 1906   200
34. Henri, *Diegito Roybal (Po-Tse-Nu-Tsa)*, 1916   204
35. Henri, *Figures on Boardwalk*, 1892   212
36. Henri, *A Normandie Fireplace*, 1897   215
37. Henri, *A Profile*, 1895   217
38. Henri, *A Boulevard, Paris*, c. 1896–1897   218
39. Henri, *Fourteenth of July—Boulevard Saint-Michel*, 1898   219
40. Henri, *Fourteenth of July—"La Place,"* c. 1897   221
41. Pierre Bonnard, *Le Moulin Rouge (Place Blanche)*, 1896   222
42. Edouard Vuillard, *At the Pastry Cook's*, c. 1898   223
43. Henri, *The Man Who Posed as Richelieu*, 1898   225
44. Edouard Manet, *Portrait of Roudier*, c. 1860   226
45. Gustave Courbet, *Portrait of Max Buchon*, 1854   227
46. Henri, *Cumulus Clouds—East River*, 1901–1902   230
47. Henri, *Derricks on the North River*, 1902   231
48. Henri, *Landscape at Black Walnut, Pa.*, 1902   233
49. Henri, *Maine Coast*, 1903, repainted 1908   234
50. Henri, *Old Brittany Farmhouses*, 1902   236
51. Henri, *Portrait of W. J. Glackens*, 1904   239
52. Henri, *Young Woman in White*, 1904   240

53. Henri, *The Working Man*, 1910   242
54. Henri, *Segovia Girl, Half-Length*, 1912   243
55. Edouard Manet, *Torero Saluting*, 1866   245
56. Henri, *Antonio Banos (Calero), Picador*, 1908   246
57. Henri, *Menaune Cliffs*, 1913   248
58. Henri, *Himself*, 1913   250
59. Henri, *Herself*, 1913   251
60. Henri, *Patrick*, 1913   253
61. Henri, *Chow Choy*, 1914   255
62. Henri, *Julianita*, 1917   256
63. Henri, *Ruth St. Denis in the Peacock Dance*, 1919   258
64. Henri, *Figure in Motion*, 1913   259
65. Henri, *Edna Smith*, 1915   261
66. Henri, *Summer Storm*, 1921   265

ROBERT HENRI
AND HIS CIRCLE

1

The Man
and the Milieu

TOWARD THE end of the last century, the arts in America underwent a profound change in scope and emphasis, thanks, in large part, to the influence of Robert Henri. It was a case of the right man at the right time and the right place. Historical circumstances favored the emergence of a pioneer with the energy and vision to guide his countrymen into new, unexplored artistic territory and, in the process, to challenge the academic establishment. Henri's story is that of a strong individual who reacted vigorously to the conditions of the period in which he grew up. To understand his position in the history of art, we therefore have to look both at the man and at his artistic and cultural milieu.

It is always difficult to make brief (and valid) generalizations about any period in the history of art. Yet generalization must be attempted for the late nineteenth century if we are to evaluate Henri's achievement. American art then, as now, cannot be reduced to any single current, but rather appears in a multitude of parallel and overlapping styles. Some of these may be closely related, others may seem totally at odds with each other. Several general trends may, however, be discerned in the period between the Civil War and the turn of the century.

Looking at the period broadly, we may discover two major currents: one that valued native or national American traditions and one that favored a more international, cosmopolitan approach inspired by European art. Both currents have been present in American art since the eighteenth century, and the pendulum of taste has swung back and forth between them from one generation to the next. If in the second quarter of the nineteenth century the Hudson River school exemplified a new American consciousness of national themes and values, the period after the Civil War witnessed a definite resurgence of interest in the art and culture of Europe. Such painters as William Morris Hunt, John La Farge, and John Singer Sargent—to mention only a few major names—found the lure of European art irresistible. Their outlook was, in different ways, unmistakably colored by their intimate acquaintance with the styles then in fashion among contemporary artists abroad. And, in each case, their artistic language was enriched and given greater sophistication by their long study of the work of the old masters in the galleries of Europe. Although this group of painters studied under various academic masters, they each retained a large measure of individuality in style and expression. Unfortunately, this was not true of the mediocre, run-of-the-mill academic artists whom Henri quickly learned to despise. These painters catered to the tastes of a rising commercial middle class, many of whom, like their counterparts in Europe, were just as happy not to find their lives (and perhaps their humble origins) honestly mirrored in the art of their time. If one may generalize, they preferred to escape from an accurate reflection of the contemporary world to a more remote, more agreeable, and often more entertaining realm. The styles of these painters in turn were borrowed largely from currently popular artists who exhibited in official academic exhibitions in Paris, London, and Munich.

The academic approach that flourished between the Civil War and World War I did not produce one uniform style that can be identified as "academic." Contrary to much that has been written on the subject, the styles accepted by the academic establishment during this period were quite varied and included such disparate idioms as those of the Barbizon school, the classical-linear tradition of Ingres, adaptations of the seventeenth-century styles of Hals and Velázquez, sentimentalized versions of the Pre-Raphaelite mode, and composites based on sources from Renaissance and Baroque Italy. The common denominator that unified all these acceptable styles was the belief in "tradition," specifically, a tradition that looked back to those artists and theorists who were recognized as worthy examples by such institutions as the Ecole des Beaux-Arts in Paris, the Royal Academy in London, and their counterpart in New York, the National Academy of Design. While there was no such thing as a single academic style, the artists of this persuasion did subscribe to a series of tenets that affected their painting and teaching. In general, they insisted on artistic discipline in the form of correct drawing, especially of the human figure, and a thorough grasp of "technique." This concept of discipline also extended to the composition of the picture, which had to be approached as a considered, rational process in which spontaneity and personal impulse had little place. In subject matter and content the academic artist usually adhered to several unwritten rules. The painting, it was felt, should illustrate some morally instructive event from the recent or distant past or, failing this, should present a comparable edifying message in contemporary guise.

The origins of this view may be traced to the Royal Academy of Painting and Sculpture founded under Louis XIV. By the late nineteenth century, however, a great deal of academic art had degenerated into mere sentimentality, cuteness, and visual storytelling. By the same token, the artist's technique frequently became an end in itself, either in terms of brilliantly executed virtuoso brushwork or as a demonstration of his skill in showing how realistically he could depict a subject.

Academic art was a commercially successful commodity in late nineteenth- and early twentieth-century America. As such, it made sense for academic artists, juries, and teachers to lend each other support. Financial advantage and public acclaim, though not of course the only considerations that motivated the academicians, were major factors underlying their efforts to maintain a position of power in the world of American art. That power was concentrated largely in the National Academy of Design's annual exhibitions and in its school, whose aims closely reflected the norms of acceptability promulgated by the Academy's juries. Both the school and the exhibitions, as we shall see, eventually became primary targets for Henri's attacks during the first decade of the twentieth century.

Another target was the art-for-art's-sake point of view. To Americans, James McNeill Whistler was by far the best-known exponent of this approach, and by the 1890's his influence had reached the United States through his paintings and writings and through his many followers in the Aesthetic movement. Early in his career Whistler had insisted that the artist should be free of any social or moral involvement with his subjects so that he could dedicate himself to his proper concern—the creation of harmonious (and often decorative) arrangements of color, tone, and pattern. Art thus became answerable primarily to itself, to its own formal and structural problems, not to questions external to it. In his own painting, Whistler's philosophy of art bore fruit; in the hands of his followers, it tended to degenerate into sheerly decorative aestheticism practiced for its own sake. It was just this that irritated Henri. In the 1890's, however, he was perfectly willing to admire Whistler's work.

One major offshoot of the art-for-art's-sake approach is represented by the art of William Merritt Chase. He accepted the premise that the artist's role was to imitate nature's appearances rather than consciously seek decorative effects. But he became increasingly fond of showing off his phenomenal technical skill in representation at the expense of any deep involvement with the subject. Thus Chase exemplified a variation that might be called "technique for technique's sake." Although Chase befriended Henri in the 1890's, perhaps because he saw something of his own image in the younger man, Henri broke with him in 1907 as the result of a bitter disagreement over the philosophy of teaching in the New York School of Art.

In Henri's youth the most progressive current in American art was Impressionism. The style was practiced in the late eighties and nineties by such artists as Theodore Robinson, Childe Hassam, and John Twachtman, who closely imitated the French Impressionists while preserving a discernible American flavor in their work. If the American Impressionists lacked great originality, they were at least honest and diligent painters capable of portraying contemporary American themes. And they fulfilled an important function by introducing an almost undiluted form of Impressionism to this country. Significantly, they did this in the 1890's, when the original Impressionists were still fighting for acceptance in France. Henri, as we shall see, briefly worked in a highly colored Impressionist style in the early 1890's and often proclaimed his admiration for the work of John Twachtman. But when Impressionism in America became sentimental and academic, as it did with Frank W. Benson, Willard Metcalf, and Frederick Frieseke in the nineties and early 1900's, Henri vehemently rejected the style.

Two major artists, Winslow Homer and Thomas Eakins, countered the tide of European fashion by emphasizing indigenous American subjects. In both cases, their artistic language resulted from a direct and honest transaction with the subject, without close imitation of European styles. However, their realism—their artistic candor, one might say—alienated a large sector of the American public in the generation after the Civil War. Thus Homer and, to a greater degree, Eakins failed to reach the pinnacle of popularity enjoyed by their contemporaries who followed the fashionable academic trends. Yet from our present vantage point in history, it becomes clear that Homer and Eakins effectively translated into pictorial terms much of the essential nature of the American experience in the late nineteenth century. Henri early recognized this and in his teaching pitted Homer and Eakins against the academicians, who shied away from any deep involvement with the character of their native country.

Such were the major trends of American art that Henri confronted. Just as important for an understanding of this period is knowledge of his personality, for the body of the text will deal in large part with the interaction of the man and his artistic milieu.

The key to Henri's personality is his belief in the freedom and inherent dignity of the individual. This conviction did not stem from any religious dogma but from a deep humanistic faith in the innate value of man as a unique being. Henri's ideal was the self-reliant individual who searched honestly within himself for the answers to the central questions of art and life. Such a view meant that unthinking allegiance to convention or tradition (especially as supported by institutions) should be avoided at all costs. Henri's convictions thus led him to distrust the entrenched power of the juries of academic exhibitions, political parties, and traditional art schools. All these, he felt, limited the natural growth of man's innate creative ability by imposing fixed standards from above. For Henri, the expressive forms of art must develop organically out of each individual's unique transaction with the world.

For almost a generation Henri fought a series of battles as an individual revolutionary against established organizations. In the process his adversaries accused him of anarchy and lawlessness, and in certain respects they were correct in doing so. Henri rejected laws and rules whenever they called for blind obedience. And he was certainly a philosophical anarchist in his celebration of the supremacy of the individual's freedom to act without having to be shackled by established institutions and formalized codes of behavior. Though a liberal and a democrat at heart, he never became entangled in politics; his role as revolutionary and reformer was enacted on a broader plane, involving art, aesthetics, education, and ultimately a whole outlook upon life. During a large part of his career, he fought an uphill battle. But because Henri's individualistic philosophy took root among his friends and students, he eventually succeeded, with their help, in revising American attitudes toward the fine arts.

Because he believed in progress in the arts, Henri championed a variety of avant-garde styles and theories of art. In the 1890's and 1900's he was the chief American painter to espouse Courbet's and Manet's Realism along with its parallels in the work of Homer and Eakins. Furthermore, in this same period he also preached the Symbolist aesthetic as practiced by the French Post-impressionist painters and, to a lesser degree, Whistler. Henri's own painting, which drew upon these sources, was considered radical during his first twenty years of artistic productivity. In these ways, then, he identified himself with

5

several major currents of rebellion and innovation, which, in turn, he communicated to a circle of followers. In the process he tried to clear away the debris of the academic approach and fought to liberalize the policies of art exhibitions in the United States.

Although Henri considered himself a painter before anything else, he could not resist the opportunity to proselytize; as a result, he is as important historically for his influence as for his painting. His influence, as suggested in the Preface, cannot be evaluated merely by surveying the many roles he played. It is probably most accurate to say that he was the central motivating force for artistic progress in his generation. He was the leading channel through which recent innovations in European painting were transmitted to the United States, and he was widely read in art theory, literature, and philosophy. Thanks to his innate gifts as a teacher, he was able to digest this material and recast it in a way that his students found thoroughly absorbing. And, above all, he was convinced that Americans must nurture an art of their own, drawing upon the essential qualities of the people, the time, and the place. This did not mean that European art should be rejected but, rather, that it should be used for whatever value it might have in fostering the expression of distinctly American values.

We will be concerned in the following pages with Henri's life and influence, his own painting and attitude toward the arts, past and present. A word of explanation is necessary: because his life from 1886 to 1900 has been touched upon only superficially in previous writings, considerable emphasis will be placed on this period in the present book. To some readers the accent on his formative years may seem to throw the book out of balance; but his biography has been handled in this way intentionally to complement the image of Henri presented in previous writings on his life.

2

The Early Years,

1865-1886

PRIOR TO the publication of Van Wyck Brooks's *John Sloan: A Painter's Life* in 1955, the facts of Robert Henri's early life were a closely guarded secret. Historians in search of information about the period before the artist reached eighteen found that the traces suddenly disappeared. There seemed to be no such person as Robert Henri on record before 1883. To those who wrote about him during his lifetime, he gave only a few scraps of information: He had been born in Cincinnati in 1865 of American parents, allegedly named John and Theresa Henri, who traced their origins to French, English, and Irish ancestry. The family had lived for several generations in Virginia, Kentucky, and Ohio, and as a boy he had spent a number of years traveling in the West. He had attended school in Cincinnati, Denver, and New York. Essentially those few facts are all he revealed about his early life.

The mystery can be solved if we realize that the surname he claimed for his parents is fictitious. Their actual names were John and Theresa Cozad, and their younger son was originally called Robert Henry Cozad. Because his father killed a man in Nebraska and was a fugitive for years before he was cleared of murder, Robert, his brother John, and his parents assumed different surnames before they moved to New Jersey in 1883.

Robert Henri's forebears came from hardy pioneering families, emigrants from France and the British Isles, who established homesteads in Virginia, Ohio, and Kentucky.[1] His ancestors on his mother's side had sailed from England early in the eighteenth century and settled for a time in what is now West Virginia. His mother's maternal grandfather, John Jones, was born in Maryland in 1777 and served as commissioner in the War of 1812, after which he settled in Kentucky. Later he sold his homestead there and moved with his wife, the former Segus Forquereau, and their children to Kanawha

County, Virginia (now West Virginia). His daughter Julia Ann (1813–1909) married Robert Burke Gatewood (1808–1884), who had been born in Amhurst County, Virginia, and operated a saltworks in the town of Malden. The couple had four children—three sons and a daughter, Theresa, who was to be Robert Henri's mother.

Henri's paternal grandfather, Henry Cozad, was of French Huguenot ancestry and counted a line of ministers in the family tree. Like the Gatewoods, he too belonged to a pioneering family. A native of Upshur County, Virginia, he had served in the War of 1812 and then settled in Vinton County, Ohio, where, on his own land, he established the town of Allensville in 1837; being a faithful Democrat, he had voted for William Allen and named his town after the Ohio congressman.[2] Here a son, John Jackson Cozad (Robert Henri's father), was born on November 9, 1830.[3] The boy's education was typical of most small communities of the time—he was taught the "three R's" and religious principles; there is no record of his receiving a higher education. His mother, Margaret Clark Cozad, had died shortly after he was born, and his father subsequently remarried. As the high-spirited youth grew older, he found life with his stepmother difficult, so he left home at the age of twelve to seek his fortune in Cincinnati, a move that marked the beginning of an adventurous and romantic career. He found a job there as a cabin boy on a river boat making the run between Cincinnati and New Orleans, and on shipboard he grew fond of watching the planters, merchants, and professional gamblers play at the gaming tables. Growing up in this environment, Cozad chose to take up gambling as a career, and with his quick eye and prodigious memory he became a masterly player. His favorite game was faro, in which he was reputed to be unbeatable. He was often referred to as "King of Gamblers," and became so skilled that many casinos barred him from playing. Much of his early life was spent traveling about the United States and South America successfully practicing his profession. It should be remembered, however, as John Sloan later observed, that "back in the sixties and seventies this kind of gambling was an honorable profession and recognized as a gentleman's prerogative."[4]

Cozad was a man of commanding aspect—tall, slender, and distinguished in appearance, with jet-black hair and sharp, deep-set black eyes (Figure 2). John Sloan compared him to an El Greco and remarked on his "courtly manners and great straightforwardness."[5] An immaculate dresser, he was frequently seen wearing a Prince Albert coat, high silk hat, and kid gloves. He was strong-willed, fearless, and determined, but to those close to him he showed an almost feminine tenderness.

8

Figure 2. Robert Henri, *John Jackson Cozad*, 1903. Oil on canvas, 32 x 26″. Collection of Mrs. A. B. Sheldon, Lexington, Nebraska, and Sheldon Memorial Gallery, University of Nebraska.

On one of his trips through Virginia, Cozad stopped at a hotel in Malden operated by Mrs. Robert Gatewood and here met her attractive daughter Theresa (Figure 3). For the nineteen-year-old girl it was a case of love at first sight, and after going through the customary formal courtship they were married at her parents' home in an elaborate ceremony on June 13, 1857. After their wedding trip, the Cozads settled in Cincinnati, where, at Plum and Fifth Streets, two sons were born: John A. on November 29, 1862, and Robert Henry—named after both his grandfathers—on June 24, 1865. Subsequently, the couple had three other sons, who died in infancy.[6]

The birth of his children brought an end to Cozad's career as a professional gambler, and he turned to real estate promotion. One of his major enterprises was the founding in 1869 of a town he named Cozaddale on the outskirts of Cincinnati.[7] Cozaddale prospered briefly, but it failed to become an important resort like Saratoga or Long Branch, as Cozad had hoped. Nor could it compete with Cincinnati in attracting manufacturing industries, so the founder was eventually compelled to devise more ambitious building projects farther west.

Much of Robert Henry Cozad's childhood was spent in Cincinnati and Cozaddale. He was educated at the Chickering Classical and Scientific Institute in Cincinnati, a private school for boys, where he did better than average work, excelling in declamation and composition and receiving lowest marks in Latin and spelling. In school he wrote plays for his class, in which he also acted, electing to play the part of "the bloody villain." His mother, a sensitive, thoughtful woman endowed with a love of good books, supplemented his school work by assigning additional readings in history and literature. Determined that her sons should grow up to be great men, she bought them books and regularly took them to galleries, operas, concerts, and the theatre. On their birthdays, Mrs. Cozad gave the boys scrapbooks, which she helped them fill with clippings about historical and current events culled from newspapers and magazines.

In 1872, John Cozad became intrigued with the idea of founding a new community in the West. The Union Pacific Railroad had announced the sale of millions of acres of land along its right of way in the state of Nebraska, providing a perfect opportunity for building a town in virgin territory. A man of quick decisions, Cozad went to Nebraska and selected a promising site on the prairie along the north bank of the Platte River where a wooden sign—"The 100th Meridian"—announced the beginning of the West. He undoubtedly had visions of a great city that would rise in this fertile farming

Figure 3. Theresa Gatewood Cozad. Photograph.

and stock-raising country. And with the coming of a major railroad, large fortunes could be anticipated. With these thoughts in mind, Cozad took an option to purchase 50,000 acres and returned to Cincinnati to advertise for colonists to settle the area.

The first immigrants arrived in December, 1873, and within a year a flourishing community named Cozad had grown up on his tract of land.[8] John Cozad took naturally to the role of leader and adviser and readily gave direction to this largely agricultural settlement. It was not long before a hotel, a school, a depot, and several business buildings were erected and a newspaper, *The Hundredth Meridian*, was published in the town. After a propitious beginning, however, the founder's ambitions were frustrated by a series of harsh winters, grasshopper plagues, and bitter disagreements with local cattle barons, who feared that their ranges might be obliterated.

Robert was seven years old when the family first came to Nebraska, and here he spent many months during the formative years of his childhood (he returned to Cincinnati to attend school in 1875, 1877, 1878, and 1879). In a number of ways his early life must have been the fulfillment of a typical American boy's dream—riding, fishing, swimming, and an occasional glimpse of a Sioux or Pawnee Indian. At the age of eleven Robert gave an informative description of some of his Western adventures in "A Letter from Young America," published in the Cozad newspaper:

I have a horse and saddle, and have a good time riding over the prairie. . . . We see a great many herders and hunters here. They are fine riders and have beautiful ponies. Some of the hunters wear pretty suits of buckskin with fringe all around. I saw one who had rows of gold dollars on his suit for buttons. They wear their hair very long and a belt around the waist filled with pistols and great spurs on their boots. They raise fine crops here, but the [grass]hoppers do most of the harvesting. It's thought they will not be here next year.

The air is very pure and it's very healthy. Nobody ever gets sick, but sick folks who come here get well. The winter is mild, only once in a while the wind blows a *little hard.* . . .

We have a nice two story school house furnished with Excelsior seats, desks, large globe, maps all around and a large black-board in the wall at each end. Our teacher is a pretty little lady, and wears a gold watch, a fine ring, and a little bit of a foot, and we love her dearly.[9]

Robert and his brother John continually witnessed their father's day-to-day struggle to build his ideal commonwealth—a struggle that included the large-scale manufacture of bricks and an ambitious attempt to bridge the Platte River. The boys' affection for their father was deep and enduring, and they were raised in an atmosphere of love and understanding, seasoned by paternal firmness.

Photographs taken when he was a child show that Robert Cozad inherited some of his father's features: a broad forehead, dark glossy hair, and the same intense glance (Figure 4). But even as an infant he exhibited a characteristic quasi-oriental look in his almost slanted eyes and high cheekbones, inherited from the Gatewoods. As he matured it became apparent that he would share his father's tall, lanky frame, and eventually he grew to a height of six feet, one-and-a-half inches.

A brief autobiographical note that Robert Cozad wrote on his fourteenth birthday tells us something of his activities at the time: "I am in better health than I ever was now and am a great boy for hearty playing as well as a great story reader. I love to write and draw. I am left handed." [10] When he was asked, in later years, when he first began to draw, he replied: "As far back as I can remember." [11] As to the exact date when he definitely decided to become an artist, he said, "I never had any other idea, but for a time it was mixed up with writing. . . . I thought it would be great to be a picture painter, but as practically all the accounts I read or heard were to the effect that artists surprised their parents and the neighbors by doing masterpieces in infancy, I supposed I was not in that class." [12] Conditions on the frontier, of course, were not conducive to the production of great art, but Henri admitted that "the stimulating influences of my mother who had a natural love for books and painting and the constructive enthusiasms of my father counted favorably against an environment—the far West, cowboys, etc., etc., in which there was no association with artists." [13] Yet Henri did not regret growing up under these circumstances: "I am rather glad that it all happened as it did, for that boy's life is part of my experience—my storehouse—and it does not matter to me at all that I didn't paint a picture when I was in the cradle." [14]

We do not know when he made his first picture, but it was undoubtedly at an early age. As he once wrote, "I remember . . . doing what was considered a good deal of damage, by my teachers, to the books I was supposed to study and which I so hated to study. The fly leaves and the margins were very inviting when pencils were at hand." [15] Soon after he arrived in Nebraska, he made colorful pencil-and-crayon drawings of a multitude of subjects, some taken from his imagination, others suggested by his new environment.[16] Some of these drawings appeared in his notebooks and diaries as

13

Figure 4. Robert Henry Cozad (Robert Henri). Photograph.

illuminated initials and marginal illustrations, or they adorned his independent prose writings. His talents soon earned him the job of designing posters advertising the Cozad colony, and he made extra money by painting and selling greeting cards and operating his own printing press.

During his childhood, Robert amused himself by writing and illustrating numerous fictional stories. His favorite task was composing his two-volume "Runty Papers," to which he devoted innumerable hours, but he also produced such prose works as "Dan Dover," "Abe, Boy Detective," and "Irish, the Boy Inventor." The boy was also an active diarist, having formally begun to keep diaries, or "note-books," at the age of fourteen. Although days sometimes went by without his making an entry, the surviving diaries comprise an invaluable record of his daily activities, as well as of local events in Cozad. Written in simple yet colorful descriptive prose, they are marked by a strong historical sense and an abundance of factual detail. And the diaries tell us much about the boy's literary tastes around 1880; some of his favorite writers, he confessed, were Dickens, Sylvanus Cobb, Jr., Jules Verne, Mrs. Mary J. Holmes, and Mark Twain. Specifically, we know his readings included John McElroy's *History of Andersonville Prison*, Dickens' *Nicholas Nickleby* and *Oliver Twist*, and Cobb's "The Forest Champion" and other stories from the *New York Ledger*. Robert liked Cobb because he was "a good lively writer" and admired Dickens as "a great describer of characters"; but he was impatient with authors who "spend so much time describing, etc., and cause the points of the story to be so far apart that I get tired out before I get to them." [17]

Further evidence about his tastes and interests may be found in his scrapbooks, which he kept concurrently with his "note-books," beginning in 1879. Along with the usual personal memorabilia—report cards, commencement programs, and the like—he preserved clippings on such subjects as the death of William Cullen Bryant, speeches by DeWitt Talmage, reports on the shooting of President Garfield, and various articles about and illustrations of great men and important historical events. But the scrapbooks were not always serious in tone; their pages were punctuated by clippings of comic poetry and sayings, anecdotes by Sylvanus Cobb and Josh Billings, and popular cartoons. It was cartoons such as these that served as the basis of Robert's youthful style of illustration, for we can find his own imitations of them scattered throughout his scrapbooks and diaries. From magazines he also cut out and saved numerous wood engravings depicting great men and important events, along with anecdotal, realistic illustrations of stories. Popular chromolithographs of sweetly sentimental cupids and scenes from antiquity likewise attracted his attention.

Having finished his schooling at the Chickering Institute in June, 1879, Robert took on increasing responsibilities at his father's side in Cozad, Nebraska. At fifteen he was placed in charge of baling operations at the Cozad hay farm, supervising the workers on the hay press and keeping accounts. He took to these duties willingly; as he confided in his diary, "It revives me up and makes me feel like I am some body to have a responsible position and be depended on. . . . No one knows how much good this does me. It makes me want to do something." [18]

John Cozad's hay business had often taken him to Denver, and in 1880 he rented a warehouse in the city, where he frequently stationed his older son, John, to oversee the receipt of shipments. With the boys growing up, their father thought seriously about sending them to school in Denver. Although the residents of Cozad were proud of having a school that was open nine months of the year—in contrast to the usual two or three in most frontier communities—the Cozads' ambition to prepare their sons for college could hardly be realized in this remote rural environment. So, in the summer of 1881, the family decided to move to Denver. Shortly before leaving Cozad, Robert wrote in his diary about their plans: "We will perhaps go into the Real Estate Business—on our own capital—and partly into the Hay & probably feed commission business. We expect to make Denver our permanent home and try to build up a fortune there." [19] Upon their arrival, the elder Cozad opened a real estate office at 636 Larimer Street under the name of John J. Cozad & Sons and shortly thereafter invested in a mining company in Leadville. Although his legal residence was Denver, family records indicate that he spent some of his time traveling to and from Cozad and Cincinnati, presumably on business.

After a year in a Denver public school, Robert returned to Cozad for the summer, where he spent much of his time in the saddle managing his father's hay farm. By this time, Cozad's leadership of the community had been seriously challenged by a group of ranchers, who had done their best to intimidate the settlers by threats of violence. In October, 1882, his difficulties with the cattlemen culminated in a bitter argument with one Alfred Pearson, a disgruntled herder, who in a drunken state attacked the founder with a knife. Drawing his pistol in self-defense, Cozad shot and mortally wounded Pearson. Anticipating mob violence and possibly his own murder, Cozad secretly fled from the town that night, never to live there again. Pearson died two months later. (Eventually, through the efforts of Mrs. Cozad's brother, a coroner's jury cleared Cozad of the murder charge.) Shortly after the shooting, having hurriedly sold her husband's property, Mrs. Cozad gathered a few belongings and with her son Robert quietly left the community. Later, the family was reunited in Denver.

Although John Cozad's business in Denver prospered, he and his wife knew that the city would afford few opportunities for their sons' education and future development. They therefore decided to move to New York; the East promised a new prospecting ground for the elder Cozad, better schools for the boys, and a complete break with the past. To be free of any lingering scandal surrounding the shooting at Cozad, Nebraska, John Jackson Cozad decided that he, his wife, and the children should change their names. He adopted Richard H. Lee as his pseudonym, probably from a prominent West Virginia relative on his wife's side of the family. His older son John was called Frank L. Southrn, and his younger son, Robert Henry Cozad, became Robert Earl Henri—adopting his middle name as a surname, but changing its spelling to reflect his French ancestry.[20] (Proud of his American origins and disliking affectation, Robert later insisted that everyone pronounce his name Hen'rye, in the American rather than the French manner). To conceal their true identity, the boys were passed off as adopted sons and foster brothers.

The effect of this environment—both parental and geographical—on the formation of Henri's personality was undoubtedly considerable. Although we cannot prove conclusively that his Western environment decisively shaped the young man's character, everything points to its making a strong impression which was never eradicated. For a period of ten years, from 1872 to 1882, he was intermittently exposed to the rigors of frontier life in Nebraska, far from the sophisticated, cosmopolitan atmosphere of the large Eastern cities. And as a boy, he often traveled through the West and Middle West, where he could witness at first hand the life and landscape of the growing nation.

At an early age he was thrust into contact with vast expanses of raw, unspoiled nature; to escape it on the frontier was impossible. This experience undoubtedly helped him to conceive of nature as an insistent vital force which man should seek to embrace for his own betterment. His attachment to nature remained with him throughout his life; as he remarked in *The Art Spirit*, "I find nature 'as is' a very wonderful romance and no man-made concoctions have ever beaten it either in romance or sweetness."[21] Just as he found an unspoiled landscape in the West, so too he encountered the Indian as a primitive, natural being living in harmony with nature. For many Americans of his time, Indians were merely storybook characters remote from their own experience. But to Henri, they were real people engaged in a different way of life—individuals whose freedom and naturalness carried important lessons for the overly sophisticated city-dweller.

It may seem a cliché to attribute his democratic spirit, his individualism, and his suspicion of external controls to an upbringing in a pioneering community. But if we accept Frederick Jackson Turner's classic thesis on the effect of the frontier upon the American character, then much of Henri's personality can be explained by the fact that he spent his formative years in the West. Indeed, Turner's summary of the influence of the frontier could almost read as a résumé of Henri's character: "That coarseness and strength combined with acuteness and inquisitiveness; that practical, inventive turn of mind, quick to find expedients; that masterful grasp of material things, lacking in the artistic but powerful to effect great ends; that restless nervous energy; that dominant individualism, working for good and for evil, and withal that buoyancy and exuberance which comes with freedom—these are the traits of the frontier, or traits called out elsewhere because of the existence of the frontier." [22] Not all of this applies precisely to Robert Henri, especially Turner's remark about the artistic sense. But its general tone does sum up much of the personality Henri evidenced as a mature man.

Many of the personal qualities the frontier evoked in Henri were reinforced by the influence of his father, who, in turn, was also well acquainted with the frontier and had traveled across the country during the Gold Rush of 1849. He was a typical American of a type now almost extinct: an individualist, an adventurer, and a speculator. Yet he was also something of an idealist, as his plans for building communities testify. In these activities all reports lead us to believe that Cozad was a model of independent action, fighting fairly but vigorously for his beliefs against seemingly insurmountable obstacles. Young Henri doubtless also inherited his father's visual acuity and deft hand.

Late in 1883, Henri and his family moved to New York City, but after a brief stay there they established themselves permanently in Atlantic City, New Jersey. Once again John J. Cozad, now Richard H. Lee, invested in real estate and, with his acute sense of property values, purchased a choice tract of land where Texas Avenue meets the beach. Because the property was largely under the waters of the Atlantic Ocean—an ideal site for a pier, which he later

18

built there—he worked hard devising breakwaters and jetties to preserve the beach front. He also erected several houses. Before enrolling in art school in 1886, Robert Henri spent much of his time helping his father with these building projects. And when he was not painting houses or reading Thackeray, he and his brother operated Southrn and Henri's Cigar Store.

Robert's interest in art continued to grow during his residence in Atlantic City, and he found time to paint and draw, sometimes taking subjects from life around him, sometimes copying prints and illustrations. It was here, in 1885, that he did his first painting, a copy of a wood engraving from *Harper's Magazine*, which he executed in the medium of dry color and beer. This effort was followed in the same year by his first painting in oil, a copy of a chromolithograph of a landscape.[23] He also utilized his talents in decorating the interior walls of his family's house with original compositions and copies from popular chromos.

Once again his scrapbooks give us a good indication of his tastes at this time. Into a volume started in 1884 he pasted innumerable political and non-political cartoons, by such artists as Gillam and Opper, clipped chiefly from the magazines *Puck* and *Judge*, along with engravings after paintings by the favorite academic masters of the day, such as Cot's *The Storm*. Scattered through these pages were many of Henri's own early drawings and water colors—some original compositions, others copies. His original illustrations were based on the idiom of popular cartoons, but his copies of 1885–1886 show that he was experimenting with a wide variety of styles—those of Walter Crane, Kate Greenaway, and the decorative manner of William Morris and his followers, as popularized by the magazine *Art Interchange* and such books as Marion Kemble's *Art Recreations: A Guide to Decorative Art* (Boston, 1884).

One of Robert's murals caught the attention of his friend and "first art critic," [24] James Albert Cathgart, champion pedestrian racer and a former student at the Pennsylvania Academy of the Fine Arts. Cathgart's enthusiasm for his work precipitated a family conference which gave a definite direction to the young painter's future. His mother and father had recognized his literary and artistic talents without forcing him to develop one field at the expense of the other, believing that he would eventually make the right choice by himself. So with Cathgart's encouragement and his family's support, Robert Henri finally decided to enroll at the Pennsylvania Academy of the Fine Arts in Philadelphia, the country's oldest and most famous art institution.

Henri and his brother left Atlantic City for Philadelphia at the end of September, 1886, each to register in a professional school of his own choice. Frank enrolled at the Jefferson Medical College. Robert presented samples of his work to the Academy of the Fine Arts; after a few days' wait he was delighted to learn that he had been admitted to the antique class. Living together in the same boardinghouse on South Ninth Street, John Jackson Cozad's sons must have looked forward with high anticipation to life and study in one of the country's great educational centers. On the eve of this new adventure, Henri wrote: "I am well pleased with my situation and expect to do well." [25]

3

An Art Student in
Philadelphia, 1886-1888

THE ACADEMY of the Fine Arts that Henri entered in the fall of 1886 was unquestionably the leading school of its kind in the country. Its only serious competitors were the National Academy of Design and the Art Students League, both in New York City. Thomas Eakins, one of America's greatest painters and teachers, placed the Academy well ahead of any other American art school during the ten years he served on the faculty. The New York academies must have envied the elaborate new brownstone and marble building on North Broad Street that was completed in 1876. In that year, Eakins began to teach there, and after the death of the old life-class teacher, Christian Schussele, he became professor of drawing and painting. During his last three years on the faculty he served as director of the school.

Eakins, Anshutz, and the Academy

When Eakins gained control of the Academy, he instituted new educational policies that were considered the most progressive in the United States. With the backing of the chairman of the school committee, and to the chagrin of many of the directors, he shifted the emphasis from drawing casts of antique sculpture to the intensive study of the nude human figure. This was a unique and revolutionary step in American art training, but one that attracted more students than ever before. Pupils were graduated quickly from cast drawing to the life class as soon as they showed signs of promise. His attitude toward drawing was also unorthodox: he permitted students to begin by painting in oils, to work in tone and color rather than starting with a line drawing, believing that "the main thing that the brush secures is the instant grasp of the grand construction of a figure." [1] Moreover, he taught sculptural modeling to prospective painters to aid their understanding of form. "If you do good modeling," he claimed, "it follows that you will do good painting." [2]

The students learned dissecting under Eakins' supervision, and twice a week they could attend Dr. William Keen's lectures on artistic anatomy. They worked not only with the human body but with animals as well, in order to comprehend the principles that underlie muscular construction. Eakins felt that "to draw the human figure it is necessary to know as much as possible about it, about its structure and its movements, its bones and muscles, how they are made, and how they act." [3] In his teaching he also advocated the study of still and "motion" photographs of figures and animals (some taken by himself, some by his friend Eadweard Muybridge); he gave lectures on scientific perspective; and he encouraged his students to study higher mathematics because he thought it was so much like painting.

When some people argued that Eakins' emphasis on anatomical knowledge of the human figure might threaten the aesthetic ends of art, he countered by stating: "For anatomy, as such, we care nothing whatever." [4] His goal was to have his pupils study the figure intensively so that they would fully comprehend its beauty—a beauty that resided as much in construction as in form. At the Academy, however, little was offered beside the study of the figure; in his teaching Eakins practically ignored the aesthetics of composing paintings. In reply to those who criticized this policy, one of his spokesmen argued: "The objection that the school does not sufficiently teach the students picture-making, may be met by saying that it is hardly within the province of a school to do so. It is better learned outside, in private studios, in the fields, from nature, by reading, from a careful study of other pictures, of engravings, of art exhibitions." [5] Eakins thus emerges as a Realist who would not try to teach others the technique of composing paintings. He probably hesitated to do so because he did not wish to set up a formula, an aesthetic code that students could follow by rote. Scientific laws were acceptable because they comprised the general grammar that each individual could use as his point of departure. For a man of Eakins' beliefs to guide them beyond that point was unthinkable.

Eakins inherited an organized, practical, and realistic mind from his father. But his objective outlook was surely nurtured by the scientific culture of the mid-nineteenth century and by the intellectual climate of his native city, Philadelphia, then, as now, a center for scientific investigation. Shortly after graduating from Central High School in 1861, he became a student at the

Pennsylvania Academy of the Fine Arts. Here he heard lectures on anatomy and entered the recently established life classes after a rigorous apprenticeship of drawing from casts of antique sculpture. Advanced students were also expected to copy pictures by old and living masters displayed in the Academy galleries. To supplement his school training, Eakins took courses in anatomy under Dr. Joseph Pancoast at the Jefferson Medical College, where he gained a knowledge of the subject more extensive than that of any other American artist of the 1860's.

After about five years of studying art in Philadelphia he realized that he had exhausted the resources of that city and that to obtain full professional training he would have to go to Paris. So, in 1866, Eakins sailed for France to become a pupil at the leading academy of that era, the Ecole des Beaux-Arts, where he enrolled in the ateliers of the painters Jean-Léon Gérôme and Léon Bonnat and of the sculptor Augustin-Alexandre Dumont.

Beside studio work, the chief courses for prospective painters were anatomy and perspective. In addition, many of the teachers advocated photography as a means of study. Eakins, as we have seen, shifted the emphasis at the Pennsylvania Academy from drawing casts and copying pictures to painting the nude figure; this, together with a thorough knowledge of anatomy, became the main basis of study in a curriculum that was strongly influenced by his own training at the Ecole des Beaux-Arts. His belief in scientific perspective and photography as valuable aids to the student may also be traced to his Paris experience. True, Eakins' systematic temperament often led him to carry the scientific side of these disciplines further than at the Ecole. And it is also clear that he grew skeptical of the academic practice of copying the surface appearance of the model and searched instead for broader means of grasping its general construction.

Like many other painters who made the pilgrimage to the Beaux-Arts in the sixties and seventies, Eakins gradually became disillusioned with the sterile and artificial aspects of the school: sentimentality, the emphasis on overblown mythological and historical subjects, and slavish allegiance to the classical past, especially in the linear tradition inherited from Ingres and carried on by Gérôme. As Eakins said after he left the Ecole, referring to his teacher Gérôme: "I had to decide never to paint like the *patron*." [6] A trip to Spain was the catalyst that made him realize the serious limitations of the academic approach. Here he spent six months painting and studying the work of the masters, particularly the seventeenth-century Spaniards. It was in Spain that he discovered the admirable qualities of Velázquez and Ribera, painters who represented the antithesis of the French academic point of view. From the work of the Spaniards, and of Rembrandt and Titian, he learned to conceive of painting broadly, tonally, in terms of large masses of dark and light, to lay in the picture in oils without a preliminary drawing, and to ignore details until after the composition had taken shape. It was a change, in short, from a linear to a painterly approach, following a course that closely parallels Edouard Manet's change in style after his discovery of Spanish painting.

While Eakins enjoyed a successful career as a teacher after his return to Philadelphia in 1870, serious criticisms of his policies developed that were eventually to force him to resign from the Academy in 1886—one of the tragedies in American art education. His frankness in using the undraped human figure in his teaching, which involved manipulation of the muscles and photographing nudes (including some from the student body), stirred up protests among the more prudish women in the classes, as well as among local groups devoted to the protection of public morals. And, under the leadership of one of his former students, several young men in the Academy who did not fully agree with his ideas tried to halt "the abuse of his authority" [7] by spreading rumors of his allegedly immoral use of the nude. The friction between Eakins and the Academy came to a head in January, 1886, when in demonstrating the action of the pelvis before the women's life class he removed the loincloth from a male model. This shocked several young ladies, and they promptly reported the incident to the directors, who appointed a committee to investigate. After weighing the evidence, the committee decided that he must agree to be more judicious in posing the nude model or else leave the Academy. Believing he was the victim of a conspiracy, but steadfastly refusing to change his teaching methods, Eakins resigned.

Robert Henri enrolled in the school in the fall of 1886, eight months after Eakins' departure. Although Eakins remained in Philadelphia and continued to teach and paint, he never rejoined the faculty of the Academy. Thus his beneficial influence did not reach Henri directly. But the Eakins tradition remained strong in the school for a few years. His pupils who continued to study there spoke with authority about their former teacher, and Henri was intrigued by what he heard. He later recalled:

It was an excitement to hear his pupils tell of him. They believed in him as a great master, and there were stories of his power, his will in the pursuit of study, his unswerving adherence to his ideals, his great willingness to give, to help, and the pleasure he had in seeing the original and worthy crop out in a student's work. [8]

Some of his teachings also came to Henri secondhand through Thomas Pollock Anshutz, Eakins' former pupil and assistant, who took over the master's classes in February, 1886. Anshutz was an extremely able, if little recognized, painter whose early style grew out of mid-nineteenth-century naturalism, as exemplified by the Hudson River school, Winslow Homer, and Eastman Johnson. During the eighties, he came under Eakins' influence and executed works—primarily portraits—that reflect the master's dark palette and concern for anatomical correctness. But he never imitated Eakins literally —witness his remarkable *Iron Workers' Noon-Day Rest*, also known as *Steelworkers—Noontime* (c. 1880) (Figure 5). Although Eakins had concerned himself with life's gentler labors—fishing, sailing, hunting, and so on—Anshutz searched out the sinewy ironworkers of West Virginia, who stand unidealized in the broad sunlight. It is hard to find more than a passing reference to classical poses in the figures, who are casually grouped against a rolling-mill in the background. The everyday activities of washing, flexing the muscles, and dressing are sampled, almost without comment. Thus in its objective, unashamed treatment of the laboring classes, *Iron Workers' Noon-Day Rest* clearly foreshadows the approach of several members of the so-called "Ashcan school" around the turn of the century. Significantly, Robert Henri, one of his most promising pupils, was to become the leader of that group, which included Sloan, Glackens, Luks, and Shinn—young men who also passed through Anshutz' classes in the early nineties. Many years later, Henri remembered Anshutz as "a great influence, for he was a man of the finest quality, a great friend, gave excellent advice, and never stood against a student's development."[9]

Anshutz was a gifted teacher who sacrificed his full growth as a painter to a thirty-year career in the classrooms of the Pennsylvania Academy of the Fine Arts. A thoroughly sincere person and modest about his own abilities, he gave himself untiringly to his pupils and thereby earned their deep respect and admiration. He imposed no artistic formulas on the students; rather, he was ready to accept all valid styles and encouraged them to develop their own individual means of expression. One of his former pupils recalled: "His influence was stimulating; his effort, to develop the talent inherent in the student, not to impose his own methods in painting. He once said that he never approached his class with thought of what he would give them, but rather expectant of what he should find there of original discovery."[10] Although some of his students remembered him as being rather aloof and distant, he was credited with an almost psychic sense for their different moods. And in spirit he remained a student himself, often joining the class in drawing from the model and entering freely into student celebrations.

Like Eakins, Anshutz believed in the future of an American art that would

Figure 5. Thomas P. Anshutz, *Iron Workers' Noon-Day Rest (Steelworkers —Noontime),* c. 1880. Oil on canvas, 17 x 24″. Collection of Dr. and Mrs. Irving F. Burton, Huntington Woods, Michigan.

not depend on European fashions and encouraged his students to paint the everyday world around them. With Eakins, he shared a belief in close observation of the subject and rigorous study of anatomy as the basis for good art. And both men disdained the senseless competition between artists for medals and prizes. Thus we may regard Anshutz as an important carrier of many of Eakins' teachings to Henri and his friends who studied at the Academy.

Of the three men at the Academy who taught Henri, Anshutz was surely the most influential. But Thomas Hovenden and James P. Kelly also contributed something to Henri's development as an artist. Irish-born Hovenden was one of America's most beloved painters and a celebrity in academic circles when he joined the faculty in 1886. His famous painting *Breaking Home Ties* typifies the popular descriptive realism, infused with a dash of sentimental moralizing, which was then fashionable in official academic exhibitions here and in Europe. Henri's third teacher, James P. Kelly, was younger than his two colleagues. A Philadelphian, Kelly had studied at the Academy and volunteered his services as a teacher when Eakins resigned in 1886. He was awarded an instructorship in that year and, taking over Anshutz' former classes, became a popular member of the faculty until his early death in 1893.

Years of Study, 1886–1888

When Robert Henri entered his first class, Anshutz had him draw from casts of ancient sculpture—starting with the Venus de' Medici—following the long-established tradition of beginning with the antique. Surveying the work of his fellow students, Henri was encouraged when he found they were "no better artists than I myself." [11] From the very beginning he exercised his innate talent for leadership, proudly noting in his diary: "I claim the honor of being the revolutioniser of some parts of the Academy. It was me that persuaded W[hipple] to open the Library—was one of the agitators of the sketch class—of the opening to the Antique [Class] of the modeling room, and now of the getting of a cast for the modeling room." [12]

At first, Anshutz was unimpressed with Henri's drawings from the antique, but through hard work and a strong desire to learn, the student improved rapidly. His chief problem, he confessed, was "the mechanicalism in my work that has always been there." [13] Recognizing the difficulty, Anshutz adopted an Eakins-like strategy in suggesting that he step back from the casts and try to achieve broad effects by painting them in oil. By the middle of November, Henri had won Anshutz' confidence and, to his great relief, was accepted in his and Kelly's life classes: "To say the least I *like* drawing from life," he announced. "I never liked drawing from the cast. I will progress here!" [14] Anshutz gave him numerous suggestions about representing action, recording proportions, and modeling the human figure. The essence of his message was: "Don't *copy* shades but put shades on your paper so as to make round things round. Every line and every shade on a drawing should *mean something*. The shade on one part of the body must be studied with relation not only to the shades next to it but all over the body." [15]

Anshutz also taught Henri in the modeling class, where the students worked from the nude model, building up human figures out of clay. During Henri's early months in the class, Anshutz criticized him for working "too much by outlines" [16] and advised him to work all around the figure. Eakins would have approved when Anshutz told the student: "Get the big things first, then the little ones." [17] Responding to Henri's determined efforts to succeed, his teacher gave him extra help and spent hours talking with him outside the classroom.

In December, Henri entered Thomas Hovenden's life class, a definite step forward in his career as an art student. Comparing his own work to the rest of the class, Henri observed: "My drawing of one day was as good (better than one) as many of the drawings of five days, not that it had finish—mine was rough but looked like the man." [18] Here we already have a hint about the path Henri's art would follow—toward the general grasp of essentials, not picayune details. He was delighted to find that Hovenden liked his manner of working and praised him more than Anshutz had in all his previous criticisms. But his faith in Hovenden was soon shaken when he learned that he could be a caustic critic of students' work. After a few weeks in his classes, Henri observed: "There is very little to learn from him I am beginning to think. My present opinion is that his criticisms are regulated by his liver. . . . Today he booms you, tomorrow he sends you down below. . . . I do not think he is a man of fixed ideas." [19] By the end of the spring term, he was to look more favorably on Hovenden's teaching, but Anshutz still remained his favorite. "Anshutz is a daisy!" [20] he remarked.

Henri spent much of his first year probing the complexities of human and animal anatomy (Figure 6). Dr. Keen's lectures on that subject, which he attended at the Academy, were a model of scientific thoroughness and exacti-

Figure 6. The dissecting room, Pennsylvania Academy of the Fine Arts, c. 1886–1888. Photograph. Henri is the third figure from the left.

tude. That he filled his diaries with extensive illustrated notes on the course testifies to the high value he placed on the doctor's teachings. Henri had early realized the importance of anatomy—believing it to be "a great profession" [21] —and gave many hours to study of the subject outside the classroom. Through his brother, Frank, a medical student, he was allowed to observe operations and dissections at the Jefferson Medical College, just as Eakins had done a generation before.

When the Academy's composition class opened, Henri had a chance to test his skill in devising original designs. He and his friends spent much of their spare time preparing works on such themes as "Silence," "Discord," and "Harmony," to be exhibited and judged by the faculty. While his fellow students often turned to history or allegory, Henri usually drew his subjects from the everyday world, reflecting at this early date a taste for real life as the basis for his art. Others frequently surpassed him in these exercises, but characteristically he attempted to overcome his shortcomings by dogged hard work.

Henri's mode of thinking about painting at this time is illustrated by his remarks about how he would treat Sikes's murder of Nancy, from Charles Dickens's *Oliver Twist:*

The murder done—Sikes looks with *fear*, horror, regret on the prostrate form. Hand clutches his breast, blood on his hands & clothes, long bushy hair in disorder. . . . Furniture, etc., must suit the time and condition. He [is] a dark powerful man. Sikes stands with body facing, head turned toward body. He is filled with dread and fear. The deed done, he feels his guilt, remembers his love, etc., etc. He cannot—dare not—take his eyes off her, his body slightly bent forward, muscles distorted.[22]

This statement is highly revealing of Henri's views about composition, reflecting, as it does, his close acquaintance with academic storytelling art that he must have seen in original paintings and in popular illustrations in magazines. His debt to the theatre is evident, too, in his selection of a spectacular moment in the tale. But he planned to cast the scene in a realistic setting contemporary with the event, thus combining the dramatic and commonplace in a way that typified so much official, academic art of the period.

Early in 1887, Henri was required to join Anshutz' perspective class, which he found thoroughly disagreeable: "I don't like perspective. I hate it. I understand it but can't take interest. It's like chopping wood." [23] Coming from Henri, these remarks are understandable; yet his distaste for perspective is curiously inconsistent with the Eakins tradition, to which he otherwise gladly allied himself. In most respects, Henri's approach to art at this time was rationalistic, doubtless a reflection of Anshutz' influence. "There is an immense amount of brain work in art," he avowed. "The mind should direct every movement of the hand. Not a mark should be made without first knowing what it will effect." [24] This attitude (which corresponds closely to Eakins' views) led to frequent disagreements with Hovenden, who regarded Henri as a "theorist" and told him: "Don't think, just paint" [25]—a clear echo of the popular academic adage, "Copy nature stupidly." But Henri held firmly to his own view: "Good theory with earnest practice is what I want." [26]

In 1887, Henri again became the prime mover behind classroom innovations. In February he and several friends organized a portrait class at the Academy, early evidence of his strong interest in this genre. In the following months he helped to initiate a sketch class, in which an Italian model posed in a variety of different costumes. And after the portait class disbanded, "something new, my own invention," [27] replaced it—a ten-minute sketch class. The class was not organized; it simply ran of its own accord. He reported: "Any student that wants to sketch proposes a class at any time. Those present wishing to sketch agree and every one takes his turn at 10 m[inute] poses till the class is tired or it is too late." [28] It would be going too far to read into this plan the germ of Henri's later philosophical anarchism, as applied to teaching and art organizations. But this scheme was, nonetheless, an exceptionally early reflection of his penchant for democratic, unregimented instruction. Significant, too, is his interest in the rapid, quick sketch, later an essential part of his art and teaching.

Near the end of the spring Henri found his niche in the portrait class, a definite forecast of his later eminence in his field. Here Hovenden responded to his work with enthusiasm: "All the students were called around to see my improvement and the good things I had done. Wasn't I as happy as a clam at high tide when I opened the door and saw Hovey lecturing over my study to all the other students! . . . To me this boom was stimulating!" [29] His progress was not confined to the portrait class: "I received encouragement from all. Anshutz' much prized and seldom given praise made me happy. Kelly gave me great encouragement." [30]

In his first year, curiosity about contemporary and earlier artists drew him to the works of art displayed in public and private collections in Philadelphia. He became a regular visitor in the city's leading commercial galleries, Earle's and Haseltine's, where he viewed the works of European and American masters, including some by contemporary artists. And he occasionally went to see the paintings in Memorial Hall in Fairmount Park, then the city's art museum. As is often the case with first-year art students, Henri and his friends attacked the obvious faults of other artists. After a visit to Earle's, he confessed: "We tore everything to pieces." [31] A trip to Memorial Hall evoked the following: "Tore the old masters out. Laughed at the drawings from the Kensington schools, England." [32]

But he took seriously the work of many fashionable academic artists, and in this he shared the conventional (and largely middle-class) tastes of his day. Munkácsy's *Christ before Pilate* earned his praise, and he thought his *Last Days of the Condemned* was "great genius work." [33] Canvases by such French academic painters as Bouguereau, De Neuville, Detaille, and Renouf, along with works by the Barbizon master Millet, he regarded as "fine pictures." [34] And among the Americans, he favored Edwin A. Abbey, John Sartain, and Cecilia Beaux, all products of the Pennsylvania Academy. Curiously, he disliked the first work he saw by his favorite instructor, Anshutz, but was quite impressed by Hovenden's *Breaking Home Ties.* What about Eakins? His pictures, being out of favor with the Philadelphia public, must have been difficult to see. By good fortune, Henri was taken to the Jefferson Medical College by his brother Frank, and there discovered Eakins' monumental *Gross Clinic* (Figure 7)—one of the most important canvases in the history of American art—which he regarded as "the most wonderful painting I had ever seen." [35] Thus Eakins' art (as distinct from his philosophy of teaching) entered Henri's consciousness as a single thread almost lost in the fabric of academic art. But his influence on Henri was to grow, especially after 1900, until he emerged as one of the younger man's great heroes.

Henri became an avid theatre-goer in Philadelphia, attending performances at least once a week, following a taste for drama initiated by his mother, who introduced him to plays in Cincinnati. By 1886, Philadelphia had become a major center for the theatre, and for a slight charge he could witness the performances of the great, as well as not-so-great, players of his day. Thanks to his catholic tastes, he was just as willing to attend popular spectacles such as the Hanlon Brothers' *Fantasma* and Harry E. Dixey's *Adonis* as Sheridan's *The Rivals* or Shakespeare's *The Merchant of Venice.* He identified himself as much with the actors as with the plays, finding the lure of the profession almost irresistible. "Every time I see such an actor [Coghlin]," he wrote, "I think that art is cheating the stage of an actor by gobbling into me—if I

32

Figure 7. Thomas Eakins, *The Gross Clinic*, 1875. Oil on canvas, 96 x 78″. Courtesy of the Jefferson Medical College of Philadelphia; photographed by the Philadelphia Museum of Art.

wasn't to be an artist I'd be an actor." [36] For Henri, the theatre was a valuable adjunct to the study of art, a belief that he maintained throughout his life: "I do not think that time spent at a good theatre is wasted. Good actors can present to the artist's eye scenes that in life are only once in a lifetime." [37]

After an undistinguished beginning, Henri made remarkable progress during his first year at the Academy. His friends told him of the improvement of his work, and his teachers continually reassured him through the winter and spring of 1887. Anshutz, he noted, "gave me to understand that my improvement was faster than usual. . . . I have worked hard and it appears that I am getting some reward." [38]

When the school closed, Henri returned to live with his family in Atlantic City. Searching for a way to earn money during the summer, he decided to enter the hand-painted clam-shell business but soon abandoned it in favor of making signs for shops and painting new houses which his father had recently erected. Although these activities left little time for the study of art, he managed to do some drawing and painting, making a few sketches out of doors of local landscapes and seascapes.

Early in September he focused his attention on a project that has remarkably close affinities to one of Eakins' favorite subjects: a painting of a medical clinic. Henri's fascination with anatomy and his realistic cast of mind probably attracted him to this subject, but since we know he saw Eakins' *Gross Clinic*, there can be little doubt that it influenced his choice. During the school year, a photograph had been taken of Robert, Frank, and several medical students performing a staged operation on the arm of a patient. This became the basis for a small painting entitled *The Clinic*, on which he worked intermittently until his return to the Academy in October. The ultimate fate of the picture is unknown.

As the end of the summer approached, Henri grew impatient to get back to school. In his second year he continued to work under Anshutz and Hovenden, carrying forward his study of the nude and of portrait painting. His interest in anatomy remained undiminished, and in December he made his "debut" in the dissecting room. Shortly thereafter he was appointed assistant demonstrator of anatomy, a minor position he shared with four other students.

Henri's friends were busy during the winter painting pictures for the 1888 exhibition at the Academy, but with characteristic independence he did not go along with the crowd. He wrote his parents: "I am not painting an Exhibition picture and I do not intend to until I can do something *good*. It is the worst thing a fellow can do to exhibit a poor or ordinary picture to start with." [39] Hovenden, though satisfied with his work, prodded him on, saying: "Now is the time to study your hardest." [40] He must have taken his teacher's advice to heart, for he wrote his parents: "If I work hard and constantly for a few years I will have a profession. Whatever my fears were before, now, I believe that there is nothing but hard work between me and success." [41] Yet despite his will to excel, he sometimes experienced spells of discouragement and depression that were so severe as to prevent him from painting.

In his first two years at the Academy, Henri gathered around himself a large band of students, some of whom became friends of long standing. Many have been forgotten today, while others achieved fame as artists, albeit within an academic framework: the sculptors Charles Grafly and A. Stirling Calder (father of Alexander Calder) and the painters Hugh Breckenridge, Henry McCarter, Edward Redfield, and Augustus Koopman. Edward W. Davis, later a cartoonist and art editor (and father of Stuart Davis), was also a member of his entourage, as were Harry Finney, James Fisher, William Haefeker, William E. Parker, Edward R. Coleman, and Benjamin Fox. At the school Henri was invariably found in the midst of student pranks and celebrations, which he often helped to organize. His gifts as a leader were also revealed in academic matters: he collected students' signatures for a petition to extend the hours of the afternoon class and was named treasurer of the committee in charge of festivities at the end of the school year. Once again we have a taste of Henri's characteristic penchant for leadership in the arts motivated by his firm belief about what was beneficial to himself and his fellow artists.

During the few hours of each week when he was not occupied with school work, he continued to attend the theatre, read serious literature—Dickens, Thackeray, and Daudet—and visit art galleries. He often obtained relief from high art, however, by going to comic operas and variety shows, believing that "once in a while a little rot is worth while seeing." [42] He was also a regular visitor at the exhibitions at the Academy and in local art galleries and gave much thought to the strengths and weaknesses of what he saw. Although his taste continued to run in the academic vein, he now began to admire such masters of the Barbizon school as Millet and Dupré. And at the 1888 student exhibition he took particular notice of the work of a young member of the night antique class, William Glackens, who was later to become a close friend and a loyal member of "the Eight." "Glackens," he observed at the time, "is one of those fellows who make splendid illustrations without the use of models, and makes nothing at all *with* models. . . . His work is *very good*." [43]

In some of his free evenings, Henri and his schoolmates thrashed out the tenets of the Swedenborgian church. These discussions were a significant step in the development of his religious thought, for they introduced him to an unorthodox Protestant sect in which Anshutz was also to stir his interest. His open-minded curiosity about a variety of liberal religious beliefs also led him to investigate Universalism and to hear Mangasar Mangasarian, the "rationalist" and independent Christian, preach a sermon on Henry Ward Beecher. The writings of Swedenborg and Mangasarian undoubtedly stimulated Henri's skepticism about traditional Christian beliefs and the organized church. Explaining his religious views for his parents' benefit, he wrote:

I dashed into action with my pen and rattled off two or three pages which were to convince you that first of all there is a God, proven beyond doubt of all reasoning beings by Nature itself, and secondly that what I objected to was not the belief in and worship of a God, but the fact that the worship is not simple and direct enough—that I would have God proven by nature—Nature is the book—there is no other—nature has proven the existence of a supreme power to all the world—to those who have never been reached by printed books.[44]

Though his parents had come from a Protestant background, they paved the way for his free inquiries into religion through their belief that the sincerity of a minister counted as much as his creed—which meant that, as a boy, he was regularly exposed to the services of many different Christian denominations.

By the middle of Henri's second year at the school, a strong trend developed among the students to go to Paris for additional training. Several of his friends had already left to enroll in the Académie Julian, a favorite school for Americans, and they repeatedly stirred his interest in studying there by sending letters praising the teachers, Adolphe William Bouguereau and Tony Robert-Fleury. During one of his moments of "Paris fever," he cited the virtues of studying at Julian's: "They work 8 hrs. a day on one model there—only three here. They have old students who do excellent work there. We have none here. . . . I can't learn much from those about me in drawing. At Paris they have their 'atmosphere' and their great masterpieces." [45] Early in 1888, Henri and a group of friends discussed the feasibility of going to Paris, where they could share an apartment and study at the Académie Julian. By the middle of May, James Fisher, Harry Finney, William Haefeker, Charles

Grafly, and Henri finally made up their minds to quit the Academy and embark for France at the end of the summer.

Two years at the Academy had given Henri a thorough grounding in the disciplines of drawing and painting. Considering the limitations of his background in the Middle West and West, his artistic horizons were greatly expanded by this experience. Yet however broadening his study in Philadelphia must have been, he was still subject to the provincial tastes of that city and, on a larger scale, the aesthetic provincialism of the United States in general. Like so many serious art students of his generation, he sensed acutely the artistic limitations of his native land and consciously tried to broaden his knowledge by making the pilgrimage to Paris.

At the end of the school term he returned to his parents' home in Atlantic City, where he painted a few portraits of his family and, more important, prepared for his impending journey to Paris. Reservations were made on the S.S. *Queen*, which sailed from New York early in September.

4

Study in Paris,

1888-1891

DESPITE HIS spell of seasickness during the voyage to Europe, Henri enjoyed the crossing. He occupied his time by sketching, reading, and keeping an extensive log, in which he recorded a number of sensitive observations about his fellow passengers. The voyage also gave him an opportunity to review his tastes in art:

There are none or few of the works of the [old masters] that are equal to the moderns according to my way of seeing. Now all the world says there is nothing like the old masters and that none of the moderns can compete with them. What I have seen makes me think the opposite and I place the painters of today ahead of all others. I think that the old masters were very great for their time—probably many of them were very much greater *for their time* than any of the moderns are for theirs. In this I am going against the "good" old laid down beliefs.[1]

This viewpoint was exceptional for an artist of the time. Academic opinion favored the traditional and the allegorical; Henri, however, at the age of twenty-three, had already made his commitment to the contemporary, at any period in history. Not even Europe was to shake his conviction, although it was to teach him to appreciate some of the old masters whose best works he had never seen and to confirm his belief in their importance "for their time."

The sources of Henri's viewpoint cannot be traced exactly. Some credit undoubtedly should be given to his upbringing in the West, far from the works of the old masters, to his taste for recent fiction, and to his reading of John Ruskin, then at the height of his popularity on both sides of the Atlantic. Important, too, was the influence of Anshutz and Hovenden, both of whom were committed to contemporary genre scenes.

After eleven days at sea, the travelers sighted the coast of Ireland, and

38

Henri immediately fell in love with the landscape, forming an attachment that may possibly have influenced his decision to spend the summers of his last years there. On September 17 the S.S. *Queen* finally docked at Liverpool, where he and his friends, tired but delighted to be on dry land, made their way to the London train.

To Henri, London was a revelation. He could hardly believe he was there, "gazing at these wonderful landmarks of history—at the very things themselves!" [2] It was a Dickensian city, he thought, rich in associations with the past: "One can get himself mixed up in old rookeries, tangled and narrow, antiquity and picturesqueness at every step—forget that he is in the 19th Century—wander about the haunts of Dickens and all that great list of English men of letters, perfectly out of the world of today, lost in delightful reveries of the past." [3] These romantic musings were not inconsistent with his taste for the tangible and contemporary. He was enchanted not only by the idea of historical distance, but also by the reality and physical presence of the sites that had inspired the authors of an earlier day.

With his friends he followed the traditional tourist's route to view the sights of London—the Houses of Parliament, Westminster Abbey, the National Gallery—trying to cram as many experiences as possible into a few days. The National Gallery, of course, was more than a tourist attraction; it was an art-pilgrim's shrine. There, Raphael's work attracted him, but not favorably; the Renaissance master was overrated, he felt, and if the *Madonna Ansidei* "had not had that magic name [Raphael] on it we would have passed it by with a glance." Turner was disappointing, too, because he failed to live up to Ruskin's praise. Van Dyck and Rubens left him unimpressed; he was sorry to see in the latter's large paintings "such flabby, boneless figures and contortions." About the Spanish school, however, he was much more charitable, finding the work of Murillo, Ribera, and Velázquez "very great." And Rembrandt's portraits he regarded as "the greatest things in the collection." [4]

His suspicion of Raphael and the Flemish Baroque was not unusual in 1888. Such an attitude had already been manifested in France by such Realists as Manet and Courbet and was reflected in America by Thomas Eakins. Henri's distrust of the aristocratic art of the Catholic countries may well have been the result of his reading of Ruskin, not to mention the natural instincts of an American born in the Middle West. That he expressed these tastes, which were to persist throughout his career, should come as no surprise; they are to be expected from a student trained in Philadelphia in the Eakins tradition. Indeed, Eakins himself might easily have made the comments just quoted.

Henri and his friends ended their brief stay in London on September 22, when they crossed the English Channel to Dieppe. If his first contact with England delighted Henri, his reaction to France was ecstatic: "Oh, what a place!" he exclaimed. "Eureka! I have it! This is what I have longed for!" [5]

Paris, 1888–1890

In Paris, Henri, Grafly, Finney, Haefeker, and Fisher tramped the streets for several days before they secured a suitable fifth-floor apartment at 12 avenue Richerand, a ten-minute walk from the Académie Julian. They agreed to do their own cooking and share the housekeeping duties, and they furnished the four-room suite without delay, decorating it with photographs, engravings—including a Rembrandt—and "copies of great mens' works and some more humble things, our own handiwork." [6] From the contents of their bookshelf, which Henri enumerated, we can gain some idea of their literary and artistic tastes: "A Duval and a Marshal treat of art anatomy, and Chapman on Physiology, a few books on art, a Ruskin, and Mythology, some books on French and one on German language, one of French history, and a variety of dictionaries, catalogue of the Louvre, a novel, a Century, a Lippincott, a Harpers and some illustrated papers—and room for plenty more." [7] Comfortably settled in a place he could call home and full of optimism about his prospects for a great future, Henri asked himself: "Who would not be an art student in Paris?" [8]

At the time that he and his friends enrolled, the Académie Julian was the largest, most popular private art school in Paris (Figure 8). Founded in 1868 by a minor painter and former wrestler Rodolphe Julian, the academy catered to foreigners, who often had trouble getting into the Ecole des Beaux-Arts, the official government school. Julian's was, for some, a relatively liberal alternative to the Ecole; for others it was a proving ground where they could master the skills needed to pass the Ecole's stringent entrance examinations. Significantly, in the late eighties the Académie Julian was the breeding ground for the group of Symbolist painters later called the Nabis—Bonnard, Vuillard, Denis, and Roussel—who met at the school while Henri was a student there. We have no evidence, however, that Henri mingled with them.

The Académie Julian offered a certain freedom from regimentation—a freedom that was decidedly absent at the Ecole des Beaux-Arts. The instructors permitted the students to work very much on their own and appeared

Figure 8. Studio at the Académie Julian, Paris, 1889. Photograph. Henri is seated at the far left in the second row.

only a few times to give criticisms. Moreover, the size of the school—some two hundred men—ruled out lengthy critiques on the work of each individual. To some, this was an advantage, not a drawback.

Rodolphe Julian was primarily an administrator who left the job of teaching to others. The faculty of the main school at 48 rue du Faubourg St. Denis —there were several branches—included Adolphe William Bouguereau and Tony Robert-Fleury, under whom Henri studied painting and drawing. A student of François Edouard Picot (trained in David's atelier) and winner of the Prix-de-Rome, Bouguereau was a highly successful academic painter who had earned an international reputation through his historical and religious canvases, which he showed regularly at the Salon. In the seventies and eighties he satisfied official as well as popular taste with his penchant for "literary" and moralizing subject matter. His style, like that of most academic painters of his time, was based on the masters of the Renaissance and Baroque periods revered by the classical tradition—with a heavy dose of realistic detail and seasoned by a sweet, sentimental mood. As a teacher he was a sincere and fair person who was considered great by many of his students. Henri, who shared this opinion at first, described him as "a little ball of a man," who was "soft of speech and gesture but appears to be a most decisive man at the same time." [9] His classroom manner was marked by his "bonhomme way, his sarcastical little laugh, his little round fat back and short arms, his long drawn sigh before an unhappy drawing, his 'pas mal, mais——'(not bad, but——), and his way of jumping about over the drawing here and there and picking out little planes." [10]

Tony Robert-Fleury also enjoyed a secure reputation as a painter of dramatic historical scenes, which he exhibited at the Salon, and like Bouguereau he had won his share of medals from the French government. A student of Paul Delaroche and Léon Cogniet, Fleury carried on the neoclassic traditions of David and Ingres in such paintings as *Le Dernier Jour de Corinthe*, which earned him a medal of honor in the Salon of 1870. Henri found him usually in a severe mood and characterized his criticisms as "direct, beautifully composed, quickly said." [11] Of the two, Bouguereau and Fleury, he preferred the former.

There have been many accounts of the academic training offered at the Académie Julian. One of the most revealing is that given by the Irish critic and novelist George Moore:

We went to France to learn to draw by the "masses," and there we heard of "solid painting," and we were told that all other painting was primitive and barbarous. The special temperament of the artist, we learnt, was nothing to the point; there was *la bonne peinture, la peinture au premier coup*, which was produced in such and such a way, and if we could not learn the trick, it was clear that nature had not intended us to be artists. And we were introduced to the nude model, propped up on boxes, or standing in a conventional pose, hand on hip. We were told to count the number of heads, and to mark them off on our paper; then with the plumb-line we were shown how to determine the sway of the figure. It drops through the ear, the right breast, the hip-bone, passing, let us say, through the heel. The leading measurements and general lines being thus obtained, note was taken how much of the body fell to the left and right of our plumb-line, and we were instructed to sketch in, drawing by the masses of light and shade. This was the way, and the only way, to learn to draw, we were assured; we needed not to think of anything but the studio model; the world in the fields and the streets, that living world full of passionate colour and joyous movement, was but an illusive temptation; the studio model was the truth, the truth in essence; if we could draw the nude, we could draw anything.[12]

The only break in the routine of working from the nude took place on Saturdays, when the students were asked to bring in compositions based on a subject (usually mythology or Biblical history) that Bouguereau had assigned the week before. These he criticized and ranked by number (1, 2, 3, and so on) according to their degree of excellence. Students receiving the higher numbers in the competition, or *concours*, were entitled to their choice of the best positions in the class for the following week. The models changed their pose once a week, and so the cycle went on throughout the year.

Henri liked the Académie Julian from the beginning; he was pleased to discover "the so much talked of 'atmosphere' here as thick as mud."[13] At the outset he made charcoal drawings from the model, which Bouguereau criticized severely at first, finding fault with the modeling and values. Unlike Eakins, Bouguereau rarely mentioned the action or "putting up" of the figure. Occasionally, Henri merited a "not badly put up" or "well enough"[14] from the master, who allowed that he improved with each figure he did. Driven by severe competition from excellent students all around him, Henri felt impelled to work. By contrast to Julian's, he observed, the assignments at the Pennsylvania Academy of the Fine Arts had been ridiculously easy, and while he retained his high regard for Anshutz, he wished that Hovenden had forced the students to work harder.

At Julian's, Henri occasionally turned to portraiture as a means of breaking away from the routine of studying the figure. He regarded the exercises in composition assigned by Bouguereau as "very beneficial" [15] and spent many hours outside of school practicing with such subjects as "the flight into Egypt" and "the sacrifice of Polyxena." Composition, as taught in the academies, was never Henri's forte, and his first attempts received low ratings. Through determined efforts, however, he often managed to earn a number regularly, though rarely a high one, in the Saturday *concours*.

Occasionally Henri succeeded in looking beyond the daily routine of hard work to glimpse a romantic, though naïve dream of his future as an artist:

I believe I could live here in this beautiful city as a home always. The art world is here, everything that is of interest in art and history is at hand. Only a step into any of the great countries—they are all at hand. I picture to my self a life of art study, tramps afoot into Italy, thro' France—into Switzerland, Germany—and on, sketching outfit on my back, stopping here and there to catch some fine old bit—visiting famous old places, picture galleries—picking up pebbles or sketching the ruins where gladiators fought, living now in the past, now in the present. A studio in Paris—big picture for the salon on hand—this dream I am indulging in, does not mean the desertion of America entirely. No, I shall always be an American and even tho' I did live here I should not be willing to do so without visiting the old place often—maybe I should want to return for good after a while.[16]

At first glance, there is little to distinguish Henri's aspirations from those of the mass of painters striving for fame within the academic mold. His artistic assumptions are those of a late nineteenth-century "romantic realist" who was stimulated by the moods of distant times and places, yet believed in concrete experiences in nature. There is no hint here, or elsewhere in his writings at this time, of a taste for the antiacademic rebels Courbet, Manet, Whistler, and the Impressionists. Nor is there any evidence that he might be dissatisfied with the Académie Julian; to the contrary, he was delighted with it. His only eccentricity was his penchant for the contemporary.

Shortly after entering the Académie Julian, Henri and his friends paid their first visit to the Louvre. Their survey of the collection, which left Henri greatly pleased, confirmed the impressions he had formed at the National Gallery. He still failed to admire Raphael, and Rubens' pictures still seemed to him uneven. As at the National Gallery, he was impressed by the Spanish painters Murillo, Ribera, and Velázquez and gave his highest praise to Rembrandt: "He stands with the modern painters untouched. Not only great for what he was—but for what he *is* as well!" Of the more recent (and academic) masters he praised Couture and Regnault and found Troyon's landscapes and scenes of cattle "wonderful." [17]

His visit to the Luxembourg Museum, the repository of recent paintings, left him overwhelmed by the excellence of the collection. The experience reinforced his belief that "the painters of the present day are the greatest that ever lived." [18] His greatest praise went to a renowned contemporary Russianborn painter, Vasili Verestchagin, a pupil of Gérôme's working in Paris. In a letter to his parents he heartily endorsed Verestchagin's conception of art, its moral bias, which could not be content with merely producing camera-copies of the subject matter, but instilled it with "sentiments that the photo could never produce." "Pictures today should be religious or moral," he asserted, "but the more advanced religion of the day of course." Henri felt that Verestchagin's style allowed the painter to make important statements about his subjects: "War has always been made glorious by literature and art and Verestchagin makes it horrible, ghastly, murder, and serves to teach us of what it really is, and that it should be avoided." [19] One of the first of the ethnographic painters, Vasili Verestchagin brought back striking pictorial records of life in the Near East and Central Asia, where he had painted for several years. These interests prefigure Henri's in kind, if not in locale. Much later the younger man was to discover a major source of subject matter in Indians and Mexicans of the American Southwest, gypsies, and Chinese-Americans.

The spring of 1889 was a particularly rich season for exhibitions in Paris. Accordingly, he paid many visits to the official Salon, which disappointed him, and to the world's fair—the great International Exposition. The latter fascinated him not only for the galleries of paintings by artists of the major countries of the world, but also for exhibits such as Edison's phonograph and the machinery for manufacturing paper, which interested him in the same way that Eakins had been intrigued by the giant American locomotive at the Universal Exposition of 1867. The paintings, of course, claimed most of Henri's attention. The Exposition opened his eyes to the art of the world, making him realize that there was something more than French painting to admire. He found the American paintings quite respectable and viewed the work of the Barbizon school with interest. But the greatest picture, in his opinion, was Bastien-Lepage's *Joan of Arc*. His liking for Bastien-Lepage marks a significant step in his developing taste for more contemporary means of expression, for although the recently deceased French painter was still more-or-less academic, he was considered "advanced" because he had utilized some of the lighter tones and broken color of the Impressionists.

Just as in Philadelphia, Henri turned to the theatre in Paris as a relief from the hard grind of studying art, though his busy schedule permitted few such diversions. He attended the Théâtre Français, as well as the variety shows, but his highest praise went to the Javanese ballet, which he saw at the International Exposition. The phenomenal grace and rhythm of the exotic Javanese dancing girls entranced him: "It was a new poetry of motion," he wrote. By comparison to Western ballet, with which he was already familiar, the performance seemed "weird, fantastic and fascinating." [20] This experience served to reinforce his faith in the dance as a major artistic medium, a conviction that persisted throughout his life, and nurtured his interest in non-Western forms of expression.

As a first-year student thoroughly engrossed in his work, he had little time to read, though he gladly received issues of popular literary and humorous magazines which his parents mailed from home. He did, however, manage to read Plutarch, Ralph Waldo Emerson's *Representative Men* and his early letters published in the *Century Magazine*, Thomas Carlyle's *Reminiscences of My Irish Journey*, and, above all, Philip Gilbert Hamerton's *Human Intercourse*. He considered Hamerton's book "one of the best things I ever read" [21] and admired the author's objectivity. Hamerton, an English painter and essayist, had been heavily influenced by Emerson, and *Human Intercourse* reveals a decidedly Emersonian bias in its plea for individualism. We know exactly what appealed to Henri from an excerpt that he copied into his diary and mailed to his parents—Hamerton's own testimonial of his debt to Emerson:

To me he taught two great lessons. The first was to rely confidently on that order of the universe which makes it always really worth while to do our best, even though the reward may not be visible; and the second was to have self-reliance enough to trust our own convictions and our own gifts, such as they are, or such as they may become, without either echoing the opinions or desiring the more brilliant gifts of others. Emerson taught much besides; but it is these two doctrines of reliance on the compensations of Nature, and of a self-respectful reliance on our own individuality, that have the most invigorating influence on workers like myself. Emerson knew that each of us can only receive that for which he has an affinity, and can only give forth effectually what is by birthright, or has become, his own. To have accepted this doctrine with perfect contentment is to possess one's soul in peace.[22]

This passage became the keynote of Henri's philosophy at that time and, as we can see in retrospect, for the remainder of his life as well. The year 1889 thus marked the beginning of his interest in Emerson's philosophy. When he returned to Philadelphia in the early 1890's, he was already preaching a decidedly Emersonian doctrine.

If Henri believed, in principle, that the individual artist should be true only to himself, as a student in Paris he was still willing to go along with the system by attempting to enter the Ecole des Beaux-Arts. Early in 1889 he and several friends decided to take the examination, although they knew it was very difficult, in the belief that, even if they failed, the experience would be good practice for their next try. For weeks, therefore, he studied the subjects he knew would be covered: history, anatomy, perspective, and architecture. When the appointed day in February arrived, he presented himself for the first part of the examination which demanded a charcoal drawing from the nude model to be completed in twelve hours. Hindered by a poor beginning, he was pessimistic about the quality of his drawing. His fears were well grounded, for his name was not posted among those who had passed, indicating that he had been disqualified from the rest of the examination.

There were, however, a few signs of encouragement during his first season at Julian's. Early in the winter Bouguereau awarded a "mention" to one of his drawings in the monthly *concours* and complimented him on the "honesty of [his] endeavor and rapid progress." [23] This praise gave Henri renewed confidence, but to keep his parents from becoming too optimistic, he told them: "The immense mountain that I am to climb to win any success appears before me with all its formidable aspect." [24]

At the end of the term at the Académie Julian, Henri and his four Philadelphia friends gave up the apartment they had occupied at 12 avenue Richerand so that each could go his own way. Henri and Fisher decided to take a small room together at 72 rue Mazarine, near the Ecole des Beaux-Arts, and to spend the summer at the village of Concarneau, a popular artists' resort on the Brittany coast noted for its varied scenery and picturesque peasant life. The summer plan appealed to Henri because living would be inexpensive and an accomplished Philadelphia painter, Alexander Harrison, whom he had befriended, had offered to criticize his work without charge.

Arriving at Concarneau in the middle of June, Henri and Fisher took a hotel room and rented a studio in the same building as Harrison's. The unspoiled Brittany countryside was a totally new experience for Henri and a relief from the stale atmosphere at Julian's. He was especially intrigued by the archaic peasant dresses with their collars and *coiffes* and found picturesque the Breton fisherwomen gathering shellfish on the beach, the sails in the harbor, and the antiquity of the walled town.

At Concarneau he divided his time between painting portraits and figures of the Breton peasants in his studio and studying light and color out of doors. In addition to sketching architectural motifs and views of the sea, he struggled with the challenging problem of painting a young girl posed on the beach under the blazing light of the morning sun. His approach to this work was basically Impressionist, a method for which his studies at Julian's offered little preparation. In working outdoors during the summer and in the studio during the remainder of the year (with occasional sketching trips to towns near Paris), he was conforming to a procedure common among students in the academies during the 1880's. But, as we shall see, he was gradually losing faith in the value of painting in the studio. Working spontaneously from nature pleased him greatly: "I'm never quite so happy as when I settle down to a sketch of a brilliant color subject when there is a strong sun and a nice sky—I forget doubts then. There is less science in my method but more heart and I generally pull out a better thing." [25]

During the summer, Henri experienced a moment of self-realization that decisively changed his attitude toward the art of painting. The incident was later recounted by Louis Bouché and William Yarrow:

One day while returning from work he passed a large granary. His eye was attracted by a crack in one of the walls which revealed an illumination. Surprised and curious, knowing that such buildings were usually kept dark, and seeing neither door nor window through which such a light might enter, he approached and placing his eye to the aperture saw that it was occasioned by a direct ray of the sun streaming through a small hole high up in the western wall. His attention, however, was immediately focused on a canvas leaning against a box. It was the study of a nude, crouching woman. He watched excitedly, for in it he seemed to see the solution of all his problems; the simple yet complete sequence of lines, the ever-changing modulation of ruddy flesh-tones, the whole painted apparently with a single broad brush-stroke which developed the form in all its details. As he stared the light gradually faded and the picture disappeared, but what he had witnessed remained with him many days. Later he had access to the granary and viewing the canvas under normal conditions, found it strangely lacking in all those qualities it had seemed to possess but it had served his purpose, for in it, achieved and definite, he had found the truth for which he had vainly sought.[26]

This incident, Henri believed, marked the beginning of his full-scale rebellion against the academic mode. It must have been crucial in the development of his art, for his work during the summer of 1889 followed the direction this vision revealed to him.

In August, Henri and his friends from the Anglo-American art colony decided to take several walking trips to see the picturesque towns and country-side around Concarneau. Sometimes sketching, sometimes examining old ruins, their hikes took them to Quimperlé and Pont-Aven, a village that supported an artists' colony populated primarily by Americans and Canadians. Here Gauguin and his circle had lived during the previous year. Although Henri and his friends spent the night in the Pension Gloanec, Gauguin's former headquarters, and visited a shop at Pont-Aven "haunted by the gaunt looking artists, impressionists and all," [27] we have no reason to believe that they came into contact with Gauguin, his followers, or their paintings. The young men did explore the town, however, and visited the studios of several American artists who showed them work that was very advanced by academic standards. These trips broadened Henri's approach by exposing him to a totally fresh environment as well as to paintings by other young artists in a variety of different styles.

His experiences in Brittany opened up many new possibilities for his development as an artist. He learned to respect the simple character of the Breton peasants, who lived far from cultivated urban society and are the spiritual brethren of the Indians, gypsies, Mexicans, and other members of the human family he painted so often in later years. The physical setting attracted him, too: Brittany was still virgin country, unspoiled by the encroachment of industry.

At the end of the summer Henri returned to Paris eager to start again at the Académie Julian; but he also promised himself time to study the paintings at the International Exposition, admitting, "I am ready now to learn a great deal from pictures." [28] To this end he enrolled in morning classes at Julian's and left the afternoons free for studies of heads, compositions, and visits to the Exposition. Pursuing this plan well into the fall, he settled into a regular routine: up at seven, breakfast at a *crémerie* near the Louvre, and then the long walk to the school. Following the afternoon's work, he and Fisher prepared dinner at home. Wednesday evenings were set aside to receive company so that the other evenings would be free for study or correspondence.

Henri was glad to find that his efforts impressed Fleury and Bouguereau much more favorably than they had during his first year. He also succeeded in winning quite a few numbers on his compositions in the weekly *concours de place*, ensuring himself good positions from which to draw the model. Many of the "big men," however, did not return to Julian's in the fall, and this disappointed Henri, since he believed that much of the school's value lay in what he could learn from the students.

He worked steadily at drawing and painting during the winter of 1889–1890 and enjoyed, as he said, "a long run . . . of very hard work and continuous progress without a collapse or falling back." [29] But, as he himself admitted, he was a slow worker, and always had been. Only by steady application to practice and study was he able to feel that he was making progress.

During the winter Henri and Fisher grew dissatisfied with their small, cramped quarters at 72 rue Mazarine and after a brief search rented an inexpensive studio nearby at 12 rue de Seine, where they could both work more efficiently. But his life in Paris was not given entirely to work. A gregarious person by nature, Henri always enjoyed the easygoing cameraderie of his friends from the American art-student colony. Many an evening he spent playing euchre or poker or attending impromptu studio parties with musical entertainment supplied by Haefeker's and Fisher's banjoes. Neither was he immune to the charms of the fashionable young women of Paris, both native and American, whose beauty he described in his letters to his family. Apparently his drive to succeed in art and his limited budget prohibited any involvement with them.

Although Henri continued to see his Philadelphia chums Haefeker, Grafly, and Redfield, he decided to take his evening meal with a group of new friends who gathered regularly at the Hôtel de Nice. His reason for joining them was more intellectual than gustatory; here he knew he would benefit from contacts with some of the strongest students at Julian's. As he expected, these meetings proved to be stimulating. During the meal the group engaged in long critical discussions of the arts, interspersed with jokes, on subjects ranging from the Prix de Rome to the merits of Byron, Burns, Milton, Shakespeare, Dante, Dickens, Zola, Daudet, and Victor Hugo. Realizing the benefits of these sessions, he began to give more time to open-ended discussions of art and philosophy with his friends in the privacy of his studio, thus initiating a practice that he maintained throughout his life.

Henri and his friends also amused themselves watching bullfights, joining in the all-night revelry of the Julian Ball, and attending the Comédie Française and the performances of dancers at the Exposition. Whereas in the spring he had been entranced by the Javanese ballet, during the fall he was no less fascinated by the grace and rhythm of the exotic, sensual displays of the Egyptian, Algerian, and Spanish dancers. He also enjoyed seeing Sarah Bernhardt for the first time. Always a connoisseur of fine drama, he was thoroughly captivated by her graceful movements and expression of deep feeling in *Joan of Arc*, a play that held "a great lesson for the art student." [30]

By this time, Henri's French had improved to the point that he could understand most of his teachers' comments without the aid of a translator. As an aid to learning the language, he began to read the novels of Paul de Kock, which he valued because they were full of ordinary, daily conversations. For the same reasons he read Emile Zola's *Nana*, followed by *L'oeuvre* and *Pot bouille*. Among American writers, he continued to delve into Emerson's *Representative Men* and read Bret Harte's *Captain Jim's Friend* and *Argonauts of North Liberty*. His reading of selections from Thomas Paine's *Age of Reason* impressed him, though he felt "we are past his object now. With Emerson we do not try to bring people to Reason by disproving the Bible, but by looking clear of everything straight at truth, and letting the big fact stand out for itself." [31] His interest in modern art was reinforced by the French periodical devoted to that subject—*La Vie moderne*—which he collected avidly, as much for the literature as for the illustrations. Founded by Renoir's patroness, Mme Charpentier, the magazine appealed to him because it celebrated themes from contemporary, everyday life as interpreted by Realist and Impressionist writers and artists.

He continued to work hard at painting early in 1890, though his spirits were dampened by a second failure in the entrance examination for the Ecole des Beaux-Arts and his inability to complete a portrait for the Salon. At Julian's his teachers consistently criticized him: "Not painted solidly enough. Planes uncertain. Too many little touches of indecision." [32] Yet he remained true to his goal of gaining a thorough foundation in art without giving in to cleverness, or "chic," to use the term then in vogue. "I'm content to plod along," he admitted, "and hope to do something good after a long time. 'Chic' is like a woman's fickle smile." [33]

His views about painting, however, were undergoing a significant change that reflected the increasing influence of Impressionism. During the winter he discussed Impressionism sympathetically with one of his more artistically advanced friends, who claimed him as a convert to the new style. "The summer work outdoors," Henri came to believe, "is of the greatest importance—it is then that the winter's grinding is put to a test, and the artistic faculties are cultivated. It is then that one studies to paint pictures." [34] In the spring he traveled to the tiny village of Brolles, near Bois-le-Roi, in the forest of Fontainebleau, where he again put his ideas into practice by painting directly from nature, as he had during the summer at Concarneau. Although his verbal comments about the landscape betray a lingering sentimentality typical of the Barbizon school, he adopted an attitude close to the Impressionists in executing his paintings. When he compared the work he brought back from Brolles with what he did at Julian's, he found the former much stronger. Looking over the last study he executed at school he vowed: "Will not paint like that again—more solid, fuller." [35]

Although Henri was now able to admire Millet, Impressionism, and Japanese art, his taste during the winter and spring of 1890 was still cast partly in an academic mold. It was the more liberal wing of the academy that he preferred, however, and he had little use for Bouguereau's commercially successful "swishy-swashy subjects in such swishy-swashy sentiments." [36] He was also suspicious of the poor academic work cluttering the Salons, which he visited repeatedly in the spring. (There were now two Salons—the "new" Salon under Meissonier's leadership having seceded in 1890 from the original, or "old," Salon associated with Bouguereau and his circle.) [37] The new Salon appealed to Henri more than the old, for there were fewer paintings and they were more tastefully arranged. Some of the artists who exhibited there—Sargent, Carolus-Duran, Puvis de Chavannes, for example—were relatively progressive, another reason why he was more sympathetic toward them.[38] In his comments on the new Salon, Henri showed that he was drawn to those artists who handled color and atmosphere skillfully. For Meissonier and others whose works were encumbered with microscopic details he had nothing good to say.

While he considered it his duty to attend the Salons, his innate curiosity and liberal outlook also impelled him to look tolerantly at the current avant-garde styles in Paris. He rebelled, however, at the Salon des Indépendants of 1890, a vast jury-free exhibition of radical, avant-garde art, which included Neoimpressionist and Symbolist paintings along with much incompetent work. Feeling that the insurgents had gone too far, he could not bring himself to identify with them, despite his increasingly advanced tastes. Henri Rousseau's work he compared to that of a little schoolboy; Van Gogh's conception of beauty aroused his skepticism, although he expressed an interest in talking with the artist as a "study of human nature." But he did realize that the show repesented a serious attempt to display new, nonacademic art: "It is no joke—it's life, human nature as seen in the extreme." [39]

Henri's comments on the exhibition show some acquaintance with Impressionist procedures ("Impressionist pictures should only be seen at a distance" [40]), as well as with the tenets of the recently established Symbolist-Synthetist group that had grown up around Gauguin in Paris and Pont-Aven. To his parents he passed along an account that a representative of the Pont-

Aven "impressionists" (that is, the Symbolist-Synthetists) had reportedly given of his method:

I go out and look about me and take in nature but I leave my paints at home. After I have been out and studied the nature about me for an hour or so I return home, take a rest, try to think of something else and forget all about what I have seen—then I am in proper condition to work and I get out my canvas and go to work in my atelier and paint my picture.[41]

Henri's exact reaction to this method is unknown, but he certainly did not adopt it immediately in his own painting. He could hardly have believed in 1890 that he would some day champion the work of Van Gogh and Gauguin, among other Postimpressionists, and would be a major force behind the first Exhibition of Independent Artists in 1910, which in turn influenced the Society of Independent Artists, founded in 1916 after the pattern of the Salon des Indépendants.

Although he could not follow the extremes of Postimpressionism, he had come to ally himself with Impressionism, which was still regarded as an advanced style, particularly among students in the academies. Impressionism symbolized the triumph of artistic innovation over academic tradition, and at this point Henri was more than willing to attack the defects of his teachers and the more conservative salon painters. His dream of success as an academic artist was fading rapidly, but in its place no clearly defined alternative had appeared.

Thus he entered a phase of life common to most young artists who cast their lot with the vanguard movements of their day—a phase dominated by uncertainty about themselves and their future. This uncertainty was compounded by the dissolution of the tightly knit group of friends who had accompanied him from Philadelphia. Fisher was called back to the United States to join his father's coal business; Grafly returned to Philadelphia to execute a statue of William Penn; Finney, still in Paris, had long since deserted the group to paint fashionable pictures on the right bank; Haefeker had decided to study in Germany. Though not one of the original five, Edward Redfield, a talented, fun-loving student from the Pennsylvania Academy, had become quite friendly with Henri during the year, and with the others' secession their ties were to become even closer.

Redfield became Henri's closest ally during their summer campaign at the Mediterranean port of St. Nazaire, near Toulon. The town and its environs appealed to Henri as a colorful site for painting out of doors, and he responded favorably to its beautiful palm trees and sunny, southern climate. After exploring the wealth of motifs along the Mediterranean coast with Redfield, he set up his easel and umbrella to tackle the problem of recording his impressions of color and value *en plein air*. At first he was troubled by the wind and the rapid changes of the sea, but through persistent efforts he managed to do several oil studies that satisfied him. Beginning with small, broadly brushed sketches, he eventually progressed to work on several larger landscape paintings. But he soon tired of prolonged work on the same canvas and, responding to the appeal of countless fresh motifs around St. Nazaire, returned to rapid sketching.

In both large and small works there was much of Impressionism in his approach to nature during the summer of 1890. He almost always painted out of doors, often under the protective shade of an umbrella, and conscientiously waited for the proper "effect" in the passing spectacle of nature: "One gets the effects by always working—and being there with sketch started at the moment that the good effect appears. Perhaps it will not then be too fleeting for one to grasp it." [42] In his diary, too, he often recorded his frustration when faced by constant changes in the weather, a common complaint of Monet and Pissarro. Occasionally he sketched landscapes with human figures, but following the Impressionist method, he executed them quickly—sometimes with a palette knife—under the full light of the sun. More often, he studied momentary effects in nature and tried to attain "freedom and color" [43] in his work. Even his visits to museums in nearby Toulon were motivated by a desire to discover how other nineteenth-century painters of the Midi, especially Dauphin and Montenard, had captured light and color in their canvases.

When bad weather prevented him from painting, he passed some of the time chatting in French with his many acquaintances among the townspeople, or he retired to his room to read Daudet, whose realism he admired, and Tolstoi's *Kreutzer Sonata*. He admitted that he did not understand or agree with all Tolstoi's conclusions, but he heartily endorsed the author's views that true religious progress should be guided by inner consciousness instead of external forms and rituals.

His painting went smoothly for two months at St. Nazaire. Then self-doubts and discouragement set in. He saw his friends, particularly Redfield, doing work he thought better than his own. And he was continually confronted by the dilemma of whether to paint colorfully and spontaneously like the Impressionists or to preserve the precise drawing, compositional order, and firm value structure he had been taught in Philadelphia and at the Académie Julian. In one painting—a landscape—he attempted, without success, to fuse both approaches. In his desire to solve the problem he fell back on the practice of making repeated oil sketches of the subject. His inability to "finish" a painting, his harassment by the winds of the mistral, and the increasingly dark, cloudy weather combined to plunge him into periodic spells of depression.

By the middle of October, bad weather had made regular painting out of doors impossible, his friends had left, and a mood of deep despair came over him. One ray of hope, however, presented itself: the possibility of a visit to Italy. Reasoning that it would be a mistake not to take advantage of the low rail fares from the south of France, Henri decided to make the trip: "I shall go there and spend enough time to study the world's greatest masters—the pictures and the sculptures that are held up as models by all our modern masters." [44]

The Italian Journey, 1890

After a brief excursion to Monte Carlo, where an evening's play at rouge et noir added 450 francs to his holdings, Henri proceeded to Rome by train, taking the coastal route via Genoa and Pisa, arriving at his destination on November 9. He spent the next fifteen days sightseeing and visiting museums, galleries, and churches. Following his Baedeker, he discovered most of the city's great Renaissance and Baroque paintings and sculptures, which he studied as carefully as his limited time permitted. Unquestionably the high point of his trip was his experience of Michelangelo's frescoes in the Sistine Chapel. These moved him to write:

It gives me new light[,] a new understanding of art. It will influence me—with this alone should I see no more I would be repaid for my trip—I can't describe— One feels himself in the presence of the most profound art, grandest conception, drawing, color, all—the color is magnificent.[45]

Henri spent hours by himself contemplating Michelangelo's ceiling, and as he continued to study it, his respect for the Renaissance master grew: "This ceiling so wonderful and so inspiring at once placed Michael Angelo on the pedestal that no copies or reproductions could do for me before." [46]

He was equally impressed by Raphael's Stanze. The frescoes were a revelation that forced him to revise his previous low opinion of the Renaissance master:

There is freedom, there is most beautiful color, such atmosphere, there is such masterly drawing (not so general as Michael Angelo—not in everything—but yet enough) and he has dealt so finely and so delicately—at the same time so strongly with his subject that he is to me a great old master—a wonderful artist.[47]

Unable to resist the lure of these masterpieces, he returned day after day to probe the secrets of Michelangelo's and Raphael's greatness.

His pilgrimage to the Roman galleries took him to the Doria Palace, where he admired Velázquez' portrait of Pope Innocent X: "He might have been painted five years ago. He grows greatly on one. He lives. And how he is modeled! . . . It holds a modest dignity that when once understood is all the more striking. I call it the best Velasquez I've seen." [48] After the Doria gallery he went to the Palazzo Colonna, where he found the finest pictures in Rome: "There is scarcely one that is not worthy of study. In the realm of portraits Titian, Tintoretto, and Veronese are all at their best." [49] The collections in the Barberini and Corsini palaces disappointed him, but the pictures in the Borghese Gallery "are all interesting and some are very great." The two outstanding canvases in that gallery were by Titian, his *Cupid Equipped by Venus and the Graces* and *Sacred and Profane Love:* "Its color is so luminous, so rich, so harmonious! It is marvelous. It is a very very great work. Color, compo—all." [50]

Fearing that he might never get to Rome again, Henri included in his itinerary the major monuments of classical and Christian architecture. Visiting the Forum, the Colosseum, the Pantheon, and other ancient sites was no chore, for he had come to Rome imbued with the romance of antiquity, thanks to early tutoring by his mother. Except for St. Peter's, whose immense space overpowered him, he could not respond favorably to Renaissance and Baroque interiors. Indeed, he attacked the more lavishly decorated examples as "cheap and gim-cracky." [51] A comparison that tells us much about his sentiments on this subject resulted from a visit to the relatively simple fifteenth-century church and monastery of S. Onofrio:

It's not pretending, very simple. Venerable. It's a relief to the gaudy grandeur down there below in the city. This old church has a charm grand St. Peter's lacks—a charm well worth the having, too—it's more the church of the old and humble follower of Christ. It's more simple [,] more genuine—I like it better." [52]

These views, of course, are not unexpected, coming as they do from a Protestant-reared American who had read Emerson. But they also reveal Henri's innate penchant for the genuine, simple, and unpretentious.

In his visits to the major architectural monuments in Rome, Henri was always careful to seek out the important paintings and sculptures that they housed, including Michelangelo's *Moses* in S. Pietro in Vincoli, which he regarded as "one of the most wonderful works of art in existence",[53] Pinturicchio's frescoes in S. Maria del Popolo, Raphael's frescoes in S. Maria della Pace, Michelangelo's *Christ with the Cross* in S. Maria sopra Minerva, and Baciccio's monumental ceiling decorations in the church of Il Gesù, "a masterly executed work—beautiful to look at." [54]

From the enthusiastic comments in his diaries it is clear that Rome was a profoundly enlightening experience for him. As a student who had spent his early years in America, he was driven by an insatiable desire to learn from the masterpieces of the past. But it was their formal and technical side that appealed to him; he paid little attention to the subject matter and original symbolic content.

On November 25, Henri left Rome for Florence. Toward the end of his stay, he had become jaded by repeated exposure to painting, sculpture, and architecture, and in his diaries we can almost hear a sigh of relief as he prepared to leave the city. When he arrived in Florence, he went directly to the Uffizi, where the masterpieces assembled there overshadowed anything he had seen in Rome. After surveying the collection rapidly, he crossed the Arno to the gallery of the Pitti Palace, where the endless walls of paintings made him exclaim, "It will take a lifetime to see all this!" [55]

Fortunately, he wrote detailed comments in his notebooks about his reactions to many of the paintings and sculptures he saw in Florence. At the Uffizi he marveled at the subtlety of Titian's color and simplicity of the effect in the *Venus of Urbino*. He praised, among others, Bronzino, Michelangelo, and Botticelli. Throughout his visits to the Uffizi, he still maintained his admiration for Rembrandt and Velázquez; yet he was tolerant, even appreciative, of the work of the pre-Renaissance Italian "primitives" he saw in Florence. Realizing that they should not be judged by modern standards, he called them "the first stepping stones of art taken by serious, deep feeling men, whom at first sight we do not appreciate but who, after study, earn our respect and now and then most profound admiration." [56]

His wanderings through Florence took him to the Museo Archaeologico, where he enjoyed the Egyptian and Etruscan antiquities, and to the church of SS. Annunziata to see Andrea del Sarto's frescoes, which he thought so fine that they rivaled Raphael's in the Stanze. At the Bargello he lingered over Donatello's sculpture, but concluded that he was not the equal of Michelangelo, whose Medici tombs moved him deeply as a work of art and as an expression of an enlightened Christian philosophy:

There's no creed, no petty glittering tricked out crowned Madonna—it is the Madonna of a nobler and a broader—a simpler mind—such a mother as might bear such a man as strove for light and truth and liberty, Christ. A man of mind and character who preached his philosophy fearlessly and never was the soft, meek, driveling character some men have painted him.[57]

This comment, of course, is more revealing of Henri than it is of Michelangelo. Typically, the former read into the art of the past those values which, as a nineteenth-century liberal, he cherished.

As the end of his stay in Florence approached, Henri realized that it had been an experience of inestimable value. He departed from the city reluctantly, for unlike Rome it had completely won his affection.

On the next leg of his journey, he traveled to Venice, where he responded enthusiastically to the city's color, which was evident despite the gloomy December weather. "I shivered but I was happy," he noted in his journal. "Venice is all I can ask—all pictures—by ways—palaces. . . . Everyone is picturesque—everywhere are artistic bits and motives for pictures."[58] S. Marco was his first stop; from there he moved on to the Doge's Palace, where he saw pictures by Titian, Veronese, and Tintoretto. The next day he went to S. Maria della Salute and the Academy, but the latter was so cold, he confessed, that the impact of the great Venetian masters was lost on him. This was his introduction to Venice: a three-day visit plagued by cold weather. But the city so impressed him that he decided to return the following summer.

Next he toured Milan. On his first day in the city, he raced to the Brera, where he gazed admiringly at Raphael's *Sposalizio* and Leonardo's *Head of Christ* (a study for the head of Christ in *The Last Supper*)—"the finest by far of all I've seen of Leonardo."[59] Then he hurried off to find that master's celebrated *Last Supper*. Its deteriorated surface disappointed him, but in spite of this he liked the work, finding much to admire in its composition and the sense of individuality in the heads. His brief stay in Milan allowed time for only one other major sight, the Cathedral. The Gothic interior pleased him immeasurably: "No church has ever been so noble, so fascinating [,] so truly impressive as this to me." [60]

While Henri was enthusiastic about much of what he saw during his trip to Italy, his character as an artist was already too well formed for him to become a convert to Italian Renaissance and Baroque art. In studying these works, he kept them at arm's length, so to speak. Important lessons were to be learned about how to put a picture together, and no finer examples of artistic integrity could be found. But Henri never became Italianate in his own painting and thinking. Even in his Italian diaries a definite "northern" or "gothic" current is evident; he consistently admired the Rembrandts he saw and praised the Milan Cathedral more highly than any other Italian building.

On December 16, Henri left Italy. He took the train from Milan to Basle and, after a long trip through the snow-covered countryside arrived in Paris two days later. He was delighted to be there again, for after living in Paris for two years it had become his second home.

Paris, 1891

A few days after his return, Henri rented a room where he lived alone—a studio was too expensive. It was a cozy, comfortable place in the house where Redfield lived, 1 rue Bourbon-le-Château, near St. Germain-des-Prés. He liked it better than any of his previous lodgings: "I have never felt more content in my life, with my den," he wrote. "I am like a lord in his castle up here, very content to be all by myself. I have lots to do and I am all the time busy." [61] A year or two earlier he would have been depressed by enforced solitude; but he had now become far less dependent on others for day-to-day companionship. As it was, he spent many of his evenings playing cards at Grafly's and Redfield's; occasionally he entertained them in his room or accompanied them to the Moulin Rouge, Folies-Bergère, the Chat Noir café, or the Eden-Concert. In 1891, Henri's circle of friends from the art-student colony in Paris grew in number, and he often took his meals or exchanged visits with a circle of some fifteen of them, including Ernest Seton Thompson (later a celebrated naturalist), Redfield, Calder, and Grafly.

For Henri the days of dutiful plodding in the academic tradition were over. He became more and more interested in exploiting Impressionism as a valid style of painting, experimented with pastels, and placed great value on his regular evening discussions of art, politics, religion, and the problems of mankind. Compared with these new interests, the Académie Julian could no longer hold his undivided loyalty. While he still prepared compositions for the weekly *concours* and realized the importance of supervised work from the model, he increasingly disagreed with Bouguereau and Fleury, who tried to dissuade him from his Impressionist leanings. The latter attacked his excessive use of violet in painting the model, and Bouguereau, seeing one of Henri's colorful studies, "drew a long breath and then gave me the devil. 'All those purples!***!' said I was going the wrong way." [62] Although Henri respected his teachers' opinions, he maintained:

I think I am nearer right than ever before. . . . It is a matter of color. Bouguereau is not a *colorist* either in combining color or reproducing it. His color is harmonious and in some cases very fine but he is never a *colorist* and as for reproduction of color, he never does that. It is always the same waxy, angel like color—just a little insipid—so from this I am not inclined to put the same confidence in his criticisms on color as in the other branches. [63]

Bouguereau's severe criticisms stimulated him, because he regarded his teacher's "*interest* . . . as the best sort of praise." [64] Responding to Bouguereau's accusation that he belonged to the "modern school," which would not last, Henri elucidated his views about art and nature in a revealing letter to his parents, which reflects a distinctly Emersonian bias:

One must work after the manner his own mind and nature leads [*sic*] him if he wants to "last"—what he says and does must be the result of his individual contact with nature—Ancient [,] modern and new schools will teach him but to last he must belong to none of them—[bound] by no creed. His nature may tend him so that the world will call him one of some set—if he inclines towards the New School—then he will be classed among them—but he to himself [illegible word] be free and follow only what nature dictates to his peculiar sensibilities. [65]

We have in this passage a trenchant summary of his philosophy as it evolved during his third year in Paris. And the germ of much of the advice he gave in *The Art Spirit* can be found in this early statement.

Henri also grew disillusioned with the Académie Julian because the quality of the class work had declined—and because he had developed better judgment. Early in 1891 he found himself the American who had been in Bouguereau's atelier longer than any other of his countrymen, and as such he was qualified to say: "The best of the old fellows are gone. The place which once seemed to reach the very utmost in everything, noise, work and smoke

[,] is no longer in its full bloom. The old leaders have been replaced by most inferior ones." [66]

The challenge of entering the Ecole des Beaux-Arts, however, still attracted him, and in February, 1891, he struggled through the examinations in drawing, history, modeling, perspective, and architecture for the third time. By the end of this ordeal he was exasperated by the uselessness of subjects such as history and architecture that seemed totally unrelated to painting:

When I am in need of these things I will look them up [;] until then I don't want to be worried more with modules and T-squares. I don't ever expect to paint Academic architectural historical subjects. I hope I may never have any more use for a T-square than a fiddler has—pure go easy unplumbed nature's enough for me.[67]

When he had given up all hope of being admitted, Henri learned that he had passed the examination. Surprised and pleased, he decided to attend the *cours de soir*, "where the work is very strong and where the best artists take turns at criticizing." [68] For the remainder of the year he divided his time between Julian's, where he painted in the mornings, and the Ecole, where he drew from the model and from casts of antique sculpture in the afternoons. Occasionally, too, he would spent Sundays sketching with his fellow students at St. Cloud, on the outskirts of Paris.

To rest and recuperate from the Beaux-Arts examination, he spent the first few weeks of March in Brolles, where he found many of his friends, including Redfield, Williamson, and Ernest Seton Thompson, in residence at Mme Deligant's inn. Here, in the forest of Fontainebleau, Henri's morale soared. He enjoyed himself thoroughly discussing "art, humanity, and other interesting matters" [69] with his companions and established a close alliance with Thompson, with whom he "talked art and nature until we became very strong friends." [70] It was through Thompson that he became interested in the utopian ideas of Edward Bellamy, whose *Looking Backward* was the theme of the group's discussions at Brolles and in Paris. Thompson sent him a copy of the book in the summer of that year.

Shortly after returning to Paris, Henri decided to submit to the Salon two of his paintings, *Les Rochers* and *Paysage*, landscapes painted at St. Nazaire and Brolles, respectively. Most of his friends had spent the winter painting Salon pictures; after two years of concentrated academic study in Paris, this was the normal course to follow. Acceptance meant official recognition for the aspiring young artist. As he said, "The success or failure of these first

'Salons' [referring to the paintings] is a turning point in life—it will make [a] grand difference." [71] He was apprehensive, however, when he learned how strict the jury would have to be, owing to the large number of artists who were *hors concours*—accepted without entering the competition. When the day of judgment arrived, Henri's work was rejected, along with that of many of his friends. Disappointed, he submitted the same pictures to the "new" Salon in the following month, but they were refused once again. His pride was undoubtedly wounded, but by 1891 he had built up enough self-assurance to continue working without the pangs of depression that had plagued him during the past two years.

If Henri was sometimes uncertain about the merits of his own work, there was little doubt in his mind at this time about whom he admired among contemporary French artists: Puvis de Chavannes, a rebel within the academic tradition whose work enjoyed a large following among the Symbolists, and, even more important, Albert Besnard. When Henri saw Puvis's murals at the Sorbonne, he described them as "the most complete, perfect beautiful deco[ration] I believe I ever saw—none excepted." [72] And Besnard he regarded as the greatest living French painter. Trained in the academic tradition under Cabanel, Besnard had skillfully taken over some of the tools of Impressionism and with his Salon paintings and murals had won phenomenal popular success. Scorned by the avant-garde in Paris, he earned Henri's praise for his Impressionist selectivity in painting the human figure—"his impressionism does not consist in peculiar technic but it is impressionism genuine." [73] From this point on, Henri allied himself increasingly with progressive movements in art, though with his devotion to portraits and the human figure he was never to become a full-fledged Impressionist.

Late in the spring of 1891 he gave almost unqualified praise to a series of Monet's *Haystacks* (exhibited at the Durand-Ruel gallery), thus revealing his close rapport with Impressionist landscape painting. Although he regarded the canvases as "demonstrations," he praised Monet's ability to capture the changing seasonal character of the landscape and found that the rough execution disappeared when the paintings were viewed at a distance: "What realism!—and too it is not brutal realism—it has the sentiment of nature which is never brutal." Monet had courageously opened new vistas in painting; in Henri's judgment, "all will be affected by the new light he has cast on the art of painting and painting will be the better for it." [74] But all Henri's lingering conservatism was not swept away immediately. He continued to visit academic exhibitions, and Dagnan-Bouveret's and Carolus-Duran's portraits still warranted his praise.

Although Henri's parents wanted him to come home in May, he talked them into letting him paint in Venice in company with Redfield until September. The picturesque quality of the city had attracted him during his visit the preceding winter, and in this sunny climate he hoped to paint the successful Salon picture that had eluded him the year before. Bidding farewell to his friends in Paris, he departed for Venice late in May. He soon met Redfield and arranged to rent a room next to his with a view on the lagoons below. The city still proved to be very much to Henri's liking: "Love and admiration for Venice grows—it is a wonderful and beautiful place, and a place full of things to paint." [75] He was also glad to be surrounded by a small group of congenial friends, including Redfield, a pair of Italian students from Julian's, and an older and rather eccentric American watercolorist, William Gedney Bunce, who offered the younger men some questionable "advice" about how to succeed in art.

At first Henri was afraid that he might succumb to the sentimental, dreamlike spell which Venice cast over him and fail to get down to work, but he soon collected himself and wandered about the city sketching a variety of architectural motifs. However, the indescribable, ever-changing hues of the city and its waterways often eluded his attempts to capture them in paint—a source of frustration for the young artist. For his larger works he painted on sunny days, which were all too rare; but he did not waste the typically misty days of Venice, drawing on them, too, as subjects for small oil sketches. His chief aim, we recall, was to produce a picture for the Salon, and to this end he started a painting of a young girl posed on the terrace of the house where he was living.

Venice was a romantic spectacle for Henri. He was captivated by the myriad sights and sounds of the city, especially the religious fetes and regattas with their highly colored sails and brilliant nocturnal illuminations. More than at any other time in the past he immersed himself in the life of the common people, spending many evenings observing their customs and behavior. His cultural life was limited to viewing Verdi's *Aïda* and reading Edward Bellamy's *Looking Backward*, Rousseau's *Lettre de deux amants*, and Lew Wallace's *Ben Hur*; as far as we know, he paid but one visit to the Ducal Palace to study the work of the old masters. His only regret was that he could not share the whole experience with a pretty girl: "One ought to be in love. That would make Venice perfect." [76]

By the middle of August, Henri had come closer to finishing a formal Salon picture than any other canvas he had ever done. He had abandoned the painting of a girl on the terrace and concentrated instead on a pair of Venetian women seated beside a window opening onto the sea. To establish the pose, he caught the models at a suitable moment while they were resting, a telling reflection of his taste for momentary actions as the basis for his art. But as August wore on into September he had still not finished the canvas, complaining that "it reminds me of a chromo— Has scarcely any of the qualities that I have studied so hard, that I have sacrificed so many other qualities for. It is terrible to look at the thing and see it so lacking in what I see and feel in nature."[77]

His summer in Venice was marked by a peculiar sense of frustration because he could not resolve the conflict between the two approaches to art that dominated his thinking. The urge to get into the Salon by producing a conventional, studied picture made him feel guilty about yielding to his strong natural impulse to seize the rich effects of color and light in small, rapidly executed oil sketches. It is no wonder that the Salon painting did not come off: the multitude of engaging visual experiences in Venice seduced him from any deep commitment to the ideals of the Salon. Henri's romantic and sensual side was thus nourished in Venice, though he probably viewed the summer as something less than successful because he could not produce a single polished painting that an academic jury would accept.

With the summer's work behind him he grew impatient to get back to Paris. But his return, he knew, would be only a brief intermission; his ultimate destination had to be the United States. In Paris he reunited briefly with those few old friends who still remained; most of the men at Julian's were *nouveaux*, completely unknown to him. Though he was anxious to see his family, he regretted leaving Paris. The city had been his home for almost three years; here, among congenial friends, he had thoroughly immersed himself in the bohemian life of the art student.

Three years abroad had decisively transformed Robert Henri. He had come to Paris from an important but provincial art school in Philadelphia, full of doubts about his future as an artist. He left France well trained in academic methods, familiar with Impressionist techniques, and conversant with the styles of the old masters and the leading modern painters. During the first year of his sojourn in Paris there had been little to distinguish him from the typical American student following the academic route to success. Only his strong taste for contemporary subjects and his realistic tendencies in art set him off from the crowd. The longer he remained in Paris, however, the more his taste for Realism and Impressionism grew, at the expense of the classical approach fostered by the academies. For Henri, Impressionism was a liberating influence, and he enthusiastically adopted many of its tenets. Similarly, his

64

taste in contemporary art shifted from the conventional Salon painters to the Barbizon school and such rebels within the academic tradition as Bastien-Lepage, Besnard, and Puvis de Chavannes. He studied Monet's paintings and thought highly of Dauphin and Montenard, who painted the landscape of the Midi in brilliant colors. Eakins, however, was remote from his consciousness, though he occasionally mentioned him in his diaries and discussed his work with two of the master's former pupils residing in Paris.

As an art student in Europe, Henri's judgment about the merits of other artists' work also matured. Intolerant at first about what seemed artificial in Raphael and Rubens, he came to understand that the value of their work lay in the unity of formal elements. His trip to Italy stimulated his interest in the "primitives" and in the masters of the Renaissance, particularly Michelangelo and Titian, and reinforced his respect for Rembrandt and Velázquez.

His European study had helped Henri develop rather catholic tastes in art. Yet underlying these varied tastes we may detect two major guiding principles, which are sometimes seen separately and sometimes together: a respect for the present world of actual persons and events, whether by modern painters or by earlier artists who were "contemporary" in their own time, and a belief that, in the process of translating the raw material of nature, the artist should impose on it his own feelings and interpretation, preferably with moral or religious overtones. Thus he opposed merely photographic naturalism as well as artificial history-painting. Moved by Millet's work, he said: "Nature for me every time. The realism, outward and *inward*." [78] Like Hamerton, Henri believed that the artist must observe and work from nature, but, unlike Ruskin, he thought that just as much should be learned from studying how other artists, both earlier and contemporary, had translated their experience of the subject in terms of paint and canvas.

If we may characterize Henri's artistic development as becoming increasingly liberal, then we can say the same about his political, social, and religious beliefs. Brought up in a liberal Democratic tradition, Henri cheered the party's victories while chastising the Republicans. And in discussions with his friends, he could be found defending the Indians in their bitter conflict with Custer's forces and condemning capital punishment, insisting that the culprits "should be treated with pity—and should be put out of the way in the gentlest manner." [79]

During the spring of his second year as a student in Paris, Henri witnessed the May Day scuffles of the citizenry with the police. He did not take sides, but the Socialist-inspired violence and disorder disturbed him because he feared a full-scale riot. And he had little sympathy with an Austrian student at the Académie Julian who he thought was "a nihilist or socialist—the dangerous sort." [80]

In his personal life, Henri thoroughly enjoyed the freedom of a bohemian existence: "There is a charm about this Bohemian life, this giving up of comforts and pleasures that other people think so indispensable, this living in the roofs of houses and being happy there in order that one may follow the nobler pursuits, and get the best of life." [81] Living on five hundred dollars a year, which his parents provided, Henri had little cash left over for luxuries, but this did not trouble him. In fact, one of his letters warns of the dangers of too great an attachment to money: "Money is only of use just so long as it feeds, clothes, and keeps a man comfortable—more than enough for that is superfluous. The American craze for amassing wealth is a brutal passion. A finer world would amass knowledge." [82]

Having been influenced by reading Tolstoi, Emerson, and Hamerton and witnessing the power of the Catholic Church in Italy, Henri rejected a religion based on convention and the repetition of outward rituals. "It is a pity," he wrote, "one cannot be an unquestioning believer. It would be so nice— would take so much responsibility off one's shoulders." [83] He rebelled, too, against the secular authority imposed by the Church, especially the seemingly unreasonable Sunday laws in England. And his experiences in Paris quickly swept away any lingering Puritan sense of modesty about the nude human figure. The innate frankness of the Parisians, plus his exposure to the life of an art student at the Académie Julian, gave him reason to complain of the false modesty about the female body that prevailed in the United States.

Henri was sympathetic to Christ as a great humanitarian and teacher, but, like Emerson, he found solace in nature, believing that the spirit of man— particularly the city-dweller—would be nurtured by association with the natural landscape. For Henri nothing matched the "real pleasure which one gets out in the *free* woods. It is as important to our lives as sunshine is to the lives of plants." [84] At Brolles he felt the impact of nature on his own being: "The walks in the woods grow more and more interesting all the time and . . . one can lose himself from the signs of humanity and enjoy a real wild woodland—full of mystery and sentiment." [85] Furthermore, he rejected the artificial "glitter and gold" seen at such royal palaces as Fontainebleau, following an Emersonian and nonaristocratic belief that "the hunter in the woods with his hut should be the happier man. His house is nature—and the decorations are God's own works." [86] There was also in Henri's philosophy a good measure of Emerson's spirit of self-reliance, in which the individual must utilize his native talents to the highest degree: "I think it is every man's duty to make the most of the mind and body God has given him—so I'm in for the struggle and if I fail to get glory I will at least have the satisfaction of having done all that was in my power to do." [87] He unquestionably exercised a measure of leadership within his circle of friends by virtue of his almost religious devotion to art, his deep involvement with recent literature, history, and social thought, and the firm conviction with which he expressed his opinions. At the same time, his diaries and letters indicate that he derived much from discussions with his fellow art students. Recalling their many talks, which must have constituted a liberal education for the group, he confessed: "I have learned from the others much that I did not know and they have made me haul together and *know* what was already lodged but unlinked in my mind." What did they discuss? "Art, life, chaff. One relieves the other." To Henri some great thought or truth, difficult to name, lay at the basis of all things—"the theory of painting and the theory of life and of all good things is the same" [88]—and it gave him the greatest satisfaction to delve into these questions in the company of his friends.

It is not surprising that he should occasionally turn to his associates for counsel, because in the competitions at the school and for the Salons they often surpassed him. Fortunately, by the end of his three-year stay in Paris, he had also learned to have confidence in his own aesthetic judgments, even in the face of his friends' successes. Though candid in his opinions of his contemporaries' work, he never begrudged their accomplishments. Indeed, he was usually sympathetic to, and proud of, any American who won recognition by the French.

Henri could look back with satisfaction on three years of hard work studying art, a period in which he tried to probe every resource that France and Italy offered. He had no illusions that his study abroad had made him a finished artist. At this point he was not even certain of his ultimate success, believing that only time would tell: "At present I feel that I have a possibility as a student. There is promise in the work—but it is only study, and as yet I can do nothing beyond that—study." [89] Henri's modesty about his progress was admirable but exaggerated. At twenty-six his achievement in the arts surpassed that of most of his compatriots of the same age, if we judge him not by the standards of clever, fashionable, academic painting, but in terms of his deeper understanding of the nature of art and its underlying philosophy. In France, of course, he was justified in feeling overwhelmed by the excellence of the art and artists around him; but to his friends in Philadelphia, as we shall see, he seemed a fully developed painter ready to take up his position as leader and prophet.

5

Life and Work in
Philadelphia, 1891-1895

AFTER VISITING his parents in Atlantic City, Henri decided to establish himself in Philadelphia, where he planned to paint and continue studying art. He moved in with his brother Frank, who had graduated from Jefferson Medical College in 1889, had married, and was successfully practicing medicine. In Philadelphia, Henri re-established his ties with the Pennsylvania Academy of the Fine Arts and renewed old friendships with his teachers Anshutz and Kelly and with former students, including his Paris companions Grafly, Redfield, Coleman, Parker, and Fisher. Here, too, he struck up a close friendship with Henry McCarter, an avowed Impressionist recently returned from Paris and now teaching at the Academy.

Study, Painting, and Teaching

Henri believed that he still had a long road to travel as an art student, and accordingly in early December he entered the classes of the Academy. Here he studied under Robert Vonnoh, among other teachers. Vonnoh had joined the faculty in 1891, the year Henri returned, and, with his Impressionist leanings, represented one of the more progressive currents in American academic painting during the early nineties. Many years later Henri was to look back on Vonnoh as a good teacher, but, as we shall see, he rebelled against Vonnoh's version of Impressionist painting.

At the school, Henri's work immediately earned the approval of the faculty and students; but he was not unduly swayed by this favorable reception: "I know from experience that my strength is only made by the absence of strength about me."[1] Looking over the work he had done in Europe, Anshutz and Kelly were quite complimentary, and Kelly suggested that he submit several of his sketches to the forthcoming exhibition at the Academy. Naturally, Henri was flattered by this praise, but realized that it was "productive of a large head."[2]

Once he was settled in his brother's home at 628 North Sixteenth Street, Henri's regular routine consisted of painting at the Academy in the afternoons and drawing there, often from the antique, in the evenings. He soon became deeply involved in the artistic life of the school, serving on the jury and hanging committee for the students' spring exhibition and showing pictures at the Academy's annual exhibition in the winter of 1892. The Impressionist style employed by Henri and several other younger artists in the exhibition—Kelly, Frank W. Benson, Edmund C. Tarbell, and Henry McCarter—placed them at the center of a bitter controversy with the traditional painters, some of whose canvases had been rejected by the jury. Many critics and artists were agitated, too, by the prominent display of a group of apparently incomprehensible landscapes by Claude Monet. Henri was branded an Impressionist, and his high-keyed work, he reported, was hung alongside Monet's: "It's rather a lucky thing," he added boldly. "I don't care how much kicking they do . . . the more noise the better, and being in it I am in it."[3] One of the more conservative reviewers obliged by declaring that Henri's pictures (*Venetian Canal* and *Venetian Girl*) showed "faulty exaggerations of an extreme mannerism in color."[4]

When the excitement died down, Henri had an opportunity to assess the public's response to the exhibition, and his verdict was disheartening. Philadelphia, needless to say, was completely different from Paris, as he soon discovered, residing, as he did, in "this miserable place where art is the least interesting thing in the world." Although *he* found the show stimulating, he observed, "Philadelphia people care and know so little about it that if it were not for the nudes to get shocked at they would never know an art exhibition was on."[5] The apparent hopelessness of the struggle of the young artist for recognition in Philadelphia, typical of many American cities in the 1890's, weighed heavily on Henri: "There's no wonder Philadelphia artists are lifeless—lack of public interest makes them ask themselves if it is not an idle fancy that theirs is a great art—and perhaps some begin to wonder if their lives are not wasted. How different in Paris where the Artist is the *Great Man*."[6]

The city slowly awoke to his presence during the spring of 1892. He was awarded a commission to paint a group of murals in the Chapel of Our Lady in the Episcopalian Church of the Evangelists, on Catherine Street below Eighth. The rector, Dr. Henry H. Percival, a cultured amateur of the arts, had traveled and lived in Italy and, in his recently erected basilican-style church, hoped to recreate the spirit of the Romanesque ecclesiastical architecture of Tuscany. Henri decided to adopt his decorations freely from Benozzo Gozzoli's frescoes in the Palazzo Riccardi in Florence in order to make them harmonize with the interior. On the southern wall he painted an original composition, *The Flight into Egypt*. This was his first and only venture in religious painting and, as far as we know, the only mural paintings he carried out. That they succeeded as well as they did may be the result of Henri's still fresh memories of his Italian journey.

In the spring of 1892, through the influence of his friend McCarter, Henri's services as a teacher were requested by Miss Emily Sartain, principal of the Philadelphia School of Design for Women. Although he had been looking forward to returning to Paris in the fall, this opportunity forced him to think seriously about postponing the trip. He reasoned that, as a teacher, he would be assured of a financial footing—financial independence was always one of his major concerns. But the lure of Paris remained, and he did not decide to accept the post until he had discussed it with his family. Finally, in June, he agreed to remain in Philadelphia to teach three mornings a week at the School of Design for Women, beginning in the fall of 1892. The decision launched his career as one of America's most influential teachers.

After having worked conscientiously on his murals for the Church of the Evangelists in the late spring and early summer, he was anxious to get out into the country to do some pictures for the exhibitions of the coming winter. He realized, however, that he would have relatively little time to paint out of doors owing to the impending demands of teaching in September; so far as we know, he completed only two landscapes of Atlantic City during the summer.

The Philadelphia School of Design for Women was America's first school of industrial art established for women. Founded in 1844, it had earned an excellent reputation under the energetic and progressive leadership of Emily Sartain, friend of Thomas Eakins and daughter of John Sartain, a noted engraver and former officer of the Pennsylvania Academy. Although the school offered courses in decorating china, industrial design, and the like, there was a full curriculum in painting, modeling, and drawing, and the faculty included three of Eakins' former students, including his close associate, the sculptor Samuel Murray. At the beginning Henri taught classes in drawing from the antique, anatomy, crayon portraits, and composition; later a course in portrait painting was instituted.

A born teacher, Henri enjoyed immediate success at the school. Although he was confined largely to routine instruction in the fundamentals of drawing, his weekly classes in composition gave him an opportunity to stimulate his students' imaginations. Following the practices of the Pennsylvania Academy and the Académie Julian, he required his pupils to make original sketches based on themes announced in advance, though he later broke from tradition in allowing them to choose their own subjects. Themes ranged from Biblical stories and fairy tales to the works of Poe and Maupassant and were executed as rough sketches in charcoal. Although no students' notes from the period have come to light, Henri's aims in teaching at this time were recorded in several articles based on interviews with him. One reporter, writing about the composition class, observed: "The aim has been to bring all that is noble out of a composition, aiming as high as possible, and striving never to let anything commonplace pass; not to finish up the work by putting in the small details, but to give a suggestion to make one feel the subject, and besides all this, to make a picture that will be as beautiful without the literary adjunct as with it." [7] From this account it is clear that in his early teaching he discouraged the tight drawing and finish typical of such academic masters as Bouguereau and Gérôme and placed the emphasis instead on devising formal arrangements that would underline the emotional content inherent in the subject. Significantly, he was not satisfied with mere storytelling; his pupils' sketches had to stand as artistically valid compositions, independent of literary associations. Even in his teaching of the antique class, a dull chore by usual standards, he encouraged the students to approach drawing in more than a factual way; one reporter, writing about the antique and portrait classes, noted that they were "rapidly advancing, the work in both cases being free from detailed treatment, but, instead, looked at in the biggest, broadest sense." [8] One of his students recounted in more detail the unusual nature of his teaching:

His lectures are spiritual as contrasted with the material view of art. . . . He also tries to put something of the sort into his "antique" teaching, but it is either below my ken or so far above it I can't reach up. . . . He told me the other day he liked the intellectual grasp I had of the subject—a bust—and always liked the spirit in which I saw the cast, but that I did not always draw what I betrayed to him (in words) that I had seen.[9]

Henri supplemented his teaching at the School of Design by conducting summer classes in landscape, an area that he was exploring in his own painting. The first of these was held at Darby, Pennsylvania, in June, 1893, shortly after the close of the school's spring term. Here his students—chiefly young women—were expected to work out of doors, according to his belief in the plein-air methods of the Impressionist painters. Criticisms were given for "the general benefit of the class," [10] an early statement of what would become Henri's characteristic method of teaching in later years. Although he urged his pupils to study drawing before taking up oils, he must have encouraged his summer students to combine their knowledge of chiaroscuro with the intense color-sensations typical of the Impressionist mode of vision, since one writer reported that the work of the class was "excellent, there being brilliancy of color and light, truth of values and a good choice of subjects." [11] In his summer teaching Henri undoubtedly guided his students along the lines he followed in his landscape paintings, which at this time were often in high-key colors, but were based, more than was Monet's work, on a "correct" framework in drawing.

After the conclusion of his Darby class, Henri traveled to Avalon, a seaside resort on the New Jersey shore, which was promoting a Chautauqua-like summer cultural program. Along with courses in literature, science, and education, the Avalon Summer Assembly offered training in art, and Henri had agreed to serve as "instructor in oil," teaching an outdoor sketch class, along with his own private class, three afternoons a week. Here, on the sunny beaches of Avalon, Henri's pupils painted from nature. Although he started with only a few students, by the end of July he was able to announce that his class was flourishing.

Henri also exercised his talents as a teacher during the informal gatherings of a Philadelphia group called the Charcoal Club, a cooperative composed of forty-three artists who were, or had been, students at the Pennsylvania Academy of the Fine Arts. Its headquarters were located in a photographer's studio on North Ninth Street. The Club had been established in March of 1893 as a result of a meeting held in the studio of the illustrator John Sloan, whom Henri had met late in 1892. One of the reasons for its founding was to combat the high cost of tuition at the Academy—1893 was a year of financial panic and depression in the United States. Three nights a week the members drew from the nude model; the remaining nights were devoted to sketching. Every Monday evening the members submitted their work in composition—based on such subjects as Dawn, Spring, and Ophelia—to be judged by all present, the best work being selected by the vote of the club. As the Phila-delphia *Times* reported: "Criticisms are freely given and the interchange of ideas kindles and sustains a lively interest." [12] There were no instructors. However, Henri, who was president of the club (John Sloan was secretary and the illustrator Joseph Laub was treasurer), periodically commented on the group's work, as did Sloan.[13]

The Charcoal Club's role was not purely educational. The studio served as the setting for the revelry of the high-spirited members of the club, who fre-quently held small banquets, with improvised music and entertainment, in connection with exhibitions of the group's work. Though far from France, they tried to infuse the studio life of the Quaker City with some of the *esprit* of the Parisian ateliers. These efforts, however, were short-lived; at the end of the summer the Charcoal Club disbanded, never to meet under that name again. But the close ties between Henri, Sloan, and their friends from the Academy and the Philadelphia newspapers were to be renewed in the fall of 1893, when Henri established a weekly open house in his studio.

Although he had secured a studio of his own at 806 Walnut Street in the fall of 1892 (beginning in October, 1893, he shared it with Joseph Laub), the responsibility of teaching five mornings a week and continued study in the evenings at the Academy left him little time to paint. Thus his artistic output in 1892–1895 was relatively small. In this period he executed several portrait commissions and painted a few likenesses of his friends and various members of his family. He also hired a Cuban gypsy to pose in the studio and occasion-ally painted behind the scenes at the ballet. During the summers he executed landscapes, primarily of subjects at Atlantic City, where he often visited on weekends or when the school was not in session. His most productive summer was that of 1894, which he spent painting in Concarneau, France, free from the responsibilities of teaching.

Despite his limited output, he managed to scrape up enough work to show in the regular exhibitions of the leading art organizations of Philadelphia—the Academy of Fine Arts and the Art Club—as well as the World's Columbian Exposition in Chicago. On the whole the critics responded favorably to his work, and he was regarded as one of the city's promising young artists. The critics' only reservations were brought on by Henri's Impressionism, a style that was anathema to the more traditional writers on the city's newspapers. And at the hands of the conservative jury of the Art Club, his and other works of the "new school of idea[,] color and noble sentiment" [14] were skyed" (hung well above eye level) on the gallery walls.

Henri continued to study the work of contemporary and earlier artists, both of the Western world and the East. We know that he was a regular visitor to important shows held in Philadelphia, took his class to the Widener Collection in that city, and traveled to New York occasionally to see exhibitions of old and modern masters. In 1894 he considered paintings by the American Impressionists Theodore Robinson and John H. Twachtman "agreeable" and admired the work of Arthur B. Davies, whom he had come to know through the critic and author Sadakichi Hartmann and who was soon to become his good friend and an influential member of the Eight. He found visits to the Metropolitan Museum most enlightening and spoke of the pleasure he had in viewing the Tanagra figurines, Manet's *Boy with Sword* and *Girl with Parrot*, and the paintings by Rembrandt, Hals, and Van Dyck.

The pictures Henri saw at the National Academy, on the other hand, thoroughly disgusted him and moved him to denounce the traditional approach of the academic artist: "Oh! What abyss. There was good there[,] too[,] somewhat repeated from the past, but what [an] array of ignorance, presumption[.] Old academicians—aristocracy of art—art even is not free—liberty only a dream[.] Man must think[.] Man does not[.] When he does[,] then he is free. Out with these schools, these cemeteries of natural art instincts! Galleries of imitations[,] fads! Commonplaces!" [15] The situation in the Academy that engendered these bitter accusations deserves some comment, since that institution was increasingly to become the target of Henri's attacks in the early 1900's.

Founded in New York in 1826, the Academy had become the most influential art organization in the country by the middle of the century. As the first professional organization of American artists, it fulfilled a dual role: it conducted an art school and it presented annual exhibitions. Shortly after the Academy was established, the officers installed a jury of selection to judge the works acceptable for the exhibitions. There was nothing wrong with this method, in principle. But as the Academy grew into middle age in the latter part of the century, the jurors (academicians themselves) tended to perpetuate their own approach to art, essentially ignoring the rising generation of American artists. Conservatism alone might have been excusable; when combined with absolute power over the fate of the young artist, it became intolerable.

In his violent denunciation of the Academy, Henry called for a reform not only in art but in intellectual and social attitudes as well, linking conservatism in painting with aristocracy, lack of freedom, and thoughtless adherence to past modes of behavior. What he proposed, in this revolutionary frame of mind, was a return to non-Western art, especially from early civilizations, to serve as an antidote to years of accumulated academic tradition. "More art," he wrote, "on a page of good Japanese rice paper than on yards and yards of Academy canvas. Back, back to Japan, to old Indian vases, to Egyptian hieroglyphs." [16] In embracing Japanese art, along with that of India and Egypt, Henri followed a course which closely parallels Gauguin's interests at the same time. Both rebelled against the excesses of academism and had sought new and more direct means of expression outside the timeworn traditions of European art. Gauguin, as is well known, incorporated elements from these exotic styles in his own work; for Henri, except for a brief period of Japanese influence, these were styles to be admired, not imitated.

In the fall of 1893, Henri's interest in oriental art was kindled once again— he had discovered Japanese art in Paris in 1890—through a trip to the World's Columbian Exposition in Chicago, where he saw the famous building erected by the government of Japan, the Ho-o-den, or Phoenix Hall, which was profusely decorated with Japanese paintings and screens. At the exhibition he also visited the Java Village, with its displays of native costumes and decorative arts, as well as the Javanese theatre, where he saw the dancing girls perform in a spectacle that must have reminded him of the International Exposition of 1889.

At this time Henri served as host to the noted Japanese artist and lecturer Beisen Kubota, a representative of Japan at the Columbian Exposition, who gave a demonstration of freehand drawing in India ink at the School of Design and visited Henri's studio several times. Kubota also spoke at the Academy of the Fine Arts, and here elucidated the aesthetic and technique of Japanese painting, emphasizing the role of harmony and balance in art. For a brief period in the mid-1890's Henri's work reflected the direct influence of Japanese art; from Kubota he and John Sloan learned to carry around a brush and bottle of ink to make on-the-spot sketches.

Henri and His Growing Influence

Robert Henri was ideally suited to become the leader of a small group of talented Philadelphia painters and illustrators, for he had been a model student at the Pennsylvania Academy and had had three years of intensive study in Europe. Meeting at a weekly open house in his studio (Thursdays at first, then Tuesdays), those who were interested could absorb his philosophy or bring their work for criticism (Figure 9). Discussion within the group was encouraged, but Henri ultimately held the floor with his eloquent and impassioned discourses on art and life. John Sloan, who attended these gatherings regularly, later evaluated their impact on himself and his friends:

In Philadelphia in the nineties, there was a group of newspaper artists, plain and rather normal young men making their livings as craftsmen—and we became painters because Robert Henri had that magic ability as a teacher which inspires and provokes his followers into action. He was a catalyst; he was an emancipator, liberating American art from its youthful academic conformity, and liberating the individual artist from repressions that held back his natural creative ability.[17]

The meetings in Henri's studio usually were attended by from four to twenty young men, and in addition to John Sloan, William Glackens, and Everett Shinn—and sometimes George Luks—the group included Grafly, Calder, Redfield, Breckenridge, Elmer Schofield, and the illustrators James Preston and F. R. Gruger, among others. Some of the newspaper illustrators attended regularly, but those who had no desire to be real artists dropped out quickly.

Henri was unquestionably the leader in these meetings; the group gathered "to listen to his talks on art and life, occasionally disputing a point but never arguing with him. He was the master, in fact he had been called 'the old man' from the time he was nineteen." [18] The arts—painting, music, and literature —were the chief subjects for discussion, along with politics and ethics. In addition to talking about others' achievements, Henri and his friends were vitally concerned about the role of the artist in America. Believing that serious painters should not try to seek financial success through their art— perhaps because his own work sold poorly in the nineties—Henri championed Emerson and Whitman as models. As Sloan later recalled:

We came to the realistic conclusion that an artist who wanted to be independent must expect to make a living separate from the pictures painted for his own pleasure. We could attack the art academies and public taste with freedom honestly earned. And as we began to ask the right to exhibit our own work, we started to defend the rights of others to that same privilege.[19]

Whitman and Emerson (along with Thoreau) had emerged as Henri's idols in the mid-nineties and, as Joseph J. Kwiat has shown, served as the basis for many of his ideas, which in turn were promulgated in his weekly studio

Figure 9. Henri and his friends in the studio at 1717 Chestnut Street, Philadelphia, c. 1893–1894. Photograph. From left to right are Grafly, Henri,
Gruger, Glackens, Sloan, Smith, and Shinn.

sessions.[20] From Whitman and Thoreau, "Henri carried on the spirit of free-thinking and belief in individual expression, hatred of orthodoxy and suspicion of institutions." [21] Clearly, it is but a short step from the teachings of these two great American thinkers to the philosophical anarchism that Henri espoused beginning in the early nineties (he was never a believer in violent anarchism). Sloan, particularly, was strongly influenced by Henri's preaching of this philosophy, but he was later unable to convince his mentor about the advantages of socialism. Although Henri had once (in 1892) admired the reasonableness of the Socialists' platform, he would have little to do with the party or its tenets.

In the nineties Henri and Sloan and their circle revealed little social consciousness of the world around them. Their primary concern was with their own individual struggles to become artists and to live and paint free from academic restrictions. Although Sloan and his newspaper colleagues were interested in various types of socialism and he and Henri discussed the subject with their Socialist friend J. Horace Rudy, whatever radical ideas they entertained at this time were "on a purely idealistic plane and our direction was primarily skeptical." [22] Under the influence of Henri's philosophical anarchism—which was undoubtedly reinforced by his reading of Bakunin—the group remained aloof from the labor movement and Populist ideas. Sloan pointed out, apropos of the muckraking movement and reform in city government, that they "took no part in these things and were little interested." [23] Edward Bellamy's *Looking Backward* and Henry George's single tax theories were discussed, along with art and religion, but the ideas were approached in a spirit of inquiry rather than in terms of practical application. "We had one cause," Sloan maintained, "art—and life, and were thinking about painting more than we had time to practice it." [24]

We have no record of the content of their religious discussions. But we know that, impatient with sentimentality, Henri "pulled [Sloan's] religious tooth" [25] and was skeptical about the value of organized religion, probably as a result of his reading *God and the State*. He introduced this book—the work of Bakunin, a professed anarchist and Marx's great adversary—to Sloan in the nineties, and, as the latter confessed later, it quite finished any religious illusions he still had.[26] Though raised as an Episcopalian, Sloan had already begun to drift away from a belief in the supernatural through his interest in Darwin's theories and, with his friends, had responded indirectly to Robert Ingersoll's ideas on evolution, which were in the air. (It is interesting to speculate on the extent to which Ingersoll influenced Henri to become an agnostic.

Henri does not mention Ingersoll in his published writings, but his 1928 diary records his sympathy with Ingersoll's antireligious views.) [27]

Though many serious discussions took place in Henri's studio, they were relieved by the boisterous stag parties in which he and his friends from the Academy staged amateur theatricals and burlesques in the manner of Gilbert and Sullivan. Such farces as *Twillbe, The Widow Cloonan's Curse,* and *Sylvester Warren Atkinson, or Soaked in Sin* from the pen of Charles S. Williamson were acted out once a year, when the studio was converted into an improvised theatre. For these productions Sloan painted the sets and Henri and Glackens prepared the costumes and make-up. Sloan conveyed the flavor of these merry performances in his recollections of *Twillbe,* their satirical version of Du Maurier's *Trilby*:

I had enormous false feet instead of the delicate little ones for which Trilby was famous; and a Burne-Jones wig. Sang "Sweet Alice Ben Bolt" in my best falsetto. My sister Marianna had made a dress for me with a Watteau pleat to mark the front, which I got on backwards and tripped over all the time. The mistake in dressing brought on other difficulties. I can remember the serene air with which Henri as Svengali kicked my false fronts into the wings, when I jumped on a table at the sight of a mouse. And we had some remarkable mosquitoes made of balloons that were manipulated like marionettes. . . . The audience was provided with beer and crackers, and there was more time devoted to intermissions than the play itself, which was part of the party.[28]

Henri invariably played a leading role as a comic. Such evenings of healthy ribaldry were made to order for his talents, for they let him combine his innate sense of satirical humor with the drive of a frustrated actor to perform on stage, even if it was before a captive audience.

Of those who gathered in Henri's studio for his weekly open house, four artists working for Philadelphia newspapers—Sloan, Glackens, Shinn, and Luks—were destined to gain recognition as painters and as future members of the Eight. Though these talented young illustrators had studied at the Pennsylvania Academy of the Fine Arts, they did not, at first, aspire to careers as serious artists. But Henri continually urged them to express themselves in paint, if only in their spare time. His innate personal magnetism and inspiring devotion to the cause of art were readily communicated to the circle of illustrators; as Sloan once said: "Henri could make anyone want to be an artist." [29] Who were they—this group that might be called the Philadelphia Four?

Born in Lock Haven, Pennsylvania, John Sloan moved to Philadelphia with his family when he was six. He early displayed a taste for art and literature, so it was appropriate that after attending Central High School, he should gravitate to the firm of Porter and Coates, dealers in books and prints, where he worked as an assistant cashier at the age of sixteen. Three years later he became a commercial artist, first designing Christmas cards, match boxes, and bookmarks for the firm of A. Edward Newton and then working on his own as a free-lance artist while attending evening drawing classes at the Spring Garden Institute, a Philadelphia trade school. Shortly afterward he enrolled in Anshutz' night class at the Pennsylvania Academy of the Fine Arts, where he learned to draw plaster casts. Bored by this type of training, he lasted only one season. In 1892 he was hired by the Art Department of the Philadelphia *Inquirer*, thus beginning a career as a newspaper artist that was to continue until 1903. It was in the year he joined the *Inquirer* that Sloan met Henri.

William Glackens was born and raised in Philadelphia and, like his friend John Sloan, attended Central High School, receiving his degree with the class of 1888. A born draftsman endowed with an exceptional visual memory, he found his niche after graduation as an artist-reporter for the Philadelphia *Record*, the *Press*, and the *Public Ledger*. From 1892 to 1894, while employed by the newspapers, he enrolled as a part-time student of painting at the Pennsylvania Academy of the Fine Arts, working under Henry Thouron and, briefly, Thomas Anshutz. In 1894 he became a close friend of Henri's, sharing a studio with him at 1717 Chestnut Street.

Everett Shinn, a native of Woodstown, New Jersey, came to Philadelphia at fifteen to study mechanical drawing at the Spring Garden Institute. After two years of classroom training he landed a job with a manufacturer of lighting fixtures, where he became an unenthusiastic designer of gas chandeliers. The foreman, recognizing his talents as a creative artist, advised him: "Art school young man, art school. You're no good to me here." [30] Shinn obliged by entering the Pennsylvania Academy in 1893; at the same time he joined the Art Department of the Philadelphia *Press*.

Compared with those of his three newspaper colleagues, George Luks' early life is a mystery. We know that he was born in Williamsport, Pennsylvania, and was raised in the coal-mining town of Shenandoah. He is reported to have entered the Pennsylvania Academy of the Fine Arts at seventeen; whether he actually did so is uncertain. Thereafter he traveled to Europe to study painting, first at Düsseldorf, then in Munich, Paris, and London.

Exactly what he did and what he learned during his European sojourn is unknown. He was back in Philadelphia in the early nineties working as an artist for the Philadelphia *Press* and at this time learned of the gatherings in Henri's studio.

These four future members of the Eight associated with each other as fellow art students at the Pennsylvania Academy and in the art departments of various Philadelphia newspapers—the *Inquirer*, the *Bulletin*, the *Public Ledger*, and the *Press*. More than any other paper, the *Press* drew them together; while they did not all work for the *Press* at the same time, by the mid-1890's its fifth-floor art department had become their favorite meeting place. Their newspaper work encouraged social contacts between them; Henri's weekly open house directed them toward common artistic goals.

In many ways Sloan, Glackens, Shinn, and Luks were well prepared to make the transition from illustration to painting. They were skilled draughtsmen, experienced in making rapid, accurate sketches from actual scenes or from memory. The discipline they learned in their newspaper work, which could not be obtained in any other field in the nineties, "compelled them to observe, select, and get the job done." [31] Their method of work demanded keen powers of observation and recall: "Sketches, if any, made on the scene, were hurried: usually mere markings with numerals shot off at tangents. . . . At the drawing-boards these marks would metamorphize into a scene of action." [32]

Before photographic halftones took the place of "on-the-spot drawings," the illustrator needed a camera-like memory. Shinn was particularly lavish in his praise of Glackens, who had an incredible visual memory, frequently going out on an assignment without pencil or paper and producing accurate drawings when he returned. The implications of this intensive visual training for the future members of the so-called "Ashcan school" should be obvious; in a sense, they learned to observe before they learned to paint, and they captured movement and gesture in their work before being schooled in "correct" drawing in the academic sense. Of course their style of drawing did not depend totally on observation. According to Sloan, they all studied the work of the English illustrators Leech and Charles Keene, who worked for *Punch* and the newspapers and from whom they derived some of their graphic conventions.

At the Academy, too, except for Shinn, they were exposed to the enlightened teaching of Thomas Anshutz, Henri's former instructor. Concerning Anshutz, Sloan recalled: "He had the same things [as Eakins] to say to his students about observation of life, the character of the forms, striving for solidity and plain painting without bravura." Furthermore, Henri's views on what painting should be dovetailed nicely with the skills and attitudes already held by this group of illustrators. "Paint what you feel," he would say. "Paint what you see. Paint what is real to you." He did not try to impose his own, or anyone else's, style upon them. Indeed, as Sloan observed, "one of the most valuable ideas in Henri's teaching was his contempt for 'making art' one's motive in working." For their generation, Sloan believed, "it was a good thing to be innocent of imitating any art styles. We found a reason to work in our enthusiasm for the world around us; we found beauty in commonplace things and people." And this devotion to the here and now was undoubtedly reinforced by their belief in one of Ruskin's major tenets (Henri had read Ruskin as early as 1886): "The necessity," as Sloan put it, "of working from the 'commonplace' and the familiar world of one's native land." [33]

When Henri instructed his friends "never [to] feel that you are making a work of art," [34] he was undoubtedly rebelling against the excesses of the cult of "art for art's sake," popularized by Whistler's followers, which had begun to exert a strong influence on American painting. As an admirer of painting and literature derived from the artist's personal interpretation of the natural image—an art which communicated human values—he found the self-conscious aestheticism of the *fin de siècle* intolerable. Similarly, he fought against the extremes of the academic approach in painting, whatever its manifestations might be. Such now-forgotten academic painters as Edwin Blashfield and Kenyon Cox were condemned by Henri's group for their "obnoxious kind of clever photographic painting," as well as for their entrenched art-political power. By the same token Sargent and Chase were chastised for their superficial treatment of their subjects and their "distressful technique that is known as academic." [35]

Henri had also come to feel that Impressionist landscape painting, after two decades of struggle for acceptance, had become the fashionable "modern" style—a new academicism—in the hands of such American artists as Childe Hassam and J. Alden Weir. And, as practiced by Joaquín Sorolla and Anders Zorn, the style dealt with surface appearances and clever brushwork, without revealing the artist's response to the tangible substance of his subject. As Sloan recalled: "In the nineties, we were opposed to Impressionism, with its blue shadows and orange lights because it seemed 'unreal.' We chose our colors from observation of facts and qualities of *the things* we painted, with little reference to phenomena of light effects." Sentimentality and artificial studio subject matter were equally abhorrent to Henri and his circle. In

Sloan's opinion, their revolt against Impressionism, which continued into the opening years of the twentieth century, paralleled Cézanne's transformation of the style, though admittedly following a more conservative path: "We realists . . . were revolting against the corruption of eyesight painting, along different lines than the Frenchmen who followed Cézanne's lead; we just went back to art in the direction of Manet and Goya." [36]

The stylistic guidelines for his friends' rebellion were supplied by Henri's own painting of the middle and later nineties and by the masters he admired. At various times in this period he championed the work of Hals, Rembrandt, Velázquez, Goya, Manet, Whistler, and Daumier, whose works were available for study in the Metropolitan Museum in New York, the Wilstach gallery in Memorial Hall, and the Johnson and Widener collections in Philadelphia, as well as through photographs and engravings in books. Needless to say, he did not advocate imitating these painters. They were to serve as stimuli for the growth of his own work and that of his young illustrator-friends, who were beginning to feel their way into painting.

Underlying Henri's teaching was a deep commitment to the spirit of the art of Thomas Eakins. Responding to the strength of Rembrandt's and Velázquez' tonal language, Eakins had brought about the first significant synthesis of seventeenth-century Dutch and Spanish realism with American painting. As a result of his direct and indirect influence on the younger artists in Philadelphia, strengthened by Henri's enthusiasm, Philadelphia became the center for the development of a new and distinctive realistic style of painting which could be applied to native American subjects.

While Eakins responded to the dignity and integrity of Velázquez' portraits and the compelling sense of form in Rembrandt's pictures, Henri admired these same artists for the vitality and immediacy he discovered in their work. For him they expressed the greatness of the human spirit in a wholesome, straightforward way. With a typically unsentimental approach, Eakins searched out the realities of American life, but did not actively proselytize for an indigenous art; he had created one for his own satisfaction. Henri, on the other hand, looked to the future, smashing conventions as he went along by his teaching and writing as much as by his painting, and with the example of Eakins before him, he directed his contemporaries toward every possible aspect of American life. Basically a product of Eakins' Pennsylvania Academy, he built upon the idea that life must be recorded honestly and vividly; but he differed from the older man in his insistence that the painter must immerse himself in every kind of experience. Henri hoped, in short, that life would be absorbed not only by the trained eye, but through all the senses. While he did not paint as much as he could have, as a result of his commitment to teaching, his four younger colleagues from Philadelphia orchestrated many of his principles in their work.

Those artists working under Henri's guidance in the 1890's adopted a dark, low-keyed palette which included generous quantities of earth colors and black. Firmly rejecting the bright spectral hues of the Impressionists, they occasionally turned to blue, green, and yellow "to 'kick up' neutral tones." [37] Their simple palette, which lent itself to the creation of tonal pictures, was easy to control and served as an ideal vehicle for artists moving from the limited vocabulary of black-and-white illustration to a more painterly medium.

Henri's study of the technical methods of Manet, Velázquez, Goya, and Hals led him to advocate spontaneous, rapid brushwork geared to the expression of vitality and immediacy, and his young associates—except for Sloan, a slow worker seeking "solidity"—followed his example. Though this rapid technique could easily become superficial, it was well suited to Henri's aims in representation: "Self expression, dynamic creative efforts resulting from a contact with life." [38]

Because the young artists under Henri's influence depicted the life of the urban masses in a realistic style, some writers have been led to regard their work of the nineties as dominantly "social consciousness" painting. But in his unpublished notes Sloan repeatedly declared that there was very little overt social content in his own work and in that of his friends at the time. They lived a rather isolated life, enjoying mutual companionship and mingling little with the common people. "If anything," he confessed, "we were snobs about labor." After taking up painting, Sloan recalled, "we began to paint things of the city because they were interesting as life"; it was the subject's poetic and humane quality, not its reflection of social or economic problems, that attracted the group. Their literary favorites were primarily the French naturalists and realists such as Zola and Balzac, along with Ibsen and Henri's idols Whitman and Emerson. Sloan also pointed out that there was no direct connection between their paintings of the 1890's and the writings of Hamlin Garland, Frank Norris, and Stephen Crane, the aim of the artists being to "paint the life we knew as Balzac had drawn the French world he lived in." True, there may be parallels in form and in content between the work of Henri's circle and that of the American literary naturalists and realists, but there is little evidence to support a case for the direct influence of the writers on the painters in the 1890's.[39]

6

Paris and Philadelphia,

1895-1900

WHEN HENRI agreed to teach at the School of Design for Women in 1892, he had grudgingly postponed his plans to return to Paris within a year. As it happened, he remained in Philadelphia for three years. During this period his intensive teaching schedule drained his energies and left little time for his own painting. Furthermore, by the spring of 1895, he had reached a low ebb physically—a condition aggravated by his constant smoking. Determined to advance his career as a painter, he resolved to return to France to live there for a period of two years.

Paris, 1895–1897

Early in June, 1895, at the end of the school year, he and a group of friends—Glackens, Schofield, Koopman, Cooper, and Grafly—sailed for Boulogne. Henri was anxious to see the Salons, which he visited regularly, though the "miles and miles of pictures" exhausted him. "There are many good things and hundreds and thousands of bad," he wrote his parents, optimistically adding, "there is lots of room at the top in art." [1] He was becoming increasingly enthusiastic about the old masters, particularly of the Dutch school. In order to see them at their best, he proposed a bicycle trip to Belgium and Holland with Schofield and Glackens. To his parents he wrote: "I think it will be a valuable trip for health and for knowledge gained by seeing the great portraits—. . . it is Frans Hals that I think of particularly." [2] After cycling through northern France, Henri and his friends arrived in the Low Countries, where they toured the galleries of Brussels, Antwerp, The Hague, Rotterdam, and Amsterdam. At Brussels, in addition to visiting the Wiertz

Gallery, they saw paintings by Rembrandt, Hals, and others, which he found "worth alone our coming to see." [3] In Antwerp, they discovered even better examples by these painters, but the finest collection of all was in Amsterdam, which finally satisfied Henri's search for masterpieces by the Dutch school.

He returned to Paris in the fall greatly improved in health. The city was not the place he had known as an art student in the late eighties, for both he and it had changed. At the age of thirty he had matured enough to know precisely why he had to be there: to absorb the intellectual and artistic atmosphere of the acknowledged center of the art world. Only in Paris could he develop his capacities to the fullest without the threat of provincialism. In the mid-nineties the city was certainly the mecca of the international art world—even more than it had been in the 1880's. The influence of the Symbolist painters and poets had reached its apex; Whistler's theories of art were in the air; and the Synthetist-Nabi style had become the accepted vanguard idiom of the day. We shall see later that Henri's paintings and theories reflect an intimate acquaintance with this milieu.

Taking a studio on the left bank at 49 boulevard du Montparnasse, he was closely associated with William Glackens, who lived nearby, and the young Canadian painter James Wilson Morrice. Henri, Glackens, and Morrice often painted together in the streets of Paris and in the countryside near Fontainebleau, all working in a style derived from the work of Whistler, Manet, and the Nabis. Some of Morrice's paintings of 1895–1896 can easily be mistaken for Henri's, and vice-versa, due to their common interest in the same artists as well as to influences that passed between the two when they painted side by side.

During his second prolonged stay in Paris, Henri enjoyed the diversions that the city offered in a way that had been impossible when he was a student. He mingled freely with his friends, chiefly American artists and students whom he had known before—Glackens, Grafly, Koopman, Williamson, and Frank Du Mond—spending many evenings in their company at the Closerie des Lilas café (also the rendezvous of the Symbolist poets), playing billiards with Morrice, or viewing popular musicales and reviews in Montparnasse. Still an avid reader, he delved into the writings of Flaubert, Stevenson, and Oscar Wilde.

Since few of Henri's letters have survived from 1895–1896, it is difficult to obtain a detailed account of his activities during this period. We know that he supported himself by organizing his own art school in Paris, the success of which he owed, in part, to the enthusiasm of a devoted middle-aged student Miss Emilia Cimino (later Rodin's secretary), one of his staunchest friends and supporters. His pupils were primarily American, English, and Scottish (including a few belonging to the so-called "Glasgow school"), though an international flavor was maintained by the presence of a Russian, an Italian, a Swede, and a Dutch woman. It must have been an exceptional school, quite different from the official Parisian academies of the 1890's, because the students were encouraged to develop their own individuality. As the class got under way and Henri's reputation spread, more pupils joined the group, thus assuring its financial stability. He gave criticisms to the class twice a week and occasionally took them to study in the Louvre. We know that he encouraged his students to look at paintings by Velázquez, Titian, and Tintoretto and to admire the work of Whistler, whom he regarded as a "very great artist." [4] In a statement of her aims in painting, Miss Cimino gives us some valuable clues about the content of Henri's teachings at this time: "Good drawing, a large and simple vision yet full of character." [5]

For Henri, the Louvre, the Luxembourg Museum, and commerical galleries in Paris took on increasing importance in stimulating new directions in his art. By 1896–1897, he had decisively cast aside his taste for conservative academic painters, many of whom he had praised in the late eighties. Visiting an exhibition of modern French painters at the Durand-Ruel Gallery, he found the academic Dagnan-Bouveret "vulgar and common," Girardot "too [weakly] finished . . . too feeble," Gérôme "like colored photos—and so badly colored," and many others "too miserably salonish to mention"; by contrast, he noted that a fine woman's head by Courbet stood out "in the midst of all this trash." [6] And the show made him regret the absence of the masterly Manets which had graced the gallery's walls a month before. That Manet exhibition, which included the *Bar at the Folies-Bergère*, *Déjeuner sur l'herbe*, and *Nana*, among other canvases, made a deep impression on him. He turned enthusiastically, too, to many of those painters who had helped to shape Manet's style: Velázquez, Ribera, Hals, and Rembrandt. His taste encompassed even some of Manet's younger contemporaries in the Impressionist group, Monet, Sisley, Pissarro, and Degas, many of whose pictures were contained in the controversial Caillebotte bequest just placed on view in the Luxembourg.

By this time Henri had begun to develop his characteristically rapid methods of painting. In his diary he noted that he could turn out a portrait in two hours and execute a head in forty-five minutes. The source of inspiration for this spontaneous technique is not hard to find: it is Frans Hals, whose name Henri linked with his own work in letters to his family. And like Hals and Manet, Henri introduced liberal quantities of black into his paintings, in sharp contrast to his former teacher Vonnoh's high-keyed, Impressionist palette.

He did not allow teaching to interfere with his steady ouptut of costumed figures, including some in Japanese dress, along with occasional street scenes and views of the Luxembourg gardens. Surveying his production when he returned to Philadelphia, his friends calculated that, on the average, he completed one picture every twelve days. Hard work, combined with native talent, finally earned him a measure of official recognition in the spring of 1896, when for the first time he successfully entered one of his paintings, *Suzanne*, in the Salon. Two more canvases, *La Dame en brun* and *Portrait de M. Francis Vaux-Wilson*, enjoyed the same honor in 1897. With two consecutive victories at the Salon behind him, Henri was prepared to return home in the fall of 1897, concluding a two-year period of intensive work that brought him closer to his goal of becoming a fully developed professional artist.

Philadelphia, 1897–1898

Henri came back to Philadelphia feeling that he had matured sufficiently to make his debut in that city. Accordingly, he approached the officials of the Pennsylvania Academy of the Fine Arts about the possibility of staging a one-man show in their galleries. With the support of his friend Alexander Harrison, his request was granted, and an exhibition of eighty-seven works was scheduled for October and November, 1897. The frantic weeks before the opening were spent framing the pictures with Sloan's and Redfield's help. The myriad chores and social duties connected with the exhibition kept Henri from painting during most of the fall, but he realized that a successful show would greatly enhance his reputation and, he hoped, would place him on a sound financial footing.

Comprised of about equal numbers of portraits and landscapes (including street scenes), the exhibition won the unanimous support of the critics. Henri was praised as a credit to the Academy and as a rising young painter whose future held great promise. True, there were some criticisms of the construction of his figures, but this fault was easily overlooked in the light of his skillful handling of tone and color, particularly in the small outdoor sketches. The frank, open quality of his work and his obvious sincerity, which did not bow to fashion, impressed some of the critics; but they warned (correctly as it turned out) that his style would be appreciated more by artists than the general public. Those who knew the work he did before going to Paris in 1895–1897 remarked on how he had abandoned his Impressionist manner. Now, in many of his paintings, especially portraits and night scenes, he reduced his palette to bring out sombre tonalities that reminded several critics of Whistler, Manet, and Velázquez. Not surprisingly, his full-length portraits evoked comparisons to these same three artists, along with Sir John Lavery, while his style of painting street scenes was linked with that of Jean François Raffaelli. Henri's friends were lavish in their praise of the exhibition, but the most impressive compliments came from the noted American painter William Merritt Chase, then on the Academy faculty, who asked to borrow a group of the paintings to exhibit in New York.

Unquestionably, his first exhibition was an artistic success; from the standpoint of sales, however, it was an utter failure. The dearth of buyers for his pictures troubled Henri deeply, and may have left a permanent mark on him. As he wrote to his parents: "Nobody seems to have had the thought of denying the strength or the quality, the promise or the endurance of the work but nobody has had the thought to buy." Recognizing one of the unhappy facts of American taste in the nineties—that paintings were often sold merely on the basis of the artist's reputation—he added: "There is nothing to do but attain tangible honors—a name won in Paris to make them buy . . . I believe it will only take a stroke of fame from over there to effect this." [7] Despite this financial failure, Henri was confident that one day the public would pay large prices for his work, that the merits of his painting would eventually be recognized.

After the exhibition was dismantled, he once again turned his attention to painting and teaching. With his limited income, chiefly from his parents (who were having financial difficulties of their own), Henri could not afford to take a year's lease on a studio, and so he moved in with John Sloan at 806 Walnut Street. Here and in a nearby studio at Tenth and Walnut he organized small private classes, which assured him enough income to cover his expenses but left little time for his own work, though he managed to do some painting on Sundays.

One tangible result of Henri's exhibition and his growing reputation as a painter was his entrée into the New York art world. During a trip to the city to view one of his own canvases exhibited there, he approached William Macbeth, a leading dealer specializing in old masters, who had recently begun to sell the work of living American artists, including that of Arthur B. Davies. Through Davies, a friend and admirer of Henri's since 1894, Macbeth had been favorably introduced to the latter's work and agreed to handle it, beginning with a small group of pictures from the Philadelphia exhibition.

Early in 1898, Henri sent a group of his canvases to the exhibitions of the Society of American Artists and the National Academy of Design, and though he was uncertain about how well they would be received—"one can never tell what may happen in these art cliques" [8]—several pictures were accepted and hung in the spring exhibitions. With the exception of the showing at Macbeth's, this represented the first display of his work in New York. Periodic visits to the city in 1898 in connection with exhibitions and his business affairs with Macbeth, not to mention calls on Glackens, opened his eyes to a new and more appealing environment than he had known in Philadelphia: "New York is so different from here—one feels alive over there." [9]

During the spring of 1898 his former students and friends in Paris continually urged him to return to France; Miss Cimino was particularly anxious to have him teach a class and generously arranged for studio facilities. In April he made up his mind to go back to Paris, where he was assured of having a small class and an income for the following year. The prospect of having more time for his own painting also influenced his decision, since he hoped for "the chance . . . to get to work and try to reap the harvest that I have been so long preparing— I think that when I once get at it that I will do work that will forever settle my disputed place in art." [10]

For several months he had quietly been courting one of the most gifted students in his class, Linda Craige, daughter of Mr. and Mrs. T. Huston Craige of West Philadelphia. She appears as the subject of Henri's *Lady in Black* (Figure 10), tall and dignified, with fine, delicate features. A talented artist in her own right, Linda was a sensitive, sometimes moody young woman whose chief avocation was reading the classics of English literature. While she and Henri were both devoted to art, they were opposites in many ways: her frail constitution and frequent illnesses did not equip her to keep up with the robust, Whitmanesque pace of Henri's life. Yet despite these differences, they became deeply attached to each other. After a short engagement they were married at Ashbourne, on the outskirts of Philadelphia, on June 2, 1898, and two days later sailed for Paris.

Figure 10. Robert Henri, *Lady in Black*, 1904. Oil on canvas, 78¼ x 38″. Present location unknown.

Paris, 1898–1900

Henri's first two years of marriage, spent in Paris, were among the happiest of his early life. Although he had little money and no definite prospects for the future, he believed that if he could paint steadily for a year or two in the city, he would soon make his mark. The Parisian environment suited him perfectly, and he delighted in showing Linda the sights of the capital. After a long search for lodgings, they finally settled in a studio at 49 boulevard du Montparnasse, where he had lived two years before. Here he embarked on an intensive campaign to produce a group of outstanding pictures, the best of which he planned to submit to the Salon early in the following year. At this point, success at the Salon meant everything to Henri, and hopes for financial returns hinged on the public recognition that would accompany a favorable showing there.

To this end the Henris lived a quiet, unpretentious life confined largely to their Paris studio. His winter class had not materialized—perhaps as a result of competition from Whistler's school in Paris—so his days were entirely free for painting. During the summer he divided his time between studio work and painting cityscapes and street scenes, including fetes and celebrations. In the studio Henri and his wife painted portraits and figure pieces, though Linda gave much of her time to posing for full-length portraits. When she was not posing or painting by her husband's side, she read aloud to him, often from her favorite writer, Kipling, while he worked on his pictures.

In Paris, Robert and Linda Henri eschewed the busy social life that could easily have been theirs through Miss Cimino, who had lately befriended Rodin and Whistler. To avoid unnecessary distractions, the Henris limited their engagements to weekly receptions, which they held on Wednesday afternoons, and occasional calls to the studios of fellow artists and writers. Through some of his American friends passing through Paris, as well as by correspondence with Sloan and Redfield, he was kept abreast of the activities of his comrades in Philadelphia and New York. But he had no interest in joining the American Artists' Club in Paris, believing that he should earn professional recognition first, then, "rather than join the club, I'd have the club join me." [11] When Miss Cimino invited him to meet Rodin (whose sculpture he admired), Henri declined. "Going to court," he said, "makes one a courtier. Those who want to do something themselves can't give up much time to the basking in other peoples' sunshine." [12]

For amusement Henri and his wife took long walks in Paris or on Sundays often traveled to nearby St. Cloud, where they could immerse themselves in

Figure 11. Robert Henri, *Woman in Manteau*, 1898. Oil on canvas, 58 x 38½".
Courtesy of The Brooklyn Museum.

nature and enjoy concerts of light music. Occasionally they undertook longer trips to the country—to Brolles, Moret, and Montigny—where they painted together and hiked through Millet country in the forest of Fontainebleau. Many of their hours, too, were spent in the Louvre, where Henri renewed his acquaintance with the work of his favorite painters, Velázquez, Titian, and Hals. The effect of the Louvre upon him at this time was profound and lasting: "This is one of my greatest advantages in Paris, to go to the Louvre—see what is really good and great. It is my way of study and there is nothing better or more stimulating than my visits there."[13] In addition, he studied the copies of Velázquez' work at the Ecole des Beaux-Arts, as well as paintings by more recent artists at the Luxembourg and in the hands of Parisian art dealers, paying particular attention to the work of Manet.

With the coming of the winter Henri returned to studio work almost exclusively. Painting in the morning and early afternoon before the light faded, he executed canvas after canvas from an assortment of models—old men, cleaning women, and children. Occasionally he would seek relief from the clothed figure by working up finished landscapes from oil sketches done on the streets of Paris or in the country. (At this time, he often worked from memory, carrying on his figure studies without the model or developing street scenes on the basis of brief sketches.) Surveying his results periodically, he was convinced that he was doing some of the most solid and complete work of his career. Although he was intent on being accepted by the Salon, he did not adjust his style to cater to official, popular taste. Decrying artists who followed the current vogue, he wrote in a moment of Emersonian self-reliance: "It is the strong personal prejudice which makes the individual artist, but one so influenced goes slow for it is not a matter of readily seizing the vogue with him, but he must find new ways and take more time to hunt them out."[14] Since he realized that the more liberal art he produced during the fall and winter of 1898 was "far different from what is generally done, out of the commonplace rut,"[15] he was understandably apprehensive about the jury's response, suspicious, as he was, about the politics of art and the fact that "juries have their prejudices, their indigestions, their pupils, and their friends."[16]

With the Salon of 1899 approaching, Henri worked frantically, framing and retouching his eight entries. On March 25 his pictures were sent off, and, with a justifiable sense of relief, he put aside his brushes and palette to await the jury's decision. A week later he learned that four canvases had been accepted, *Woman in Manteau* (Figure 11), *Un P'tit, L'Echarpe rouge,* and *La Neige* (Figure 12), and that the vote for them had been unanimous.[17]

Figure 12. Robert Henri, *La Neige*, 1899. Oil on canvas, 25½ x 32¼″. Musée National d'Art Moderne, Paris.

Preparing for the Salon left Henri exhausted and he realized that he needed a prolonged rest. Accordingly, he and his wife decided to spend the summer on the coast at Concarneau, where living was inexpensive and landscape motifs abundant. In Paris he had become uneasy about having to spend so much time on portraits and eagerly welcomed a chance to return to painting out of doors. Although his funds were limited (a bequest of a thousand dollars from Linda's grandmother bolstered their finances), Henri was determined to stay in France and make the most of his favorable reception in the Salon. Why not return to Philadelphia and take advantage of his recent success? He had given his answer earlier in the year: "If my more liberal art is to be appreciated it is only at the greatest center that it will have early notice, work with less pretentions to the 'Grand Style' may get on in small localities, but I have always fared better here than at home—and it is certainly here that I make my progress." [18]

Believing that outdoor air and exercise would replenish his energies, he did not settle down to work at Concarneau immediately. Instead, he and Linda explored the town, witnessed the colorful spectacle of the local "Fête de Dieu," and exchanged visits with their friends the Schofields, the Florences, and Miss Cimino. Soon, however, he returned to work and after a few weeks produced a number of successful sketches and paintings of the recent fete, views of the port, and a variety of landscapes of the surrounding countryside. He did not hurry to hire a model, and, as it turned out, he never did, for bad weather and severe attacks of the grippe forced the couple back to Paris after a month.

When they arrived at their studio, Henri was amazed to find a letter informing him that the French government had bought his painting *La Neige*, exhibited at the Salon, for the Musée National du Luxembourg. This was a tribute to Henri's artistic integrity and a high honor for an American painter; fewer than ten other Americans had been so rewarded.[19] The purchase of his painting by the state had a distinct practical value, too, in placing him before the public as an accomplished artist. As he said, "It is of more value *by far* than a medal in the old salon or an Associée in the new, and with this recognition of the first order it is now likely that those who were afraid to buy so eccentric work as mine will take the sanction and purchase." [20] The sale of *La Neige* helped Henri financially, of course, but even more important, it stimulated his confidence in himself. It is no wonder that he had suffered occasional doubts; before this he had sold only four or five pictures.

For the remainder of the year, he painted with renewed hope and enthusi-

asm, turning once again to his wife as a favorite model, particularly as a subject for full-length portraits. And, as before, landscapes claimed much of his
attention. Many of the latter were painted during his and Linda's frequent
visits to the nearby suburbs of Charenton and Alfort, where the Redfields had
recently established themselves. Although the Henris lived a restrained social
life, usually avoiding the cafés, they often saw their friends James Morrice,
Alfred Maurer, Miss Cimino, and the Koopmans, along with the illustrators
James Preston and Ernest Fuhr, who told them of the activities of the "clan"
in Philadelphia and New York.

Henri was approached by three of his former students as well as by two of
Koopman's pupils who were anxious to have him criticize their work on a
formal basis. Because it was financially to his advantage, he accepted the offer
and in 1899–1900 taught two mornings a week. His income in Paris had always been modest, and only through teaching and economizing was he able
to survive without the support of his parents, who, despite their own financial
problems during the nineties, generously offered their aid whenever it was
needed. In November, 1899, however, the situation changed for the better.
His father sold at a handsome profit his Atlantic City real estate holdings,
long the subject of a bitter legal battle, which he finally won.[21] Moreover,
twelve of Henri's paintings were purchased by a Philadelphia entrepreneur
for five hundred dollars. Further success seemed inevitable now that his pictures were hanging in the Art Institute of Chicago and the Carnegie Institute.

Early in 1900 a gift of five hundred dollars from his father enabled Henri
and his wife to make a long-awaited trip to Spain. He had been drawn to
Velázquez and Ribera while a student in Paris twelve years before, but the
opportunity to visit Spain had eluded him until now. He arranged to take up
residence for six weeks in Madrid, where he would be close to that great repository of Spanish masterpieces, the Prado. His chief goal was to study
Velázquez, and to make the most of this experience he executed five full-scale
copies of the master's paintings, *The Actor, The Surrender of Breda, Maria
Anna, Menipes,* and *Don Moro, the Dwarf.* At the Prado he also saw a great
exhibition of Goya's work that fortunately coincided with his visit to
Madrid.

He responded warmly to the courtesy and dignity of the Spanish people
and admired the striking gray-blue skies and blond light of the landscape. In
Madrid he was attracted to the bullfights, whose colorful protagonists later
became favorite subjects for his paintings. This first brief visit to Spain made

97

Henri a faithful convert to the life and customs of the country, and he returned on future trips to paint the gypsies and dancers, as well as the picadors and matadors in the elaborate costumes of the bull ring.

Toward the end of his two-year sojourn in Paris, Henri had given much thought to where he and Linda would settle after returning to the United States. Two things were certain: he wanted to be near his family (his parents were now free of their duties in Atlantic City), and at the same time as close to New York as possible, if not actually in the city. He had long since ruled out Philadelphia as a permanent home—"almost any other place would be better." [22]

This was not to be the Henris last sojourn in Europe, by any means, but by the summer of 1900 Henri apparently had decided to establish himself not in France, but in America, thus revising his earlier belief that success must be won abroad. He may well have felt that his frequent acceptances by the Salon and the honor of the Luxembourg's purchase of *La Neige* gave him the cachet of foreign approval which was so important to success in America. By this time, he had spent seven years working abroad and absorbing the beneficial influences of the great museums and galleries. Whatever the reason for his decision to return, Henri clearly intended to sink his roots permanently in his native country and to go back to Europe only as a visitor, not to live there as an expatriate.

7

Maturity and Public
Recognition, 1900-1906

IN THE United States, Henri decided to take a house and studio in New York City. With the help of his friend Glackens, he finally discovered a suitable place, an old four-story brownstone at 512 East 58th Street (now 14 Sutton Square), overlooking the East River. While the house was not in a fashionable district, it would provide a multitude of river views for him to paint. Linda described it as an "ideal place . . . right on the banks of the East River—and out of both the front and back windows that river is fine—busy little boats hurrying by—and big white river steamers." [1]

Henri's letters and diaries of the early 1900's make it clear that he intended to establish himself primarily as a painter, not a teacher. Yet he also realized that his style of painting was still far from fashionable and that he would have to wait patiently for the public (and potential buyers) to accept it after they had been exposed to its merits for a while. He could not count on sales to support himself and his wife. Therefore, he had to accept a post teaching art several days a week at the Veltin School, a private school for girls, beginning in the fall of 1900.

Believing that his success lay in what he produced as an independent painter, Henri turned out canvas after canvas depicting landscapes, cityscapes, figures, and portraits. At this time he created some of his most compelling views of New York, paintings that caught the city's shifting moods, ranging from threatening, gray storms over the East River to the spirited play of children in Central Park. Now, too, he painted countless portraits of his family and friends; paying commissions were still rare. Linda served as his favorite model, posing hour after hour for portraits and full-length figure pieces.

When he moved to New York, his magnetic personality and deep involvement with contemporary American art continued to attract kindred spirits. William Glackens and George Luks had preceded him to the city, and once Henri was established there, he kept up his close friendship with them, especially Glackens, visiting exhibitions and spending evenings with the younger man. Many of Henri's friends who previously worked for newspapers in Philadelphia—James Preston, Joseph Laub, and Edward W. Davis—had also emigrated to New York and were drawn to his circle once again. His group also included, among the artists, Van Dearing Perrine, Frank Vincent Du Mond, Alfred Maurer, Augustus Koopman, James Wilson Morrice, and Ernest Fuhr. Henri also attracted the young Cambridge poet and philosopher Carleton Noyes; Sadakichi Hartmann, poet, playwright, and critic, whom he had known since the early nineties; and Byron Stephenson and Charles Fitz Gerald, art critics, respectively, for *Town Topics* and the *Evening Sun*. Arthur B. Davies frequently visited Henri's studio, and the two attended art exhibitions and concerts together.

A native of Utica, New York, Davies had studied at the Art Institute of Chicago before moving to New York City in 1886. Here he lived a quiet life painting in a studio on the top floor of the house in which the Macbeth Gallery was situated. His style before the Armory Show grew out of the lyrical-poetic tradition of American painting exemplified by La Farge, Vedder, and Ryder, with strong influences from Puvis de Chavannes and, as a result of an Italian trip in 1894, from Giorgione, Botticelli, and Piero di Cosimo as well. While he earned a reputation as a withdrawn, mild-mannered dreamer—a painter of unicorns and maidens (see Figure 13)—Davies was known to his close friends as a determined champion of liberal causes in art. And as his presidency of the Armory Show proved, he was a man of immense organizational ability. These qualities must have made him attractive to Henri; Davies, in turn, undoubtedly regarded Henri as an energetic and influential ally in furthering the cause of progressive painting in America. As we shall see, Davies was to be one of the major powers in the group that assembled the exhibition of the Eight.

It was in New York that Henri met the painter Maurice Prendergast, four years his senior and another future member of the Eight. A Bostonian, he was a solitary, independent figure who had periodically traveled abroad to study and paint during the eighties and nineties. Prendergast surely came close to meeting Henri in France in 1898, since he was an intimate friend of James Wilson Morrice. But although Henri had heard about Prendergast and his work, they were not to meet until the fall of 1901, when Glackens brought

Figure 13. Arthur B. Davies, *Unicorns*, 1906. Oil on canvas, 18¼ x 40¼". The Metropolitan Museum of Art, Bequest of Lizzie P. Bliss, 1931.

Prendergast to Henri's studio. From this point onward, Prendergast visited Henri frequently during his periodic trips to New York from his home in Massachusetts. Shortly after their first meeting, Henri praised him to his parents, writing: "Prendergast is one of us—a very personal and original painter —quite unlike anyone else." [2]

Prendergast's manner of painting was quite different from the styles of the other members of Henri's circle. His decorative style, as exemplified by *The Flying Horses* (Figure 14), represented a marriage between the highly colored Neoimpressionism of Signac and Cross with the planar, measured processionals of Carpaccio. An early champion of Cézanne's work, Prendergast, like Davies, stood out as rare exemplar of avant-garde taste in American painting in the 1890's and early 1900's. It did not matter that his style was unlike Henri's; the latter appreciated Prendergast's originality and his willingness to defy the Academy.

Still another future member of the Eight was Ernest Lawson, who was introduced into the circle by his close friend Glackens. Born in Halifax, Nova Scotia, Lawson grew up in Kingston, Ontario, lived briefly in Mexico City, and in 1891 moved to New York, where he became a pupil at the Art Students League. Heavily influenced by his teachers, J. Alden Weir and John Twachtman, he became a convinced Impressionist. Even a year's study in Paris under Jean Paul Laurent and Benjamin Constant did not deflect him from that style. Lawson eventually established himself in Upper Manhattan close to the landscape motifs that attracted him: the Palisades, the Harlem River, and the Hudson Valley (see Figure 15).

Lawson was not typical of the American Impressionists of his generation; had he represented the academic, sentimentalized version of Impressionism, Henri would have turned him away. The very traits that made Lawson exceptional in his time qualified him to join the artistic rebels who made up the Eight. His brushwork was bold and free, lacking in "refinement." In many of his paintings, his colors were uniformly intense, in the tradition of Guillaumin —"a palette of crushed jewels," as one critic put it.[3] And he frequently painted the less genteel aspects of the urban landscape—bridges, railroads, and squatters' huts along the riverbanks. While his style was quite different from Henri's, he became a congenial, if laconic, member of the circle, remaining closer to Glackens and Davies than to Henri himself.

In the early 1900's, Henri reinforced these personal ties by visiting his friends and inviting them to call on him in his studio, where lively discussions of art and life took place. One day a week was set aside to entertain callers,

Figure 14. Maurice Prendergast, *The Flying Horses,* c. 1908–1909. Oil on canvas, 23⅞ x 32⅛″. The Toledo Museum of Art, Gift of Florence Scott Libbey, 1957.

Figure 15. Ernest Lawson, *Harbor in Winter*. Oil on canvas, 24 x 30″. Collection of Mrs. Dan Oppenheimer, San Antonio, Texas.

but his gregarious personality demanded more frequent social contacts, so he found himself receiving friends and students almost every afternoon. Entries in his diary record his myriad activities—playing billiards with Luks, talking with Perrine about the theory of color-music, criticizing the manuscript of Noyes's book *The Enjoyment of Art* (published in 1903), reading Whistler's *Gentle Art of Making Enemies,* and listening to Linda read aloud from the writings of Maxim Gorky.

Just as regular as "the gang's" visits to each others' studios were their dinners at their favorite rendezvous, Mouquin's, an inexpensive French restaurant at 28th Street and Sixth Avenue and a popular meeting place for artists, illustrators, and newspapermen. Here Henri and Linda often joined their friends in an atmosphere reminiscent of the bohemian life they had known in Paris.

The Henris' contact with their fellow artists was fostered, too, by giving up their home to live in a studio in the Sherwood Building at 57th Street and Sixth Avenue. (Henri had transferred his studio from his house to the Sherwood Building in mid-1901; they moved into the studio in September.) With its full complement of artist-residents, the Sherwood Building was a natural center of artistic cameraderie—not the equal of the Parisian ateliers, to be sure, but the closest American equivalent. Henri found it a most congenial environment.

While he cultivated a new circle of friends among artists, critics, and writers in New York, he also kept up his contacts in the Philadelphia art world. He often went to the city to view exhibitions—in which he often participated—and to socialize (and play poker and billiards) with his two best friends, John Sloan and Edward Redfield. These two often reciprocated by visiting him in New York. While Redfield had settled in the village of Center Bridge, Pennsylvania, and was rapidly gaining recognition in academic circles with his Impressionist landscapes, Sloan was still employed as an artist on the Philadelphia *Press* and with Henri's encouragement continued to paint and exhibit his work.

In 1902, Henri was compelled to make more frequent trips to Philadelphia because his wife had become dangerously ill during the winter, and the doctor had ordered her to recuperate at her parents' home in West Philadelphia. Never a healthy woman, Linda was subject to repeated illnesses during their married life. When she was away from New York, Henri wrote her long, affectionate letters during his lonely hours after coming home from Mouquin's. He described the events of the day which he knew she would want to hear: critiques, pro and con, of art exhibitions in New York; news that William Merritt Chase praised one of his pictures, calling it a "corker"; and tales of exploring the city streets and parks in search of pictorial motifs.

Because Henri had boldly established himself as a leader among artistically liberal painters, he was invited to organize a small show of pictures for the Allan Gallery, New York. This was the first of a series of progressive exhibition schemes of increasing importance which he initiated. Then, as in the future, he chose artists whose work he believed in, but who belonged to no particular school. Most of those he invited—Glackens, Fuhr, Maurer, Perrine, and Willard Price—were his friends, who had departed from the fashionable styles approved by the National Academy. In hanging the show, he violated tradition by trying to give each exhibitor a fair share of the best places in the gallery. In the academies, it was common practice to arrange pictures in a hierarchy on the walls—the best being hung "on the line" (at eye level), while the less desirable ones were "skyed." He countered this system by substituting two lines of pictures for an exclusive well-placed row. "The 'line,'" he wrote Sloan, "is hung down within about fifteen inches of the floor so that both upper and lower lines are equal."[4] Likewise, he was careful to distribute the pictures democratically, with regard to lighting: "Everybody is equally arranged half in light and half in dark."[5] This "little exhibition of our own,"[6] as Henri called it, heralded future schemes not only in the equalitarian arrangement of the paintings, but also as an early effort to provide exhibition space for more progressive art, thus bypassing the authority of the National Academy.

Henri's taste in painting grew increasingly progressive in the early 1900's, as regards both European art and that of his contemporaries in America. He shed all affection for official French academic art and its American imitations; the sight of the 1902 exhibition at the National Academy of Design moved him to write: "The prizes have gone to commonplace, to ordinary and bad things. The show a good saleable shop. . . . Superior mediocrity."[7] Among his more conservative favorites were Millet (and his American counterpart Homer Martin), Puvis de Chavannes, and Whistler. He was equally fond of those rebellious modern French masters not yet tolerated by the Academy: Manet, Monet, Sisley, Renoir, and Degas. And on the contemporary scene, he praised the work of Eakins, Blakelock, Ryder, William Morris Hunt, Chase, and Redfield, as well as of the future members of the Eight, Davies, Glackens, Sloan, Luks, and Prendergast. His admiration for these artists placed Henri in the avant-garde as far as popular American taste at the turn of the century was concerned. While Whistler, Puvis, Millet, and the Barbizon school had gradually gained acceptance by this time, the Impressionists were still largely excluded from major American exhibitions. The work of that great pair of independents, Ryder and Eakins, was shown periodically even in academic circles, but they enjoyed little popularity and few sales. As to Henri's younger friends who were to join him in the Eight, they were accepted occasionally, not regularly, in academic exhibitions and were considered rebellious individualists who had strayed from the flock. But these very qualities attracted Henri to them, and as early as 1902 he regarded his friends as the nucleus of a nonacademic group whose day would soon arrive:

I really do believe that the big fight is on and I look for a great change in the attitude toward the kind of art I have been doing in the coming year. There are a number of us here now and all working on independent and personal lines—our own individual lines. Glackens, Davies, George Luks, Redfield, and a few others, each different from the other.[8]

Henri's belief in individual expression, as opposed to the conventional formulas of the schools, led him to encourage independence and diversity of styles in his pupils. As William Macbeth wrote, apropos of his teaching: "Those who come under his influence will lose no individuality or be in danger of passing out as mere echoes of their master." [9] We can grasp the content of his teaching at this time from a lecture he delivered at the School of Design for Women in Philadelphia.[10] Here he warned the art student to avoid becoming bogged down in the pursuit of technique for its own sake. The student, he thought, should naturally cultivate personal sensations and emotions, and his means of expressing them, rather than mechanically learn the craft of drawing. Imagination and fancy, especially our inborn, childlike appreciation of the world, must not be sacrificed to mere description of things. "What you must express in your drawing is not 'what model you had,'" Henri cautioned, "but 'what were your sensations,' and you select from what is visual of the model the traits that best express you." [11] He encouraged his listeners, when painting the model, to concentrate intensely on the dominant idea that it inspired, eliminating whatever was not essential to "the greater meaning." "This," he claimed, "is selection," concluding, "the great artist has not reproduced nature, but has expressed by his extract the most choice sensation it has produced upon him." [12] After elucidating these views, he defined the role of the teacher as an "encourager"—a definition that best applied to Henri himself.

Early in 1902 the prospects for his success as an artist began to brighten. His dealer, Macbeth, offered to give a one-man show in his Fifth Avenue gallery in the spring of that year. Henri accepted eagerly and, with the prospect of an exhibition in hand, painted all the more intensively to prepare for it. At this time he must have thought of himself primarily as a painter of landscapes and city scenes, for these subjects, both French and American, along with a few portraits, dominated the show. (In 1901, Macbeth had urged him to paint New York cityscapes, and Henri may have felt that his future lay in this field, considering that it had been a Paris cityscape, *La Neige,* that the French government had bought for the Luxembourg.)

He thought the Macbeth show might be his chance to gain public recognition, though his optimism was tempered by caution born of experience with the hard facts of contemporary American taste: "That the work is good and original and worthy of any buyer I and some others know but whether the public is ready for them, yet, remains to be seen." [13] After the exhibition opened, reviews from the major New York newspapers began to pour in. The press, on the whole, was favorably disposed toward the work; however, a few critics failed to follow Henri's excursions into then unfamiliar artistic territory. To his parents, he had to explain:

Many critics as well as many artists mistake my leavings out and my accentuations and suppressions for lack of completion, they being so set in their belief that art is the business supply of reproducing *things*—they have not learned yet that the *idea* is what is intended to be presented and the thing is but the material *used* for its expression. What they mistake for my undevelopment is the very sign of development and instead of being short of the point they seem to think is attainment, I am really beyond that point, having shed the unnecessary, and passed on into the freer field of expression.[14]

Several critics who knew Henri personally from meetings at Mouquin's understood the aims outlined in this letter much better than his less sympathetic reviewers. Charles Fitz Gerald, art critic of the *Evening Sun*, wrote:

In dealing with nature he is in the habit of making a version of his own, and the results seem to be disconcerting to many minds. . . . It is a curious thing that a certain mechanical polish is commonly associated with the idea of finish, and from a few remarks dropped by casual visitors to Mr. Henri's exhibition it is evident that his landscapes are regarded by many as sketches, or thoughts half expressed. What does not seem to be understood is that the eye that saw "The Hill-Top" and mind that grasped and realized so vividly the idea of "A Sudden Shower"

. . . are worth all the hands that ever niggled over a surface for the sake of explaining and polishing what from the first conception was meaningless and worthless. The truth being that in comparison with Mr. Henri's work, most of he landscapes commended for their completeness and finish have, in reality, never even been begun.[15]

For Henri and his critics it was the old battle between academic finish and detail, so much in fashion at the turn of the century, and the grasp of simple, essential forms and the expression which emanated from them—the latter concern, of course, being more advanced and destined to overthrow the academic approach that Henri so thoroughly despised.

In a vein similar to Fitz Gerald's, Byron Stephenson of *Town Topics* tried to illuminate Henri's art by probing his motivations:

He grew dissatisfied with mere prettiness in art and started to work out his own salvation by trying to forget all he had learned and throwing technique to the winds. His work is forcibly individual, and the very strength of that individuality will make his pictures caviar to the general. He has stood face to face with Nature, and then painted as he feels. He carries away with him only the impression of what he considers worth remembering, and in placing it on a canvas employs his brains as well as his brush. That he had yet "arrived" he would probably be the first to disclaim, for he is ever experimenting with Nature and studying her infinite moods.[16]

Stephenson also warned, rightly, that Henri's pictures would not appeal to the general public. Yet two paintings were sold, covering the costs of the exhibition and netting the artist five hundred dollars. He was pleased with this, not really expecting more at the moment; but he could not resist contrasting his sluggish sales with "miserable puny little pictures, imitations of all that has been done before and of much not worth doing over again, being sold in New York every day." [17]

After the Macbeth exhibition he returned to his normal routine—teaching, painting, and enjoying the companionship of his artist-friends. In June he joined Linda at her parents' summer place in Black Walnut, Pennsylvania, a village nestled in the rolling hills northwest of Wilkes-Barre, where the landscape is nothing less than spectacular. The dramatic contrasts of light and shade, the high ridges and deep valleys, the constantly changing moods of the weather—all attracted Henri. Roaming the Pennsylvania countryside in June and July, he produced some of the freshest and most striking landscapes of his entire career. Doing one small oil sketch after another, he captured the fleeting effects of rainstorms and billowing cloud formations, his favorite motifs during the summer of 1902.

The 1902–1903 season promised Henri greater fame through additional exhibitions and a new teaching post. The proprietor of the New York School of Art, Douglas John Connah, was eager to get him to teach several night classes, starting in the fall. Henri accepted with caution, for he always harbored a fear that too much teaching would cut into his time for painting. An invitation to teach there was an honor, because the New York School of Art was one of the city's leading art academies, thanks to the spectacular popularity of the chief instructor, William Merritt Chase. The school had been founded in 1896 as the Chase School by Chase himself. Under his direction, however, it had run in the red, so after two years he gave up the management, although he remained as the leading member of the faculty. At that time the school had been renamed the New York School of Art, but many continued to call it the Chase School.[18]

On the exhibition front, Henri was also moving ahead. In the fall he was invited to present a comprehensive one-man show at the Pennsylvania Academy of the Fine Arts. Scheduled for November in Philadelphia, the show was then to go to the Pratt Institute, in Brooklyn, in December and January. With the prospect of these exhibitions before him, he kept busy during the fall obtaining frames, repainting old pictures, and executing new canvases. For this second major show in Philadelphia, he chose a wide sampling of landscapes and cityscapes, portraits and figure studies, forty-two pictures in all, which were hung in the Academy's two central galleries. Most of them were big pictures, to be seen at a distance. "My work," he said, "is of such a nature as to derive a more than usual advantage from being exposed in a large room."[19]

Artistically, the show was a success, and it earned a fair measure of praise from the critics. Again, artistically liberal critics who understood Henri's aims congratulated him; conventional writers found him a powerful but groping artist, still painting "incomplete" pictures. But one thing is certain: his style appeared advanced and individual, and it stood out sharply against the commonplace clichés of academic art. Fitz Gerald, the most sympathetic of the New York critics, pitted him against the artists who catered to popular taste, and a tribute to Henri's integrity was the result:

Mr. Henri is what admirers of the journeymen painters . . . love to call an uneven or uncertain painter. In other words, he has not invented a receipt for the manufacture of paintings. Instead of finding a public to determine his output he has become a slave to his own vision, and under its fallible guidance he has explored the world as best he could.

Then he continued with a summary of the merits of Henri's current show:

An exhibition like this is highly stimulating after the perfunctory exhibitions of the ordinary sort. The distinction is not merely superficial. We often meet with work that has an air of personality, but proves on closer scrutiny to have nothing more than style; the illusion of something deeper being due to a clever system of dodging that consists in the evasion of vital points instead of a conscientious grappling with them. It is because Mr. Henri is not content with such half measures that his work fails to satisfy the worshippers of style.[20]

Integrity, individuality, self-expression—these were the distinctive elements of Henri's work for the critics who had eyes to see them.

It is hard to realize that this was Henri's last one-man exhibition in a public institution in the New York area before the great memorial show at the Metropolitan Museum in 1931. Because the pictures from his 1897 exhibition at the Academy and the Academy-Pratt Institute show in 1902–1903 sold poorly, he probably decided that these large public displays were impractical; he certainly would have starved on the proceeds, which were negligible. This unhappy situation may also have turned him away from painting landscapes in favor of portraits. These, at least, were ordered on commission and payment was certain.

Early in 1903 there were further signs that Henri was becoming a major force in the art world. Connah asked him to teach summer school; he received several portrait commissions; and he was elected a member of the Society of American Artists. Just as important, he was invited to serve on several juries for shows at the Pennsylvania Academy of the Fine Arts—a sure sign of recognition by his peers.[21]

Henri's diary records an immense amount of activity during the spring of 1903 which must have taxed his physical stamina: teaching extra classes at the Chase School, many visits to exhibitions in the city, entertaining friends and visitors, and working steadily on his own paintings. At this time he turned almost exclusively to portraits, particularly full-length, almost life-size portraits of women—such as those of Miss Edith Dimock and Jesseca Penn—which were becoming his forte. Whistler, Sargent, and Chase had recently popularized this portrait type, following the example of Velázquez' renditions of Spanish nobility, and Henri, with his deep admiration for Velázquez, readily attached himself to his tradition.

When June arrived, he and Linda realized that they both needed a change of pace, so they decided to spend the summer with Edward Redfield and his family in Boothbay Harbor, Maine. The people and the town delighted the Henris. Boothbay Harbor was (and still is) a charming, picturesque fishing village and yacht basin, which, in the early 1900's, had begun to attract summer visitors along with a few artists who were taken by its pictorial possibilities. His letters reveal his enthusiasm about living close to nature once again, fishing in the harbor, sailing around the islands in Redfield's catboat, and going out to paint oil studies of the sea and clouds. As in the past summer at Black Walnut, Henri captured the changing character of the weather in his marines and landscapes; seen as a group, they reveal the contrasts between threatening storms and tranquil seas, brilliant sunlight and umbrageous twilight shadows.

The landscape effects of Boothbay Harbor, however, were tame when compared to those of Monhegan Island, seventeen miles from the mainland, where he and Linda journeyed in the middle of July. They were ecstatic about the place. Henri's description of the Monhegan landscape closely parallels the themes of the paintings he executed there:

You can stand near the light house and have a view of the ocean to the west and to the east—and from the great cliffs you look down on a mighty surf battering away at the rocks—or you can descend and get a side view of the cliffs from lower rocks and then you can disappear from the sea into the pine forests—they are wild. The village is on the inland side—a little harbor shielded by a small island—simply a huge mass of rock. It is a wonderful place to paint—so much in so small a place one could hardly believe it.[22]

During his six-week stay at Monhegan, he continued to produce small panels. Though the sudden changes in nature's moods had attracted him at Boothbay Harbor, the wild, untamed forces of the island landscape, the rushing currents of the ocean, and the barren cliffs roused his enthusiasm even more.

The Monhegan experience was also a tonic for Linda. She often painted by Henri's side, and their long hikes through the hills and forests helped to improve her failing health. They were so fond of the island that they persuaded Henri's father to invest in Monhegan real estate and thought seriously of setting up a permanent summer studio there. As it happened, the studio never materialized, but Henri transmitted his enthusiasm for the place to Rockwell

Kent and George Bellows, who painted some of their best-known works there. Henri did not come back to the island himself until the summers of 1911 and 1918.

But teaching also demanded his attention. He traveled to New York several times during the summer of 1903 to give criticisms to students at the Shinnecock School of Drawing and Painting at Bayport, Long Island, where the summer session of the New York School of Art was conducted. William Merritt Chase, who usually taught there, had taken a class to Holland on the first of his celebrated European study-tours, leaving the school in the hands of Douglas Connah, F. Luis Mora, and—with central billing on the school's flyer —Robert Henri.

Henri returned to New York refreshed and ready to begin a new season of painting and teaching. His schedule at the Chase School had grown to four classes: morning men's life, evening men's life, afternoon portrait class, and composition class. While the school kept him busy during 1903–1904, he found ample time for his own work. As in the previous year, he concentrated more and more on portraits such as *Lady in Black* (Figure 10), *Portrait of George Luks* (Figure 16), *Willie Gee*, and a group of portraits of Eugenie Stein, a popular model known as Zenka of Bohemia. Whereas earlier he would have spent much of the winter painting cityscapes and reworking the summer's landscape sketches, now he left many of them in their original state —small, broadly executed canvases that are fine works in their own right, despite their modest dimensions.[23]

Henri continued to send his pictures to various national and regional exhibitions, including those of the Society of American Artists and the National Academy of Design. He was elated when he heard that the Carnegie Institute had purchased his *Girl in White Waist* for two thousand dollars—his first sale to a public collection. (Unfortunately, it was destroyed by fire in 1905.) By this time his work had earned the esteem of almost every art critic on the major Philadelphia and New York newspapers. The consensus of opinion was that he had definitely arrived; in fact he was sometimes equaled to such better-known artists as Chase and Sargent as a portrait painter. Now and then one of his paintings would be singled out as the best work in a major exhibition—no small praise for the thirty-eight-year-old artist.

He enjoyed a good reputation within official circles, even in the ultra-conservative National Academy of Design, which usually (but not always) admitted his paintings to its exhibitions. Yet he also sent his work to, and participated in, the activities of the more liberal Society of American Artists.

Figure 16. Robert Henri, *Portrait of George Luks,* 1904. Oil on canvas, 76½ x 38¼″. National Gallery of Canada, Ottawa, Canada.

And, at the same time, he stood out as a leader among the more progressive, nonacademic artists working in New York, some of whom—Prendergast and Glackens, for example—were often accepted in the exhibitions of the Academy and the Society of American Artists. Others, such as Davies, Sloan, and Luks, were little known and would not, or could not, participate in the Academy's shows.

Because he believed so strongly in this group of artists, all of whom were his friends, Henri took steps to organize a major exhibition of their work, along with his own, at the National Arts Club in New York. By this means, the group could attract public attention in a way that would have been impossible through existing channels. This exhibition of forty-five pictures opened in mid-January, 1904.

The event was not universally acclaimed. One disgruntled critic dubbed it "a most lugubrious show" and then went on to attack the participating artists:

Decidedly they have a novel point of view, an outlook where nature is seen under her most lugubrious mood, where joyousness never enters, where flesh and blood are almost at the vanishing point, and where unhealthiness prevails to an alarming extent. . . . Here are the dreary, the sad, and the bitter. The commonplace mortal might attribute these things to indigestion.[24]

This critic's remarks stem from a viewpoint accustomed to academic prettiness in art, and he undoubtedly spoke for many who saw the show. But just as vocal were those who defended Henri and his friends for their healthy spirit of rebellion. "Here are men," one critic wrote, "with various creeds, all of them robust and emphatic. They know what they want to do, they are not content to drift with the majority, and are, every one, gifted in more than usual degree." [25] As usual, Charles Fitz Gerald, who knew them best, came to their rescue with an intelligent appraisal of their aims, calling Davies' *In the Valley*, Glackens' *Ballet Girl in Pink*, Luks's *Whiskey Bill*, Henri's *Portrait of a Young Woman in Black*, and Prendergast's *Promenade on the Seashore* "the most significant as representing current production that this city has seen in recent years." [26]

In the reviews of the show, Henri fared better, on the whole, than his friends; his portraits belonged to a familiar tradition. Glackens, too, was tolerated, even praised. But Luks and Sloan seemed vulgar in subject and crude in technique, while Prendergast and Davies were so individual that some of the critics were simply baffled. Nevertheless, this show, like that at the Allan

Gallery in 1901, represented one more step toward an autonomous, independent exhibition scheme, free of the ties of the Academy and the Society of American Artists.

In April, 1904, the four Philadelphia-trained painters—Henri, Glackens, Luks, and Shinn—were joined by the last of their number, John Sloan, who had lost his job on the *Press*. Henri had kept in close touch with Sloan through correspondence and by calling on him in Philadelphia. Now the two were together again and became even closer friends than before. In New York, Henri constantly encouraged Sloan. Indeed, he was one of the few who had faith in the younger man during the first decade of the century.

After the Chase School closed in June, Henri traveled to Cooperstown, New York, to execute two portraits of Bishop Henry C. Potter and one of Mrs. Potter's son, the millionaire horseman F. Ambrose Clark. Setting up a temporary studio, Henri worked at high speed, using a technique inspired by Frans Hals that he had practiced since the late 1890's. Now his skill was put to the test; as he wrote his family about the bishop's portrait (Figure 17): "I have worked with really great rapidity so far and at present as far as I am concerned I have painted a fine head, very good in likeness and with dignity and force." [27] But in this and later letters he wondered whether the things that pleased him would also please his clients—always a dilemma for a portrait painter who wants to create a work of art as well as a likeness. The art critic of the New York *Press*, reviewing the three portraits, put his finger on the crux of another dilemma that Henri faced, the conflict between honesty and prettiness:

Mr. Henri always has shown a desire to paint the truth. That quality in a portrait painter is likely to react to his disadvantage. When society folk have their faces and figures preserved on canvas they have a strong desire to "look pretty," and a man who seeks only to perpetuate the truth is likely to be out of favor with the moneyed ones.[28]

In these and related portraits. Henri managed to combine an honest portrayal of what he saw with the qualities of elegance and grace that most fashionable sitters demanded. While remaining true to his own vision, he found that he could paint portraits to the satisfaction of at least some of the elite of American society. As a result, patrons such as the Potters commissioned portraits from him with increasing frequency, though he never became a stylish society painter like John Singer Sargent.

When the New York School of Art opened in the fall of 1904, Henri re-

Figure 17. Robert Henri, *Portrait of Bishop Henry C. Potter*, 1904. Oil on canvas, 72 x 50″. Present location unknown.

turned to his job of teaching. He continued to paint from models posed in the studio, particularly Anna Maria Bustamente, the subject of *Spanish Dancing Girl* and *Spanish Dancer—Sevillana*, but this work was frequently interrupted because he was in great demand as a juror. In the fall alone he served on juries for the Pennsylvania Academy of the Fine Arts, the American Photographic Salon (where he met John La Farge and Childe Hassam), and the Society of American Artists, of which he was elected chairman of the Committee of Invitation.

His reason for accepting the Society of American Artists position should be noted: "Accepted with idea that I might get them to invite pictures by A. B. Davies who has not been sending to S.A.A. because of previous bad treatment. . . . They would do well if they but had a fair appreciation of Davies' work (which however is only appreciated by a few)." [29] This was one of the few positions in an art organization that Henri ever accepted, and it is significant that he did so to help Davies, a friend and little-recognized artist whose work he believed in. Of all the official art organizations, the Society of American Artists was, at this time, the most congenial medium through which Henri could work toward his goals. Save for the help of his friend Bryson Burroughs, later curator of the Metropolitan Museum of Art, Henri fought alone within the ranks of the Society.

Founded in 1877 in rebellion against the self-perpetuating, conservative exhibition policies of the National Academy of Design, the Society of American Artists in its early years became a haven for the more adventurous younger Paris- and Munich-trained artists. While some members of the Society belonged to and exhibited at the National Academy, the newer organization was much more sympathetic to the advanced tendencies in European painting that Americans had now learned to echo—the Munich school, Impressionism, and the Whistler tradition. To the Society the once fashionable Düsseldorf influence and Hudson River school that still dominated the National Academy exhibitions appeared hopelessly out of date. Yet even the Society of American Artists, conceived in rebellion against the Academy, had grown rather conservative and academic in its twenty-seven years of existence. As a result, Henri's group, representing a youthful and artistically liberal element, was able to gain only limited recognition from the Society. But in the absence of more suitable channels, the Society of American Artists provided their best opportunity for public exposure. For the time being, Henri was willing to work within this organization; the National Academy, needless to say, was almost out of the question for the younger men and the membership of the Ten was limited to that many artists.

The fall of 1905 saw Henri receive the Harris Prize from the Art Institute of Chicago for his full-length portrait of Linda, *Lady in Black* (Figure 10). He was also named juror for the Carnegie Institute's International Exhibition and was appointed to the hanging committee of the National Academy of Design. But late in the fall, in the midst of these activities, his life underwent a sudden change. Linda, who continually suffered from poor health, became dangerously ill in November. At first she gave signs of responding to the doctors' care, but after several weeks hope for recovery faded. She died, attended by Henri and his brother, on December 8, 1905.

Henri's sense of loss was indescribable. Although she had often been absent from New York because of illness, he was deeply attached to her and had hoped that she would eventually develop a healthier constitution so that they could enjoy life together, without interruption. Now, with Linda gone, he was desolate.

By the beginning of the new year he slowly returned to his regular routine of teaching. But understandably he was able to paint only a few pictures during the winter and spring of 1906, notably the *Portrait of Miss Josephine Nivison* (known as *The Art Student*) and several portraits of Thomas Anshutz. To escape the loneliness he felt so acutely at this time, Henri sought the companionship of John and Dolly Sloan, who invited him to countless dinners at their apartment at 165 West 23rd Street. Indeed, he became almost a permanent guest during his months of bereavement, often staying up with Sloan into the early morning hours talking, sketching, or playing euchre—then spending the night.

As if to blot out the tragedy of Linda's death, Henri immersed himself in the busy activities of his friends who gathered at the Café Francis. His diary records numerous dinners there with the usual company—Stephenson, Preston, Frederick James Gregg (a critic he had befriended), Glackens, Fuhr, Luks, Lawson, occasionally Shinn and Morrice, and, not least, the proprietor himself, James B. Moore, self-styled bohemian and amateur of the arts. Moore's four-story brownstone house on West 23rd Street, even more than the Café Francis, was a private retreat for himself and his artist-friends; here Henri played shuffleboard and poker and joined Sloan, Luks, Lawson, Shinn, Rudolph Dirks, and others in decorating the subbasement with paintings and satirical cartoons.

Henri was unquestionably the mentor of the Café Francis group:

Ever since his Paris days he has been known to surround himself with a crowd of artists, who, although no disciples, were willing to listen to his theories and criticisms, and to consider him as a sort of leader. At present he is the patriarch of the Café Francis crowd, a number of young painters, illustrators and *literati* who believe in the poetical and pictorial significance of the "Elevated" and the sky-scraper, of city crowds and rows of flat houses. To these men Henri expounds his philosophy of art, and he seems to take these monologues over his *entrée* or *café noir* as seriously as any of his brush performances.[30]

In 1906, Henri also drew closer to his former instructor, Thomas Anshutz. That painter, who continued to teach at the Pennsylvania Academy of the Fine Arts, maintained a high regard for Henri's work, and they kept in touch by writing. Now, Henri invited him to give a series of lectures on anatomy at the New York School of Art—lectures that served as solid factual discipline to supplement Henri's own inspirational teaching. These contacts, and Sloan's and Henri's regular calls on Anshutz in Philadelphia, strengthened the rap-port between the older man, who represented the Eakins tradition, and the New York group. Henri had learned the fundamentals of painting and draw-ing from Anshutz at the Pennsylvania Academy in the late 1880's; by the 1900's the younger man was capable of absorbing ideas of greater depth and sophistication from his former teacher. Evidence from both men's former pupils indicates that many of Henri's methods were inspired by Anshutz' teachings and philosophy of art.[31]

Throughout the difficult period after Linda's death, Henri worked actively for the Society of American Artists as a member of a three-man council, to-gether with Kenyon Cox and Samuel Isham, to negotiate the absorption of that society by its parent body, the National Academy of Design. Early in 1906 he attended many conferences with representatives of the Academy; finally in early March the Society agreed to rejoin the Academy, from which it had seceded twenty-eight years before. Although all members were now united under the banner of the National Academy of Design, Henri and his circle hoped that the new blood of the Society of American Artists would bring about more liberal policies. The merger, however, raised Sloan's suspi-cions. "It seems to me," he wrote, "that it narrows things down until a large new gallery is built. H[enri] thinks that no difference will be felt." [32] As it turned out, Sloan's suspicions were justified; the Academy remained just as conservative as before.

Although Henri was elected a member of the National Academy in the spring of 1906, he was also a major force behind exhibition schemes and so-cieties that threatened to undermine the Academy's authority. In May, for example, he met with a group of fellow artists at the Players' Club to establish an organization of artists of liberal tendency to hold exhibitions of watercolors, drawings, and the graphic arts. The members, to be drawn partly from Henri's circle, partly from the relatively advanced Ten American Painters, were Henri, Glackens, Sloan, J. Alden Weir, William T. Smedley, Albert Sterner, Willard L. Metcalf, and Robert Reid. In his diary, Henri noted the tenets of this now-forgotten society: "No officers. Division[,] by lot[,] of space. No enlargement of membership. Invitation of participation by unanimous consent." [33] After recording this rather democratic and equalitarian statement of policy, Henri went on to list other artists who might be invited to join: Winslow Homer, Davies, Shinn, Lawson, Luks, Childe Hassam, and Prendergast. Though founded with good intentions, the society and its liberal exhibition plans were never heard of after 1906. But by its very existence, however brief, it paved the way for the Eight in two important ways. The list of members and potential members included, among others, all of the future Eight, and its exhibition policy was remarkably close to that developed by the Eight in the following year.

Several of the founding members of the short-lived Players' Club group belonged to the Ten American Painters—J. Alden Weir, Willard L. Metcalf, and Robert Reid; Childe Hassam was also a member and Winslow Homer had once been invited to join the Ten but declined. This strong representation from one of the most progressive groups of artists in New York suggests that the Ten should be recognized as a major forerunner of the Eight. The organization had been founded in 1898 to protest the sterile policies of the Society of American Artists, "not believing," as one of them stated, "that an art show should be like a child's bouquet—all higgledy-piggledy with all the flowers that can be picked." [34] Their main purpose was to hold small, selective annual exhibitions of members' work, "following the Japanese view." [35] The rules governing these shows were most democratic. The *American Art Annual* reported: "The pictures were placed in groups, the works of each painter being hung together. The gallery was divided into ten equal spaces, and drawn for by lot, with the exception of the south wall." [36] There were no officers. Hassam was the leading organizer of the Ten, but Weir and Twachtman contributed significantly to the success of the shows, which were the real reason for the group's existence and which were repeated every spring for twenty years, the life span of the organization. The similarities between the aims of the Ten and the organization founded at the Players' Club in 1906 speak for themselves. It is important to realize that Henri helped to establish the latter group and, in doing so, absorbed some of the principles underlying the Ten.

Shortly after the merger of the Society of American Artists and the National Academy, Henri was called to Aiken, South Carolina, to paint portraits of Mrs. George Sheffield and her three children. Once again he had an opportunity to mingle with the wealthiest sector of American society, including Gertrude Vanderbilt Whitney, sculptress and collector of modern American art, who two years later was one of the chief buyers at the exhibition of the Eight. Henri was fascinated by the luxury and slow pace of life in the South and wrote long letters about his experiences to Sloan and his parents: "I have played a good deal of bridge. Have gone about somewhat in a social way. Had a touch of tennis, one of golf—horses etc.—but with all have been pretty well under the strain of the portrait." [37] Years in Philadelphia and New York had acclimated him to the bustling life of the city; thus the tranquility of Aiken was disconcerting.

With a successful pair of portraits behind him, Henri returned to New York to be greeted by an offer to take a class from the Chase School to Europe that summer. He accepted, no doubt partly out of his love of teaching and partly because he had not been to Europe in six years. The class was organized along the lines of Chase's previous summer tours, begun in 1903, but Henri's methods of teaching, needless to say, were to be quite different from Chase's. As Henri himself wrote to one of his students: "The best personal brag the 'Maestro' can make in regard to his pupils is that he gives his pupils a chance to do what they can do instead of keeping them from it." [38]

Henri and nineteen students sailed for Spain early in June, 1906. Their ultimate destination was Madrid, where the class was to work under his guidance for six weeks. Some of his pupils preferred to paint in the studio; others worked out of doors; and still others copied paintings in the Prado. Periodically, he gave criticisms in the studio and, as we might expect, often took his students to the Prado to see the work of Velázquez, Goya, and El Greco.

Henri, we will recall, had visited Spain briefly in 1900, and at that time became an enthusiastic admirer of the country. In 1906 he grew even fonder of it as a place to live and paint during the summer months. He preferred the climate to New York; but more than that, he found himself in sympathy with the Spanish people, especially the gypsies, dancers, and matadors. They, in turn, looked upon Henri with admiration and respect, giving him the honored title of "el maestro."

In Madrid, Henri established a studio separate from his students, where he painted a number of his well-known pictures of Spanish subjects: *Gypsy of Madrid* (or *La Trinidad*), *La Reina Mora*, and *Gitano* (or *Gypsy with Guitar*). Sometimes he hired people to pose, but more often his models were drawn from his circle of Spanish friends. They must have sensed his enthusiasm for them and their country, because such noted personalities as the Republican writer and reformer Don Federico Nieto Linares, the matador Felix Asiego, and the gypsy dancer Milagros Moreno, known as "La Reina Mora," extended their friendship to Henri and frequently posed for him. He was not a detached observer of their life and customs, but an active participant; from his letters it is obvious that he enjoyed every moment he spent with his Spanish friends.

He was also an avid fan of the bullfights, a medium that he considered a fine art. His letters from Spain are filled with critiques of the style and personality of the great matadors, Manolete, Possades, and Asiego. Thanks to Asiego, he was invited to mingle with the bullfighters just before they entered the ring, and here took the snapshots of Asiego that served as the basis for a full-length portrait of that matador. Henri's comments on the finished picture aptly summarize the impact the Spaniard made upon him:

He is in full costume as he appears just before the grand entry into the ring—the procession across to the president's (of the fight) box where he salutes and makes his short address (which no one hears) but which is interesting—graceful to see—and which is immediately before the blast of the trumpet which signals the entry of the first bull. . . . Before going into the fight they are all very serious and one can see in their faces that they are [*sic*] do not get over the sense that they are about to take risks that may end in death or injury of an almost equal value. My visit to them before the entry was a very interesting moment and in my portrait I think I got the sense of that look on the face I noticed particularly in Asiego.[39]

If Henri was impressed by the spectacle of human drama in the bull ring, he was no less attracted by the colorful costumes and natural simplicity of the gypsies. To his parents he wrote:

They are the most savage people in color I have ever seen—not a bit like the colorful and weakly romantic Italians—but strong—savage—positive—in their costume and in all their customs the most child like people I have ever seen and as proud as if each one was a king or queen. Always at home, feel that they are your equal and feel too that you are worthy of them—have much respect.[40]

Figure 18. Robert Henri, *Gypsy Mother*, 1906. Oil on canvas, 51 x 33″. Collection of Mr. and Mrs. John C. Le Clair, Glen Gardner, New Jersey, and New York.

Prior to this trip to Spain, Henri had occasionally been attracted by those people or races, such as the Breton peasants, who remained sincere and natural human beings and had not been spoiled by the excesses of sophisticated Western civilization. By 1906 his search for what he later called "My People" had become a creed, and the Spanish gypsies were one answer to his quest, as indicated by his remarks about the subject of his *Gypsy Mother* (Figure 18):

A gypsy with a baby in her arms came in—crossed the room to where I was seated . . . and at once sat down at my feet in front of me and began a comfortable conversation while the half naked baby slept or fed himself at a breast that was only concealed by a shawl. The gypsy was typical of the race, very large handsome eyes in a dark face—a gleam of teeth, jet black hair and much gypsy finery and flowers. She seemed as if she had never known a place better than sitting there and one would have said we were very old friends by her easy manner. . . . The mothers seem to have the mother instinct to an intensity— children themselves they seem. Good easy nature is their characteristic, and with all their irregularity of life there is from appearances a natural morality—this girl with her baby seemed to have the most perfect spirit of happiness and contentment.[41]

So struck was Henri by this experience that he had the woman pose holding the baby in her arms and, as he wrote, "painted very rapidly a thing which I think contains some of the life she made more clear to me in her conversation." [42] From the painting and Henri's comments about it, it should be evident that he was probing the essence of the sitter's life and personality, not painting gypsies because they were picturesque "characters" that would appeal to a public attuned to academic art.

Henri painted portraits and figures, as well as a number of small cityscapes of Segovia, throughout the summer of 1906, and remained in Madrid to carry on his own work after the class left for Paris early in August. At the beginning of October, however, he, too, was compelled to leave for New York.

8

Henri and the Independent
Movement, 1906-1910

In the fall and winter of 1906, Henri's schedule was filled with a variety of activities. He returned to teach a full roster of classes at the New York School of Art, painted numerous bust-length and full-length portraits of one of his favorite models, Jesseca Penn, and kept in close touch with the growing number of students and friends who depended upon him for advice. And in November he was elected to the jury for the National Academy's annual exhibition, the first since its amalgamation with the Society of American Artists. It was, he observed, "very much the same jury the Society usually has[,] only three or four exceptions in the thirty members," [1] not a very encouraging sign to one who helped bring a liberal note to the Academy.

Just as Henri was recovering from the shock of Linda's death, his father became gravely ill and died in December.[2] Mrs. Lee gave up their Manhattan apartment to live in Henri's studio until the following year, when she returned to Atlantic City to be close to her old friends.[3]

Early in 1907, after recovering from the depression that came over him when his father died, he returned to active professional life. He failed to attract enough portrait business, however, to justify the expense of his new Bryant Park studio—$2,500 a year. His failure did not reflect any lack of talent on his part but, rather, his reluctance to paint superficial, flattering portraits. "He won't do the five o'clock tea drinking that is necessary for portrait work in this country today," Sloan observed.[4]

The spring of 1907 saw Henri lash out more vehemently than ever before at the injustices of academic juries and exhibitions. The first blow in what became an open conflict with the Academy was his withdrawal of two of his paintings from the spring exhibition. As in previous years, he was appointed a member of the jury to decide which paintings would and would not be accepted. In the course of the judging he found that things were going badly for many of the young progressive painters—among them his own friends and students. When certain entries by Luks, Shinn, Sprinchorn, Kent, and Glackens were rejected, Henri insisted that a second vote be taken, this time placing the pictures in another room amid new surroundings. The jury, however, was not won over and voted them down again, much to Henri's dismay.

He was further outraged when his own pictures were reviewed by the jury in his presence. In the first round of judging, two of his three entries, *Colonel David Perry* and *Asiego*, were rated No. 1 (meaning unanimous acceptance), while the third, *Spanish Gypsy and Child*, was ranked No. 2 (a majority vote). But when the paintings were judged a second time, as was customary, the rating of *Asiego* dropped to No. 2. Chagrined by this indignity, Henri promptly withdrew the two paintings ranked as No. 2, leaving only *Colonel David Perry* in the exhibition. Such a move had sometimes been made by other artists in previous years—but never with the publicity that accompanied Henri's withdrawal of his work.

Henri's feud with the Academy became even more serious after the pictures were hung. There was not enough space in the galleries to display every painting that been accepted; some of them, therefore, had to be omitted. When Henri discovered that two paintings by his friends Luks and Sprinchorn were left out, he pointed out two empty places on the crowded gallery walls where they might fit, and the paintings were duly hung. By the next day, however, they had disappeared. One newspaper reported that "those in charge of the hanging had decided that the proximity of the two paintings in question to the other pictures detracted from the mural effect desired, and as a consequence they were taken down." [5] This move, needless to say, irritated Henri further. When he was asked by a member of the hanging committee whether it was the wall or the men he was interested in, he replied (as he wrote his mother), "It was the men I was interested in and not the wall." [6]

These were symptoms of serious rupture between Henri's group and the Academy; but the break was not yet complete. He still wanted to maintain the good will of the Academy and encourage them to recognize the newer movements in American art. At this time he saw himself as a leader who would try to point the way, within the Academy, toward a more catholic viewpoint that would encompass the work of such progressive artists as Luks, Glackens, Sprinchorn, and Kent. At the time of the furor over his withdrawal of paintings he confessed privately to his mother, "The whole matter

is the old one that I have been active in behalf of the more talented and original—and altho I have always been in perfect order according to rules and in
good humor[,] my activity has riled some of the academicians who do not
want to see my ideas succeed. . . . People want to know if I am going to
start a secession—a new society, etc., etc.—many quite worked up over it and
desirous that it come about." [7] There was certainly ample precedent for
Henri and his group to secede, but at that moment he was still willing to cast
his lot with the Academy.

The conflict between the "progressives" and the "conservatives" stirred up
a tremendous amount of publicity in the newspapers, and contrary to what
one might expect, the majority of the press sided with Henri. As the standard-
bearer of the rejected, he was expected to speak for his side. "I have been
over run with things to do," he wrote in April. "I have to do all that I can—it
is a time when while what I do has no immediate return—or almost none—I
have to do to make the road clear for the future." [8]

Several of the news articles suggested that Henri, as leader of the insurgents, might secede from the Academy and form a rival group. As a result of
two additional blows from the Academy, he was virtually propelled into
doing so. In their April meeting the Academy failed to elect as members more
than three artists from a list of thirty-six well-qualified nominees (including
Arthur B. Davies, Ernest Lawson, and Jerome Myers), "most of whom were
excellent artists—some the very best." [9] After the meeting Henri was forced
to conclude: "This action . . . shows that the academy is hopelessly against
what is real and vital in American art. What the outsiders must now do
is hold small or large group exhibitions, so that the public may see what
the artists who have something important to say are doing." [10] The die was
cast when Henri's beneficial influence in the Academy was cut off as a result
of his failing to be re-elected to the jury for the next two exhibitions. The
implications of this slight were obvious; as one artist remarked, "It means that
the progressives will stand no chance." [11] In the light of these developments,
one might have expected Henri to be gloomy. On the contrary, he felt "it is
all for the very best and the results will be very beneficial." [12]

While the Academy controversy was raging in the spring, he began to
gather his forces for a rival exhibition. Fortunately John Sloan's diary provides a week-by-week report of the evolution of their plans. On March 10
and 18, Henri discussed with several of his friends the idea of organizing a
show of their own, though no definite conclusions were reached at this point.
The next move was a formal meeting in Henri's studio on April 4 to talk over

the possibility of a show of the "crowd's" work in the following year. Six of the future Eight attended the meeting—Henri, Luks, Davies, Glackens, Sloan, and Lawson. It was decided that Sloan would manage the finances and Henri would do the correspondence. By the middle of April a plan to hire a gallery to carry a year-long exhibition materialized, but this was soon abandoned as being too expensive. After exploring several possible locations for an exhibition of shorter duration, the group settled on William Macbeth's galleries at 450 Fifth Avenue, and through Davies' negotiations, Macbeth agreed to let them use his facilities for two weeks in February of the following year.

Henri and Sloan held numerous discussions of the proposed exhibition with each other and with their friends in the latter part of April, and on May 2 a second important meeting was held in Henri's studio, where the original six associates were joined by Everett Shinn. Each man was asked to contribute fifty dollars toward the expenses of the show; Macbeth had demanded a guarantee of five hundred dollars (later reduced to four hundred) for the use of the gallery. On May 15, Davies reported to Sloan that Maurice Prendergast, the last to be invited to join the Eight, had written an enthusiastic letter of acceptance. Now that their plans had crystallized, Henri confessed privately: "It has been arranged that in February Davies, Sloan, Glackens, Luks, Prendergast, Shinn, Lawson and I will hold an exhibition of about five pictures each at Macbeth's Galleries. This is already news in the papers. Macbeth's Gallery is now—his new place—the best gallery on 5th Ave. for such an exhibition." [13]

The nucleus of the Eight consisted of Henri and the four Philadelphians, who, with Lawson and Davies, had come to be identified as the "Café Francis element." True, Everett Shinn had drifted away from his friends, but he gladly reunited with them in 1907 to fight for a common cause. Prendergast was well known and respected by Davies and Henri and, like the others, his art was moving in an original, unacademic direction. Logically, Sloan's friend Jerome Myers might have been included too. He painted scenes of city life on the East Side and also wanted to escape the domination of the Academy. Sloan always thought Myers should have been invited, but Henri blocked the idea. Myers was not a member of the circle, and Henri objected to the sentimentality of his work.

In a most revealing entry in his 1927 diary, Henri reminisced about "the two men who might have been of the '8' had one of them been younger or the other older. A. P. Ryder and George Bellows." With regard to Ryder,

Henri noted: "The only time I met Ryder he expressed himself as strong for the '8' and spoke with enthusiasm of several members of the group." As to Bellows, "George would naturally have been of the group but it antedated him. Many people now believe he was a member." [14] Apparently, in their early stages of planning, the group intended to accept additional members, "taking in anybody who has something to say about life in his own way and doesn't paint by algebraic formula." [15] The idea, however, was abandoned, for the Eight, like the Ten, never expanded beyond its original number.

The organization of the Eight was simplicity itself: there was no president and no jury—just the necessary secretary-treasurer to oversee business matters. As it turned out, Henri and Sloan, with Davies' assistance, did most of the work. Henri was the ideological leader who handled the correspondence and communicated with the press; Sloan, as secretary-treasurer, collected the money, photographed many of the paintings, and served as general manager. Davies, with Sloan's help, produced the catalogue and maintained close liaison with Macbeth.

It is hard to ascertain who first used the term "the Eight." Mary Fanton Roberts claimed priority, but Sloan asserted that Frederick James Gregg initiated its use.[16] The term first appeared in print in a short article by Gregg in the May 15, 1907, issue of the New York *Evening Sun*. Probably he and his fellow writers gravitated to the expression "the Eight" simply as shorthand for what reporters had earlier called "the Eight Independent Painters," "the Eight Secessionists," or "the Society of the Eight." Many years later Henri explained, "The title 'The Eight' was not of our making. It was applied to us from without," [17] a view confirmed by Sloan's diaries. But the group readily accepted the term, and it has remained in currency ever since. The five Philadelphia artists of the Eight who painted unidealized city scenes, sometimes including slums, also came to be known popularly as the Ashcan school.[18]

On May 14, when the arrangements for the 1908 exhibition were completed, the Eight announced their plans to the press. Since the sensationalism of some of the writing about the exhibition in 1908 tended to cloud their real purpose, we can obtain the best idea of their aims from the early articles.

" 'We've come together because we're so unlike' was the gist of their statements," the *Sun* reported.[19] While those of the group who usually sent pictures to the Academy would continue to do so, their bias was definitely anti-academic. "We don't propose to be the only American painters by any means," one member stated, "but we do say that our body includes men who think, who are not academic in the hard, unfeeling sense of the word." [20] It was clear, too, that they were not tied to any creed or school. Henri, better than anyone else, clarified this position in a letter to an editor who requested information about the group: "They have been working for years developing and producing on the same lines in which they are now found[,] each from the other very different in his way—no unity in any cult of painting—similar only in that they all agree that *life* is the subject and that view and expression must be individual." [21]

Underlying their statements to the press was a distinct note of Americanism in subject matter and in their belief in the progress of art in this country. It was probably Henri who was quoted as saying: "All are men who stand for the American idea. It is the fashion to say that skyscrapers are ugly. It is certain that any of the eight will tell you: 'No, the skyscraper is beautiful. Its twenty stories swimming toward you are typical of all that America means, its every line is indicative of our virile young lustiness.' " [22]

In their formative stage, the Eight intended to expand their influence. One reporter stated: "During the next two years they expect to secure a gallery of their own, large enough to display 200 canvases or more." [23] Other newspapers quoted a spokesman of the Eight as saying that the group would probably increase their number when a large gallery was obtained and might invite progressive artists from various cities in the United States and Europe to exhibit with them—this last point a distinct forecast of the policies of those who staged the Armory Show of 1913. And there is good reason to believe that they intended to make their exhibitions an annual affair.[24] None of these proposals was carried out under the name "the Eight," but, as we shall see, many of their number were behind the vast Exhibition of Independent Artists held in New York in 1910, itself a precursor of the Armory Show, to which they also contributed.

There is another motive behind the secession that must be recognized: this is the matter of financial support. If Henri and his friends hoped to gain a large public audience for their work, so much of which was anathema to the Academy, some alternative to the Academy's annual exhibitions had to be devised. The Eight's plan for a show was the first effective step in this direction, and Henri obviously enjoyed the accompanying publicity.

His rebellion against accepted academic norms was carried out on still another level in the spring of 1907, in his teaching at the New York School of Art (Figure 19). Henri and Chase, the leading instructors, had initially been quite sympathetic to each other, but their views on teaching and on the nature of good art had grown apart over the past four years. While Chase main-

Figure 19. Henri and the night class, New York School of Art, 1907. Photograph.

tained that "art is draughtsmanship" [25] and objected to the alleged vulgarity of the work of Henri and his students, the latter won a far greater following in the school by his vital, independent methods of teaching. In defense of the way he taught at the school, he wrote: "It is not a place where students are fitted into the groove of rule and regulation but where personality, originality of vision, idea, is encouraged, and inventive genius in the search for specific expression stimulated." [26]

Eclipsed by sheer weight of numbers of students loyal to Henri, Chase was forced to retire from the New York School of Art and return to the staff of the rival Art Students League, where he had taught previously. As Henri told the story: "There is going to be a desperate fight I guess to knock out the N.Y. Sch[ool] of Art, but I have no doubt but that if the N.Y. Sch[ool] manage[s] the business end all right that my reputation as a teacher will carry against all that they will do. It appears that Chase is very bitter about the way the students of the school have flocked to my classes." [27] Fortunately, the students remained faithful to Henri, and the school continued for two years under his leadership. When it failed, it was because he left to establish his own school.

The friction between Chase and Henri did not disrupt the latter's plans to take a group of students from the school to Holland that summer. After giving up his Bryant Park studio and renting a less expensive one at 135 East 40th Street, he embarked on a summer's journey to Haarlem, where, as in Madrid the year before, he taught a class and worked at his own painting. Haarlem was a logical choice for a summer school because he and his pupils could study the work of Hals in the museums and find countless picturesque subjects among the natives of the city and surrounding countryside.

The Dutch people, especially the children, fascinated Henri. He spent most of the summer painting a series of quickly executed informal portraits of three young girls—Cori, Martsche, and Fi. He was intrigued by the contrast between two of them: "All the time I have been here I have painted over and over again a little roistering white headed, red cheeked, broad faced girl [Cori]. I have done many heads of her, most of them laughing. I have another little model [Martsche]—just the opposite type in character—thin, pathetic— pale—very interesting and just as Dutch as the rollicking one." [28] Typical paintings that illustrate this contrast are *Cori Looking over Back of Chair* (Figure 20) and *Martsche in White Apron* (Figure 21). He worked with amazing rapidity, producing from one to three paintings a day.

When his class was over in the middle of August, a number of his students

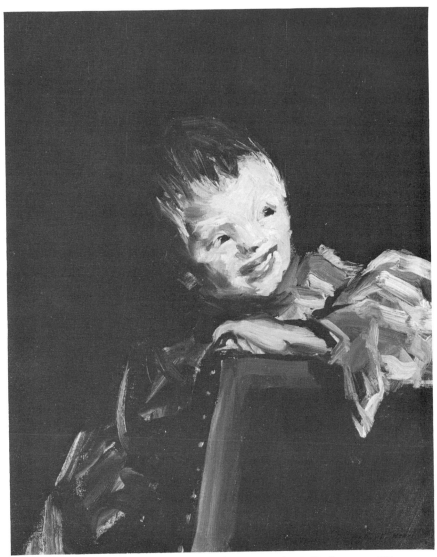

Figure 20. Robert Henri, *Cori Looking over Back of Chair*, 1907. Oil on canvas, 24 x 20″. Collection of Mr. George Perutz, Dallas, Texas.

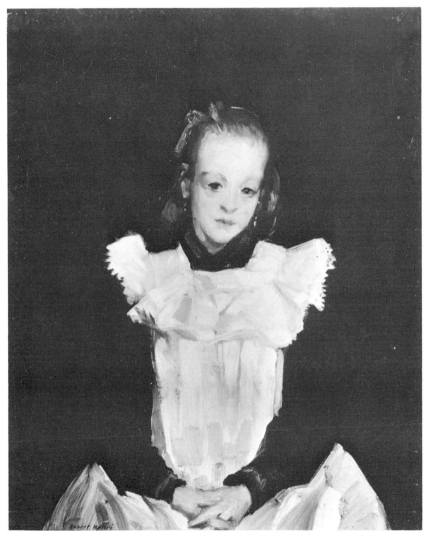

Figure 21. Robert Henri, *Martsche in White Apron*, 1907. Oil on canvas, 32 x 26″. Collection of Mrs. Howell Howard, New York.

left for Paris, while several who were close to him remained in Haarlem to paint landscapes or work beside him in the studio. "There is a value to me," he wrote, "in that several people assist in keeping the humor of the laughing girl [Cori] alive." [29]

He finally embarked for New York late in September, to be greeted by the Sloans, who had moved his belongings into his new studio on East 40th Street. He found New York depressing. He could not help looking back nostalgically to Holland as a land of "clear light sunshine reflected into those big east windows [of his Haarlem studio], sunshine in the children who posed and played, sunshine in the warm friendship." To the Dutch sunshine he contrasted the gloomy atmosphere of New York—New York, "where the $ is so important, where the light even in the big cleaned windows has so little happiness[,] where the faces of the people are so much sadder." [30]

On his return to America, he became engaged in a round of taxing activities that left him tired and depressed. But after a few weeks, he finally settled down to teaching fully subscribed classes at the New York School of Art, painting a few portraits (of Jesseca Penn and his well-known *Eva Green*, Figure 22), and working for the forthcoming exhibition. This task occupied many hours during which he met with Sloan and Davies to conclude their plans. While Sloan was photographing paintings and Davies and Macbeth were laying out the catalogue, Henri pored over the mailing lists and carefully revised a definitive article on the group, written by Mary Fanton Roberts, scheduled to appear in the *Craftsman* magazine.

The final arrangements for the exhibition of the Eight were made in January, 1908, by Henri's friends. During this period he had been compelled to make frequent trips to Wilkes-Barre, Pennsylvania, to execute portraits of Mr. and Mrs. George Cotton Smith and Miss Edith Reynolds. Fortunately, they were completed by the end of the month, in time for him to return to help his associates hang the exhibition at Macbeth's on February 1.

The walls of two galleries were divided into eight equal sections of about twenty-five running feet apiece, and each man was free to exhibit whichever pictures he thought most suitable, within the limits of the assigned space. Each member hung his own pictures, taking care not to place them above "the line." When this work was finished, there was nothing to do but wait for the opening scheduled for February 3, the following Monday. Henri, Sloan observed at the time, "seems quite nervous over the exhibition." [31]

When the show opened, it quickly became a major center of interest in New York. "The show at Macbeth's is creating a sensation," Henri reported

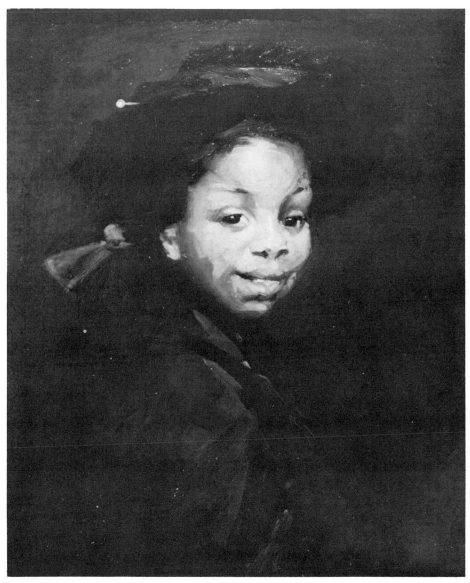

Figure 22. Robert Henri, *Eva Green*, 1907. Oil on canvas, 24 x 20⅛″. Roland P. Murdock Collection, Wichita Art Museum.

to a friend. "It was packed like an academy reception from early morning to night." [32] By the eighth of February, Sloan was able to report that about three hundred people were entering every hour, with at least eighty-five people constantly in attendance. In all, about seven thousand visitors saw the show.

The exhibition also proved to be a commercial success. Pictures valued at over four thousand dollars were sold: two Davies, two Henris, one Shinn, one Luks, and one Lawson, and of this number, four were purchased by Gertrude Vanderbilt Whitney.[33] When the final tally was made, Sloan was jubilant: "We've made a success—Davies says an *epoch.* . . . Macbeth is 'pleased as Punch.' " [34]

Part of the success of the exhibition hinged on the publicity it generated in the New York newspapers. And much of this attention was due to Henri's persistent efforts in cultivating and educating such art critics as Fitz Gerald, Stephenson, Gregg, and Luks's friend James Gibbons Huneker, who sympathetically defended the group. A major article appeared almost every day during the two weeks of the show; some critics objected to it, to be sure, but the majority, as Ira Glackens has observed, accepted and even praised the work.[35]

Those critics who attacked the Eight did so for a variety of reasons. One, for example, found fault with weak drawing and construction in Davies, Prendergast, Sloan, and Henri and scolded the first two for passing from nature into a world of fantasy: "These canvases of Mr. Prendergast look for all the world like an explosion in a color factory." [36] Another complained because the Eight pretended to discard "the conventions of mere picture-making" in the effort to express their individual personalities, but still gave the impression of "having developed their ideas within ill-lighted studio walls, under the influence of this or that foreign master," thereby falling into the trap of "mannerism." [37] Still another, understandably, objected to the painters' "unhealthy nay even coarse and vulgar point of view," coupled with an undue preoccupation with "technique" and poor drawing.[38] Although these criticisms differ from one another, they reflect a distinctly academic bias, which demanded that the artist exhibit a knowledge of correct drawing and anatomy and a fidelity to the surface appearances of his subject and, above all, that he avoid "inartistic," common themes like Luks's pigs and Sloan's tenement houses.

Almost as if to answer these objections, several writers who were sympathetic to the Eight pointed out that their styles were not so radical when compared to the work of "the men who were the rage in artistic Paris twenty years ago." [39] As one critic pointed out: "Any young painter recently returned from Paris or Munich—the Munich of the secessionists—would call the exhibition of the eight painters very interesting but far from revolutionary." [40] Others defended the right of each member to express himself in his own individual way rather than conform to a set of pre-established academic canons. "Let us try to shift the focus," one suggested, "whenever a new personality swims into our ken. Let us study each man according to his temperament and not ask ourselves whether he chimes in with other men's music." [41] As to the merit of the pictures, the critic of the *Evening Sun* saw masculinity and power in Henri's *Laughing Child* and *Dutch Soldier*, humanity without sentimentality in Luks's *Pet Goose*, and technical mastery in Glackens' depiction of a commonplace, contemporary theme in *The Shoppers* (Figure 23). The same reviewer went on to praise the "rude animation" of Sloan's street scenes and the bravura of Shinn's paintings of the ballet, arguing that many of the exhibitors had indeed responded to the challenge posed by the conservative critic Royal Cortissoz that the painters "go forth into the living, breathing world with no thought of anything save the straightforward portrayal of visible things." [42]

One of the most perceptive critics to write about the Eight was Mary Fanton Roberts, who saw their desire to portray that world as a step toward a distinctly national American art.[43] Chastising the artists who borrowed their style and subject matter entirely from European painting, she pointed to the Eight as a group who produced "a home-grown art, out of our own soil":

Any one of them will tell you that just now there is no civilization in the world comparable in interest to ours; none so meteoric, so voluble, so turbulent, so unexpected, so instinct with life, so swift of change, so full of riotous contrast in light or shade. We have vivacity and bleakness, subtle reserve and brutal frankness, gorgeous color and pathetic dreariness. We are magnetic through our great surging of life from ocean to ocean. We have grown humorous balancing our greatness against our defects. We are enthusiastic and fickle, and we are just beginning to understand our power, our beauty, and our blunders and the fact that we have just as good a right to regard ourselves as a source of inspiration as of revenue only.

She warned the reader that she did not mean that "American art should be patriotic(!), limited to American subjects only." To underline her argu-

Figure 23. William Glackens, *The Shoppers*, 1908. Oil on canvas, 60 x 60".
Chrysler Art Museum, Provincetown, Massachusetts.

ments, she quoted Henri as saying : "It seems that the basis of future American art lies in our artists' appreciation of the value of the human quality all about them, which is nothing more or less than seeing the truth, and then expressing it according to their individual understanding of it." He left it to the individual painter to discover the artistic language best suited to what he had to say. The men of the Eight, Mrs. Roberts reported, "boast no special creed for their work, they are not a school." They expressed an American point of view naturally, not self-consciously. As she put it: "They are not consciously trying to create a new art for a country that needs one; yet they are every one of them (and quite a number of others besides) doing the kind of work that is essentially creative and absolutely typical of our own racial characteristics, our social conditions, and our widely diversified country."

It should be clear from these remarks (which Henri edited and corrected in proof) that the Eight—and particularly the five from Philadelphia—did not subscribe to the strident nationalism of the 1930's regionalist painters Curry, Benton, and Wood. Nor were they using their art as a weapon in the struggle for social reform—as they so often have been accused of doing. Mrs. Roberts' statement gives us the necessary clue to their orientation: to be contemporary in their own time, as Taine had recommended in France years before. In this way the national character of their art would emerge naturally and organically, just as it had with Manet, Goya, Degas, and Renoir. It is no accident that these artists, along with Velázquez, Hals, and Rembrandt, were looked upon by Henri and his friends (Sloan, Luks, Glackens, and Shinn) as exemplary models, both in their attitude toward their subjects and in their styles. What they had in common in many, but not all, cases was a desire to depict the life of ordinary people in their normal routine of daily activity. In doing so, of course, the artists interpreted experience, rather than portraying what they saw in a photographic manner. (See, for example, Sloan's *Election Night* [Figure 24], Luks's *East Side Docks* [Figure 25]; and Shinn's *Sixth Avenue Elevated after Midnight* [Figure 26].)

The artists Henri and his circle admired not only stimulated the Americans' interest in contemporary themes but also helped them to forge a style appropriate to these subjects. While Henri objected to European art as a subject of slavish imitation, he realized that he and his friends could not risk cutting themselves off from it. Thus, he thought, the language of European art could be studied profitably, then transformed according to the needs of the individual artist, and finally turned to the representation of American subjects. In this, he was both national and international in outlook, though two of his as-

Figure 24. John Sloan, *Election Night*, 1907. Oil on canvas, 25 ⅜ x 31 ¾".
Collection of the Memorial Art Gallery of the University of Rochester.

Figure 25. George Luks, *East Side Docks*, 1905. Oil on canvas, 21 x 27". Private collection, New York.

Figure 26. Everett Shinn, *Sixth Avenue Elevated after Midnight*, 1899. Pastel, 8 x 12½″. Collection of Mr. and Mrs. Arthur G. Altschul.

sociates, Glackens and Shinn, were criticized, and with good reason, for imitating Renoir and Degas too closely.

In their first paintings done in Philadelphia under Henri's guidance, Sloan, Luks, Glackens, and Shinn adopted a dark palette, contrary to that of the American Impressionists of the mid-nineties. The palette was based, in part, on the tonalities found in the work of Velázquez, Hals, and Rembrandt, as well as Goya and early Manet. These European masters, whom Henri admired, could speak with great dramatic power, often coupled with a realistic intent, by eschewing superfluous local colors in favor of the might of arbitrary contrasts of light and shade. They did not record the optical sensations of light on surfaces but rather built imposing pictorial structures that intensified certain aspects of visual experience beyond slavish fidelity to the hues of nature. Their approach dictated that shadows need not be colored, nor must illumination be sunlight, but that everything could be subjected to the total plan—the overall visual impact—of the painting, which was geared to the intensification of whatever properties the artist wished to express. For Henri, this mode of painting was the perfect antidote to the prettiness of academic art. He and his friends forced their contrasts to the point where they shocked the public; and the earthy hues they used in the early years of the twentieth century told of a potent emotional response to life in which false gaiety and sentimentality dissolved in favor of the raucous clatter of the city and the life of the common people who lived in it. The five painters from Philadelphia knew from experience the gloomy colors of the city streets; followers of Whitman, they observed misery as well as happiness. The dark palette, the sharp contrasts of light and shade, were thus the most direct means of expressing their special experiences of urban humanity around the turn of the century. None of them, except Glackens, had pursued the delicate poetry of color before the exhibition at Macbeth's in 1908. It is not surprising, then, that they should have earned for themselves epithets such as "the black school," "the revolutionaries," and "the gang." [44]

What was the significance of the exhibition of the Eight? It proved conclusively, and for the first time in America, that a group of artists who were strongly antiacademic could attract wide public notice and financial returns —not as curiosities, but as significant artists who honestly spoke the language of their own time and place. True, the Ten had freed themselves from the hegemony of the Academy, and while they emerged as progressive artists in the late nineties, by 1908 their style appeared to Sloan "like New York taste today—like spring hats with less utility—seems so lacking in enthusiasm." [45]

There had been earlier attempts, too, by young students of Henri's to hold exhibitions outside the regular academic channels, but these were hardly noticed by the public and the press. Thus the show at the Macbeth Galleries stands as the first well-organized, successful presentation of an important new kind of American painting which seemed so radical to the established academic painters and their spokesmen that they rejected almost all of it. The Eight, then, not only broke the grip of the Academy, but also addressed the public as a united front with a distinct identity. Many of the critics, realizing that Davies' style, like Prendergast's and Lawson's, was remote from that of the five who had come from Philadelphia, tended to overlook these three men when considering the historical importance of the show. The show's core, and the part that received most attention, was composed of works of varying degrees of realism by Sloan, Luks, Glackens, Shinn, and Henri, and though they insisted that they were not a "school," their exhibition ultimately came to stand for the triumph of pictorial realism in American painting.[46] The exhibition at Macbeth's was a rallying point for those, particularly the young, who wished to see a realistic treatment of contemporary themes win out as the modern idiom; and the show's success gave courage, again to the young, to carry on the fight against the Academy by organizing larger and more radical exhibitions of contemporary American art.

After the excitement over the exhibition had died down and arrangements had been made to send the pictures to Philadelphia, Henri's life returned to normal—teaching and painting portraits. The relative calm of the late winter and spring of 1908 was interrupted by his election to the National Institute of Arts and Letters; an offer from Connah to take a class to Spain that summer; and, most important, his marriage to Marjorie Organ, a twenty-two year old cartoonist on the New York *Journal* (a portrait of her by Henri is reproduced as Figure 27).

The daughter of Mr. and Mrs. John Organ of New York City, Marjorie was a beautiful, vivacious redhead who left Hunter College in her freshman year to study art with Dan McCarthy, a newspaper artist who ran a study-by-mail school in the New York *World* Building. Recognizing her talent, McCarthy guided her into newspaper work, and when his school failed, he suggested she join the art staff of the New York *Journal*. And so she did, becoming the only woman (and a very young one) in an office of eight or ten men. Having embarked on a career as a cartoonist at the age of seventeen, she became well known as the artist of the comic strip "Reggie and the Heavenly Twins," which ran for three years in the *Journal*, and for her caricatures of theatrical personalities in the *World*.

146

Figure 27. Robert Henri, *The Ancient Dress (The Masquerade Dress)*, 1911. Oil on canvas, 76½ x 36¼″. The Metropolitan Museum of Art, Arthur H. Hearn Fund, 1958.

She was often squired about by Walt Kuhn and Rudolph Dirks, cartoon-
ists working on the *World* and *Journal* respectively; and at Mouquin's, one
of their favorite haunts, Henri was pointed out to her as the leader of the
Eight. At Walt Kuhn's urging, she attended some of Henri's lectures and was
attracted by his slight southern drawl and electric changes of manner. Finally
Dirks, himself a friend of Henri's, introduced them at Mouquin's late in
March. Two days after the meeting Henri began to paint her portrait in sittings that were kept a secret from all but her sister Violet. Indeed, few were
aware of their courtship during the spring, so their marriage on May 5 in a
civil ceremony at Elizabeth, New Jersey, came as a complete surprise to most
of his friends. Reporters on the New York newspapers did not discover the
wedding until early in June, after the couple had sailed to Spain for their
honeymoon.

The Henris arrived at Gibraltar in the middle of June and from there made
their way to Algeciras and Granada, then to Seville, Cordova, and finally
Madrid. His new bride appreciated the colorful life of the Madrid streets and
cafés, and her wit and youth added new zest to Henri's deep love of Spain.
His bullfighter friends again rallied to him and drank many a toast to their
health.

As before, Henri taught a summer class in the studio and took his pupils to
museums, while working on his own pictures in his free time. Marjorie posed
for several portraits, and once more he turned to his favorite subjects: Spanish children, gypsies, dancers, and bullfighters. Among his better-known
paintings done during the summer of 1908 were *Cinco Centimo*, full-length
and bust-length portraits of Picador Antonio Banos (see Figure 56), and several full-length portraits of the dancer Manaleta Maraquis.

In the middle of September they left Madrid to spend a month in Paris,
where he introduced Marjorie to the world of art and entertainment that he
had already come to know so well. Here they walked along the boulevards,
shopping and stopping at the cafés; and in the evenings they went to the
theatre, explored Montmartre, and attended the performances at the Bal
Tabarin and the Folies-Bergère. This was a time for enjoyment, not work,
and Henri chronicled their holiday activities in a letter to his mother:

We went into the *jardin* of the Tuileries near at hand and saw the balloons that
were grouped ready to go up and going up in the Grand Prize balloon race—18
of them—they sailed away over Paris—we took the boat for St. Cloud and went
down the river—beautiful ride late in the day—there was a fete at St. Cloud—not
very lively in itself but we took dinner at the brilliant Café Bleu. . . . At the

Salon there are many things in an effort to be bizarre[,] some good—many very bad. It is not nearly as good as I expected it to be. We have been to the Louvre and the Luxembourg and the other permanent exhibitions[,] to many theatres where the novelties of the French stage and very fine up to date costumes are to be seen—to some of the dance halls, etc., etc. Paris, if anything, looks grander than ever and it is certainly a wonderful place. . . . I have been tremendously interested in the aeroplane work of the brothers Wright. The one who is over here is doing great things.[47]

Significantly, Henri also visited the Salon d'Automne, which Prendergast and a former pupil, Patrick Henry Bruce, strongly urged him to see. Then in its sixth year, the Salon opened its doors to the most advanced forms of modern art in Paris—thirty works by Matisse, along with Fauvist paintings by Camoin, Derain, van Dongen, Friesz, Manguin, Marquet, Puy, and Vlaminck. From his diary we know he gave some thought at this time to Matisse' role as an artist, and it is almost certain that he discussed the French painter during a visit to James Wilson Morrice, who had recently become a close friend of Matisse. Henri was probably not convinced immediately of Matisse' merit as a painter (he was later to become more sympathetic to him), because when he returned to New York, he spoke of "the strange freaks" at the Salon d'Automne and said, "The Eight exhibition was much more notable." [48] History, of course, was to prove Henri wrong in this judgment.[49]

After he returned to New York, he resumed his regular teaching duties at the New York School of Art. Things went smoothly until the middle of November, when continual delays in salary payments forced him to deliver an ultimatum to Douglas John Connah, manager of the school, to recover the amount due. Finally, an understanding was reached: the money owed to Henri was to be paid in monthly installments. In December, however, the school was unable to raise the necessary funds, so he had no alternative but to announce his resignation if payment was not made by January 4. When the deadline arrived, Henri had heard nothing, so he withdrew from the school. His reason for resigning was strictly financial; but Connah gave a different story to the press, claiming that the school found Henri's influence on the students steadily diminishing. The opposite, of course, was true. After Henri's departure, a more "refined" academic regime was instituted; two of Chase's former pupils, Charles W. Hawthorne and Eugene Paul Ullman, took over his duties. A year later, the school went bankrupt.

When the news of Henri's resignation reached his students, many threatened to quit the school and urged him to establish classes of his own. On January 6 he agreed to do so and immediately secured a studio on the sixth floor of the old Lincoln Arcade Building, at 66th and Broadway. His student Carl Sprinchorn was appointed manager and caretaker of the studio; easels, chairs, and stools were purchased; electric lights were installed; and on January 11, 1909, Henri's classes met in his own school for the first time.[50]

He was optimistic about the prospects for this new venture, and his hopes were well founded; thanks to his personal magnetism as a teacher, his classes were soon crowded. Helen Appleton Read, a former student at the Art Students League who transferred to the Henri school, left a vivid account of his teaching:

> Perched on stools and lockers we listened to Henri preach a new and broader gospel of art. But in reality what was there that was revolutionary in it? He taught us again universal truths of art which had been temporarily eclipsed by a scholastic, competitive method of teaching, then current. He opened our eyes to the beauty and meaning of many things which as academic students with an academic training (which meant accurate drawings from life models) we would never have felt.
>
> The old idea was to learn to draw the figure before the student had ideas. Henri's idea was to have ideas first, paint pictures, make compositions, which is the same thing; learn to draw as you go along. He taught us to paint from the inside out so to speak, to try to find that inner thing that made one particular man or woman different from any other man or woman. He tried to wean us away from the idea that we were art students, a state which immediately causes scales to grow over one's eyes, and to see things again as ordinary human beings. There was much talk of personalities and composition and less of planes and brushwork.[51]

Henri continued to exert a profound influence on a generation of American men and women who flocked to him as the only viable alternative to stagnant academic training. In the first year alone, A. S. Baylinson, Henry J. Glintenkamp, Guy Pène du Bois, Paul Manship, Morgan Russell, Andrew Dasburg, Bernard Karfiol, Paul Rohland, and Carl Walters worked under his direction.

As a result of his marriage, Henri's social life in New York took a more active turn. On Thursday evenings (later Tuesday evenings), the Henris held weekly receptions in the studio, attended by artists, writers, editors, and students. In a sense these were the logical continuation of the regular meetings at 806 Walnut Street in Philadelphia. Absent, of course, were the pot-bellied stove, the rarebits cooked over the gas jet, and the annual satires. Still, the bohemian spirit of those earlier days was not inhibited by the modern conveniences of steam heat and an electric stove. These evenings usually followed dinner at Mouquin's (the Café Francis failed in 1908) or at Petipas, a French restaurant on West 29th Street where artistic and literary folk gathered. The presence of the New York members of the Eight usually could be counted on, along with George Bellows, Rudolph Dirks, Walter Pach, and Walt Kuhn. Frequent visitors, too, were the art critics Charles Fitz Gerald (now married to Glackens' sister-in-law), Byron Stephenson, and Frederick James Gregg; the poets Alfred Kreymborg and Vachel Lindsay—the latter a student in Henri's classes; and William Carman Roberts and Mary Fanton Roberts, both distinguished editors, he of the *Literary Digest*, she of the *Craftsman*. In the summer of 1909 they were joined by John Butler Yeats, Irish portrait painter, genial raconteur, and father of the poet William Butler Yeats. Now and then the noted dancer Isadora Duncan, whom Henri and his friends worshiped, would make an appearance at the studio in flowing robes of royal purple.

For these receptions Marjorie would provide crackers, cheese, and beer and then leave the guests to Henri. The chief order of business was talk—not only about art but, as Robert McIntyre recalled, also about "poetry, music, literature, bull fighting in Mexico and Spain, baseball, the merits of certain shaving creams, history; in a word, life and its living." [52] Art students who attended these Thursday evening sessions often brought their work, on which Henri gave criticisms for all to hear. And it was not unusual for these gatherings to end with the assembled company playing poker around Marjorie's drawing table.

Henri's myriad activities took much of his time away from painting, but he managed to produce several impressive full-length portraits of Marjorie, who was his chief model through the winter and spring of 1909. During this season his own production suffered because he gave so willingly of his energy in the fight for independent exhibitions. In December, while the original show of the Eight was still on the road—it toured Philadelphia, Chicago, Detroit, Toledo, Pittsburgh, Cincinnati, Bridgeport, Connecticut, and Newark— Henri discussed with Glackens and Sloan the possibility of a second exhibition at Macbeth's. All three favored the idea, but when Henri contacted Macbeth, he learned that the gallery was fully booked through May, 1909, and that it would be too late to schedule a show of the Eight that year. [53]

Since the plans for a second group show were frustrated, Henri and Sloan began to envision a more ambitious exhibition scheme: a permanent gallery, where the work of the Eight and artists they invited could be displayed throughout the year. After a meeting in April, Sloan recorded a proposal that he, Henri, and their business friend J. B. Lichtenstein had evolved:

We talked with Lichtenstein on the subject of a Gallery. He proposes that three or four rich men be found to furnish the funds—that they appoint a treasurer in charge of the funds, the expenditure to be only for stipulated purpose of rent, maintenance, salaries for manager and assistant, profits to go into a contingent fund. The works shown to be invited by the Eight, and subject to their judgment so that the shows will be expression of their judgment.[54]

Discussion continued into May, and in that month Henri, Sloan, Davies, and Lichtenstein explored several possible locations for the gallery. But with the coming of the summer they temporarily suspended their activities.

It was only in December, 1909, that Henri and Sloan renewed their interest in a large independent exhibition. While Henri was painting Sloan's portrait, another scheme was developed, which Sloan recorded in his diary:

I suggested another exhibition tapering from Ullman's Big Show at the Madison Square Garden [a proposal for a gigantic, spectacular one-week exhibition that one of Sloan's friends had made several days before] to a smaller affair in the big empty first floor room that Henri and I looked at in the spring on 35th St. near Sixth Avenue. This idea we worked out till it looks to me as though we could put it through. At about $5.00 a picture, selected exhibitors. A show to last a month, "The American Art Show." [55]

This proposal was the most immediate antecedent of the Exhibition of Independent Artists in April of the following year, but several abortive attempts at other schemes temporarily eclipsed this plan.[56]

A definite strategy finally began to take shape early in March, when Henri's young friend Walt Kuhn suggested to him a plan, not unlike Sloan's, for a large exhibition of short duration to be financed by a contribution of two hundred dollars apiece by Henri, Sloan, Davies, and himself, with each exhibitor paying according to his means. Sloan readily agreed to this proposal, dropped the plans he had made with Ullman, and joined Henri and Kuhn in shaping what ultimately became the Exhibition of Independent Artists. The three artists held an important meeting on March 11, 1910, and several days later arranged to rent for a thousand dollars a vacant building at 29–31 West 35th Street to house the show during the month of April. The original four who had offered to pay two hundred dollars each were now joined by several others, including some of Henri's students, whose contributions helped provide the necessary money.[57] On the basis of a list drawn up by Henri, Sloan, and Kuhn, a schedule of fees [58] was sent to those who were invited to exhibit—a miscellaneous group comprised of young, unknown artists, academicians of progressive tendency, and avant-garde artists who refused to submit work to the annual Academy shows. About half of those invited were, or had been, Henri's students.[59] The idea behind the show was simply to have no connection with the National Academy, "either in a friendly way or the opposite," but to attempt to rival its shows in size and importance. "The fact is that there are a great many good pictures painted in New York which are never exhibited. We aim to place these pictures before the public." [60]

As secretary-treasurer, Sloan spent a hectic two weeks typing and addressing announcements, receiving fees, keeping accounts, and, with Kuhn's help, compiling the catalogue. Henri, in the meantime, was preparing a definitive article on the Independents for the *Craftsman*, while Kuhn took over the management of the improvised gallery on West 35th Street. The pages of Sloan's diary for the days just before the opening reflect the spirit of excitement he and his friends felt in staging this historic exhibition: "We have done a great thing in planning and executing this project and are showing now the New York public such an exhibition of American art as has never been seen before—the best exhibition ever held on this continent (that is, composed of American art exclusively)." [61] (Early in 1910, Jerome Myers had hoped for an exhibition of international scope, a sentiment echoed later by Davies; such a scheme, however, would materialize only three years later in the Armory Show.) [62]

Sloan's excitement grew as the pictures began to arrive. He had reservations about a few of the contributions; he thought that several pictures should be withdrawn (there was no jury and no prizes were given), presumably because they were of inferior quality. But most of the work aroused his enthusiasm: "Invigorating stuff," he said, "full of force and interest." [63] The hanging of this great exhibition was undertaken by a committee composed of Bellows, the sculptor James E. Frazer, Glackens, Davies (who was too ill to attend), Sloan, Kuhn, Du Bois, and Henri, with the assistance of several of Henri's pupils. The three floors were rapidly filled with the work of 103 artists hung in alphabetical order—a total of 260 paintings, 20 sculptures, and 219 drawings and etchings, which were confined to the third floor. The rooms were equipped with electric lights and each picture was rigged with a lamp of its own—in sharp contrast to the uneven and usually poor illumination in the galleries of the National Academy of Design.

The *vernissage* and reception took place on April 1—and it was nothing less than a sensation:

In the evening came a real triumph, the three large floors were crowded to suffocation, absolutely jammed at 9 o'clock. The crowd packed the sidewalk outside waiting to get in. A small squad of police came on the run. It was terrible but wonderful to think that an art show could be so jammed. A great success seems assured. . . . There were at *least* 2000 people on hand in the evening.[64]

While the show attracted throngs of people during the month of April—it was open without charge every day, including Sunday, from 10:00 A.M. to 10:00 P.M.—the anticipated sales did not materialize. Though three small pictures were sold the first day (a Henri drawing and sketches by Clara Tice and Edith Haworth), only two more works were sold during the remaining twenty-six days of the exhibition—a drawing by Coleman and a sketch by Edith C. Barry. The total receipts amounted to only seventy-five dollars.[65] Henri must have been gravely disappointed by these poor results, in view of the fact, reported in his diary, that over two million dollars had been spent at auction in New York for pictures by the old masters and the Barbizon school during the same month that the Exhibition of Independent Artists was open. Disgruntled, he summed up the results of the show on the closing day: "The exhibition was a great success as far as general notice and attendance— The crush at the opening and continued full attendance to the last day. Financially nothing happened."[66]

Just as with the exhibition of the Eight, some critics found value in the show, while others were repelled by it. Clearly, avant-garde American art had not won over the reviewer who wrote that the exhibition was composed of "insurgents, anarchists, socialists, all the opponents to any form of government, to any method of discipline."[67] Frank Jewett Mather of the *Nation* expressed regret that aside from a few men of worth—Henri, Glackens, Sloan, Shinn, Myers, Bellows, and Davies—"there is more green, yellow and red sickness about than positive talent."[68] Not all the critics were so hesitant to embrace the new: Joseph E. Chamberlin thought the exhibition showed "a great deal of good and promising work," including some by "artists now unknown whose work some day may be famous."[69]

There is no question that the Exhibition of Independent Artists attracted a tremendous amount of public attention during the month of April, 1910. But to the organizers it appeared that there was more hue and cry than real sympathy for their aims. It was Henri's writing, more than anything else, that explained what the show meant and why it was so important for the development of American art. He defended the exhibition as giving young artists a chance to display individual and experimental work, "the independent personal evidence which each artist has to make and which must become a record of their time and a proof of the advancement of human understanding." He realized that many who viewed this new art would be shocked, but urged them to accept "those who are pushing forward, who need and deserve recognition, who must have encouragement, who should receive praise for every step of their advance." Progress, freedom, experiment: these are the keys to Henri's philosophy; and the Exhibition of Independent Artists was the medium through which the fruits of this philosophy, and those who shared it, could be judged. This is not to say that the exhibitors had to paint in a style that he approved of. On the contrary; "this is called an independent exhibition because it is a manifestation of independence in art and of the absolute necessity of such independence. It does not mean that it is an independent organization, but that it is made up of the independent points of view of men who are investigating." [70]

Henri's emphasis on freedom and independence in art, his rebuttal of everything the National Academy stood for, makes him the ideological father of the Armory Show. That exhibition, held in 1913, was a living illustration of much of the philosophy he expressed in 1910, and the major powers behind it—Pach, Kuhn, Davies, and Myers—were, in varying degrees, members of his circle in the first decade of the century. Henri himself was a member of the Association of American Painters and Sculptors, which staged the Armory Show, but as we shall see, he was overshadowed by younger and even more progressive men who embraced the work of the leading avant-garde artists in Europe: the Fauves, Cubists, Expressionists, and their forerunners. For Henri, the chief function of the Independent Exhibition was to promote American art, so that "the people of America learn the means of expressing themselves in their own time and in their own land." [71]

The 1910 exhibition was, in another sense, the forerunner of the Society of Independent Artists, founded in New York in 1916. Many who helped to stage the earlier show became directors of that society, and in many respects their policies were similar. In 1910, Henri had rejected the idea of incorporating the Independent Exhibition as a permanent organization, stating: "I can see no advantage to art in the existence of art societies. The thing that inter-

ests me in this is the idea of it, the idea of independence, the idea of encouragement of independence and individuality in study and the giving of an opportunity for greater freedom in exhibitions." [72] The independent spirit of
these beliefs, which reflect his anarchistic suspicion of organizations, was
adopted by many of his students, some of whom later took up the fight for
open, nonacademic exhibitions in this country. [73]

Although the Exhibition of Independent Artists was Henri's chief concern
in 1909–1910, he was also involved in organizing and managing his own
school and moving into more commodious quarters. His new studio at 10
Gramercy Park, where he was to live until his death in 1929, was on the top
floor of a handsome mid-nineteenth-century house on the south side of the
park—then, as now, a quiet, picturesque oasis where one can retreat from the
frantic tempo of New York City. [74]

9

Teachings and Philosophy of Art

THE EXHIBITION of the Eight and the Independent Exhibition of 1910 were, in many ways, culminating incidents in Henri's career. In a sense his life can be viewed as a "linear" development leading up to these two major events. But after 1910, the year in which he reached the age of forty-five, the nature of his influence changed. He was unquestionably a central figure in stimulating the development of the most advanced, nonacademic art of the 1890's and 1900's, but in the years immediately after 1910, younger, more progressive personalities such as Walt Kuhn and Walter Pach, along with Alfred Stieglitz, partially supplanted Henri as leader of the vanguard. When the Armory Show of 1913 made it quite clear that crucially important developments in recent European painting had gone almost unnoticed by the majority of American artists, many tried frantically to catch up with the latest trends in French, German, and Italian art. This event opened up a new era in the teens and twenties when many American artists, both good and bad, turned to Europe for guidance, largely abandoning the styles, subjects, and traditions of their native country. In this milieu it was inevitable that Henri should appear *retardataire* to some of the younger men. He continued to exert a strong and beneficial influence on American art, but because his influence was not as central as before, it seems appropriate to discuss the selected areas in which his leadership was still felt: in his teaching and philosophy of art, in the planning of exhibitions, and in his writings. The development of his style will be discussed in Chapter 12.

Henri's teaching in Philadelphia and Paris in the nineties and at the Veltin School, New York, was but a prelude to his period of greatest influence: during 1902–1909 at the New York School of Art and 1909–1912 at his own school. Although he continued to teach after this period, at the Art Students League and the Ferrer Center, a greater number of distinguished pupils passed through his classes between 1902 and 1912 than at any time before or after. Several of his most articulate students—Stuart Davis, Guy Pène du Bois, Rockwell Kent, Walter Pach, and Helen Appleton Read—wrote about their days under his tutelage, and from their remarks, along with Henri's own writings and information gathered from interviews, an accurate picture of his teachings and philosophy of art may be recreated.

It is universally acknowledged that a great measure of Henri's success as a teacher stemmed from his magnetic, inspiring personality. His very presence in the classroom stimulated his students to pour forth their creative energies with a facility that they had not imagined possible. Warm and humane at heart, he did not indulge in boisterous showmanship. Rather, he taught with a quiet, concentrated intensity of speech and gesture, though he could lash out vehemently against anything he believed was wrong or unjust. Part of his success was due to his eloquence, but this was only an outward symptom of his deep personal involvement with the issues of creativity and human emotion. Teaching, for Henri, was not just a way of earning a living; it was a duty he shouldered voluntarily because he believed he had a mission in fostering the growth of art in his native country. His profound faith in the progress of American art, both present and future—undoubtedly inspired by Walt Whitman—was readily transmitted to his students and gave many of them the courage to pursue the difficult business of painting in the face of public indifference.

Henri had definite ideas about the function and role of an art school, and in his teaching he put these ideas into practice. He deprecated those artists who studied technique as an end in itself—manual skill for the sake of virtuosity. His goal was just the opposite: to have the student develop his technique organically from the ideas that motivated him. Voicing thoughts that reflect Emerson's and Whitman's concept of organic functionalism (a principle echoed, too, in Louis Sullivan's theory of architecture), he spoke of "the need of inventing the necessary technique of the thing you have to express today, the technique that must be beautiful, that must be perfect because it is the only thing, the fittest, the shortest, plainest, *the* way of painting the idea in hand." If the young artist had something significant to say about life, about the world he lived in, then an appropriate pictorial language for his ideas would inevitably emerge. Henri insisted that the art student constantly be aware of the purpose of his work, which should be "the presentation in art of ideas of value," whether about religion, philosophy, or the "great conditions in life." Since art had a responsibility to society, not merely to itself, the art-for-art's-sake viewpoint was irrelevant and useless. The student, therefore, should immerse himself in the life and conditions of his time, absorb "the great ideas native to the country," and then learn how to express them.[1]

In his classes, Henri helped his students meet these three requirements. While the last—learning the means of expression—was thought by many of his contemporaries to be the exclusive concern of an art school, he saw his role as being much broader. Henri, his students recalled, talked not only about art, but about music, literature, and life in general, giving his pupils the equivalent of a liberal education. Whitman, Emerson, Rousseau, Dostoievsky, Tolstoi—these names were coupled, in Henri's talks, with those of Wagner, Zola, Ibsen, De Maupassant, and Isadora Duncan. He must have communicated his enthusiasm to his students most effectively, for Stuart Davis reported: "When Henri spoke of writers . . . what he did was to inspire a desire on the part of the listener to go out, to look up all this stuff and get involved with it." [2]

Henri also directed his students' interests to the world outside the classroom. Believing that painting should be a testament of the American artist's response to his immediate experience, and thus represent his nationality, he urged his pupils to become actively involved in the life of the city and country around them. Judging from their work, they often gravitated to the poorer sectors of American society, much as Dreiser had done in literature in the same period. Their attitude was chronicled by Helen Appleton Read: "Henri's point of view, which advocated all life as subject matter for art, brought in its wake the belief that the poor were nearer the realities of life and so more appropriate subjects for art. Life seemed to the Henri student to flow stronger and fuller in Bowery bars and riverfront alleys than in the Knickerbocker Hotel or in the fashionable streets of the upper east side, and the woman who wrapped her baby in a tattered shawl was, by this same reasoning, a more poignant symbol of maternity than one who could afford to buy her layette at the Lilliputian Bazaar." [3] These interests led to what Helen Read called "a species of mild socialism" among some of Henri's more politically radical students. (Later some of them contributed covers and illustrations to the Socialist magazine the *Masses*.) In his perceptive recollections of Henri's classes, Rockwell Kent (himself a Socialist) took pains to point out that "if Henri turned to labor, underprivilege and dilapidation as the subject or background for a picture it was merely because, to him, man at this level was most revealing of his own humanity." [4]

Henri also explained to his students how he expected them to experience life: not as passive observers, but with a masculine vigor that Walt Whitman would have admired. Guy Pène du Bois recalled the essence of Henri's teaching: "To find [beauty] we've got to be honest and fearless. We've got to be men first of all; the artist can come later. When he does come thus prepared, he will gain greatness." [5] These remarks contain the germ of Henri's whole philosophy. As he explained in the pages of the *Craftsman:* "A man should not care whether the thing he wishes to express is a work of art or not, . . . he should only care that it is a statement of what is worthy to put into permanent expression." [6] Just as Whitman willingly ignored poetic conventions when the force of his message burst the bonds of traditional literary form, so Henri had little patience with styles in which the niceties of pictorial form were sought as ends in themselves. Decorative art, needless to say, was beneath contempt.

By the same token, he discouraged photographic realism and despised "story-telling" in art; those who wanted to be illustrators, not painters, he cast aside pitilessly. The unconventional axiom that he handed down to his students was simply this: "It is not the subject but what you feel about it that counts." [7] In his painting and teaching he followed a personal credo that stressed expression over beauty for its own sake. Echoing views that were promulgated by the French Symbolist-Synthetist painters, Gauguin, Denis, and Sérusier, Henri wrote in 1909:

Colors are beautiful when they are significant. Lines are beautiful when they are significant. It is what they signify that is beautiful to us, really. . . . There are certain shades of yellow that are horrible to us because they relate to sickness, and if we search all the way through, we will find that all of the color that we declare as beautiful is only beautiful because it is the manifestation of the thing we most desire, the thing that we like most. Of course, the thing we desire is not always comfortable." [8]

To bring out the young artist's personal response to the subject, he created an atmosphere in which freedom and individuality of expression were nurtured. The ideal art school, he felt, should stimulate the development of each student as an individual, "recognizing in him a man, another new force; giving him the use of knowledge and experience but never dictating to him what or how he shall do." [9] For Henri, the unique personality of each student was the real source of valid art; it could not be imposed from without. Thus, under Whitman's and Emerson's influence, he would demand that the student "work both mind and body to the limit of his endurance to find in himself whatever there is of value; to find his truest thoughts and find a means, the simplest, straightest and most fit means to make record of them, to be the deepest thinker, the kindest appreciator, the clearest and simplest, frankest expressor he can be today." [10] His relationship to the student was unique in American art education; he was a catalyst, an encourager who discarded dry rules and useless laws of art. He made the aspiring painters in his classes conscious of their own innate creative ability and skillfully drew them out in the spontaneous act of painting a picture. As early as 1906 he had marveled at the miraculous potential of the subconscious, and it was this, along with the imagination, that he cultivated in those who studied with him. His preoccupation with the intangibles of expression seemingly at the expense of sound technique left him open for criticism; even some of his friends admitted that he was sometimes blind to the structural faults in work done in a spirit of fresh spontaneity.

This is not to say that he ignored discipline in his teaching. While he rejected the practice of drawing from plaster casts and, like Eakins, encouraged his pupils to take up painting without a preliminary line drawing, the majority of his time was spent teaching from the live model, both figure and portrait. To use his own words: "I am for drawing and construction, for continued and complete study, acquirement of firm foundation." [11] To implement these beliefs, he employed his former teacher Thomas Anshutz, and later Homer Boss, to give demonstrations of anatomy by building up the muscles in clay on a human skeleton. Boss's teachings complemented Henri's and contributed much to the effectiveness of the school. As one former pupil recalled, "We all felt he [Boss] was a most valuable asset to Henri's teaching as he concerned himself more with the fundamentals of technic and structural values. Henri could baffle us with a bravura technic during one of his infrequent demonstrations, while Boss would astound us with his knowledge of anatomy and sound craftsmanship." [12] As a student under Henri, Boss had been fascinated by Anshutz' method of lecturing on the bones and muscles with the aid of a skeleton and modeling clay, performances which the younger man learned to duplicate. So it was that the Eakins tradition of scientific knowledge of the human body was transmitted via Anshutz, and then Boss, to Henri's New York pupils.

Visual memory was also trained in the Friday-night classes, when Henri posed the model for half an hour, during which time the students were told to observe but not to draw. Then for an hour or more, they sketched the figure from memory. "Many of the results," Maurice Becker recalled, "were unbelievably faithful renditions of solid form in light and shade." [13]

"We were told to draw the model not according to some formula," Stuart Davis recalled, "but in terms of how it looked to us as a fresh experience. The questions of finish or prettiness were of no importance. The question was whether you could communicate some direct experience with this model in terms of its form." [14] For Henri, life drawing was not an end in itself, as it had been at the Académie Julian, but an exercise in composition; indeed, the life class, he remarked, "is a feeder to study in the composition class, they are the support one of the other." [15]

His greatest and most influential moments were in his celebrated composition classes. "I have always considered in my teaching the composition work the centre to which all other work is tributary," he said.[16] Students in the composition class were asked to make paintings or drawings of subjects from everyday life—the Bowery, Childs' Restaurant, Matteawan Asylum, prize fights, and sports of all kinds. They would work up these sketches into paintings in the studio or at home, and on Saturdays, just as at the Académie Julian, the pictures were brought to the school and hung on the walls, to be criticized by the instructor. Henri addressed the whole class, moving from one picture to the next; sometimes he would deliver a long discourse on one after another, at other times discuss a group of paintings together. As a rule he stressed the emotional impact of the picture, judging how effectively it communicated human values or the moods of nature:

I do not want to see how skillful you are—I am not interested in your skill. . . . I only want to see the things that bring to my mind the fact of life and that point a certain interest in life—That is [,] that point the meaning in life, that seem to get at the reason of things [,] at the principles of things so that I not only see the thing you have seen, but I see the deduction, or rather projection you make from that thing, the excitement, the pleasure that you have felt in the thing.[17]

When he criticized the construction of a picture, he approached it as a whole, trying to suggest ways of clarifying the total expressive message of the work. No rigid canons of form or technique were imposed on the artist; as we have seen, he wanted his students to learn to invent a fresh, new pictorial language for every new situation or subject. "Art was not a matter of rules and techniques, or the search for an absolute ideal of beauty," Davis recalled. "It was the expression of ideas and emotions about the life of the time." [18] Students with an innate sense of composition profited by the freedom Henri offered them, but the designs of those lacking this talent often became loose and disorganized—a fault difficult to avoid, given Henri's methods.

The Saturday composition class was, more than any other, the place where the students received a broad, liberal education, far transcending the limits of conventional art instruction. The stimulating effect of these classes on the younger generation was recorded by Davis:

He would talk about the paintings we brought in for three or four hours, and in the process of talking about those pictures he would criticize them not from the standpoint of some pre-established norm of excellence, but in relation to his own ideas. Or he would talk about some book he'd read and what it meant about life, and how this painting and the attitude toward it were related, or not related to the book. He'd talk about his own interests while he was talking about the painting and in that way, since he had more experience, more purposeful experience with culture in general than the crew of youths who were there, his discussions were very educational affairs.[19]

If Henri introduced his students to the painters he admired, he did not encourage them to imitate his own style of painting. "Don't paint like me," he said again and again. He did expose his students to the work of artists he believed in because he thought they could learn valuable lessons from it; the European masters mentioned in his classes most often were Velázquez, Rembrandt, Hals, Goya, Daumier, El Greco, Manet, Courbet, Degas, Van Gogh, Gauguin, Whistler, Cézanne, and Renoir. As to his contemporaries, he spoke highly of Rouault and even before the Armory Show praised Matisse' draughtsmanship. Nor did he overlook the American tradition as represented by Eakins, Homer, Twachtman, and Ryder. On the walls of the classrooms Henri posted large reproductions of works by many of these masters, and to those who were interested he lent his albums of mounted photographs and post cards that he had diligently gathered over the years.

Why study the work of contemporary and earlier artists? There were at least three major reasons, in Henri's mind, for doing so. In the cases of Rembrandt and Goya, their paintings testified to the humanity of their authors and reflected a sympathy with mankind that he wanted his students to emulate. They could find in earlier paintings, too, able demonstrations of the grammar of representation—line, color, light and shade, composition, and so on. These examples were not imitated, of course, but served to illustrate underlying principles of the visual arts. Most important, he used the work of other artists to illuminate the nature of artistic creation, the principles of which transcended any single time, place, or medium. All the arts were shown to be related to each other, and to painting, by all-encompassing basic principles, "great formulative forces, . . . of which the passing daily interests which seem all in themselves, are but results."[20] Likewise, he found

163

good art in all the epochs from ancient Egypt to the present and sought out what he believed to be the valid art of his contemporaries at home and abroad. Looking back on his years of study at the Académie Julian and the Ecole des Beaux-Arts, he bitterly regretted that his teachers had never called his attention to the best art of their own time: "We were never allowed to hear about men like Cézanne and Gauguin," he recalled.[21]

While Prendergast and Davies brought a knowledge of Postimpressionism to America, recent developments in French painting were known only to a small coterie of artists before Henri spread the word among the younger generation. Except for Stieglitz, whose influence was limited in scope, there was no one besides Henri to foster an understanding of these new currents in European painting; they were almost entirely ignored by dealers, collectors, and museums before 1913. He realized, correctly, that if America was to have an art that would draw on the best of native and foreign sources, he would single-handedly have to transmit the traditions of recent European painting to these shores. Without these influences, American art would languish in a retarded provincialism that had been its lot since the founding of the colonies.

While Henri believed in a healthy future for American art, he did not fall prey to a blind, self-conscious nationalism. "He showed them the Frenchmen," Forbes Watson reported, "but he did not encourage them to imitate the Frenchmen."[22] Henri's reason for taking this position should be self-evident: the artist, he believed, should absorb the life and spirit of his own nation; if he did so effectively, his art would naturally and organically express his nationality. Just as Manet, Courbet, and Degas reflected the life of their times, so Henri believed that American painting "demands deep roots, stretching far down into the soil of the nation, gathering sustenance from the conditions in the soil of the nation, and in its growth showing, with whatever variation, inevitably the result of these conditions."[23]

As compared to the progress of French painting in the first decade of the twentieth century, most American painting lagged behind by at least a generation. Realism and Impressionism had won their battle in France, and the influence of the Salon was gradually waning. In France these advances were made during the second half of the nineteenth century by such dedicated artists as Manet, Courbet, Monet, and Cézanne working against what seemed to be the insurmountable obstacle of the academic establishment. The same revolution had to be repeated on this side of the Atlantic a generation later. If the Academy was not as firmly entrenched in America as it had been in France, the forces to combat it were much smaller in number.

164

10

Aspects of Henri's Career, 1910-1929

Exhibition Programs

THE MACDOWELL CLUB

ALTHOUGH HENRI was unquestionably the major force behind the exhibition of the Eight and the Independent Artists of 1910, these were one-of-a-kind shows that did not allow him to realize his ideals on a continuing basis. The MacDowell Club of New York first invited him to put his theories about art exhibitions into practice, and he did so more successfully here than in any other organization. Founded in memory of the American composer Edward MacDowell, the Club served as a forum to promote the understanding of the fine arts; the emphasis was on music, but small exhibitions were occasionally scheduled in the Club's gallery.

Through his friendship with Mrs. James Haggin, patroness of the arts and supporter of the Club, Henri became the architect of a unique, jury-free exhibition scheme, the plan of which had begun to germinate in his mind after the 1910 Independents show. The aim of the plan was to provide a continuing series of exhibitions under the Club's auspices that would enable groups of eight to twelve artists to exhibit—without jury or prizes—at intervals of two weeks. Each group was to be organized by a "representative" who would select a congenial body of fellow artists; or else a group of several artists could assemble of its own accord, voting to bring in additional colleagues if they wished. These self-organizing groups were temporary and disbanded as soon as their two-week exhibition was over. Henri envisioned an open forum for different groups—students as well as older men—to exhibit in favorable company, modern as well as conservative. Beginning with the first exhibition in November, 1911, held in the clubhouse at 108 West 55th Street, the shows became a continuing event for the next eight years.

Henri's scheme combined a democratic, nonjuried process of selection with a measure of control to rule out unsympathetic elements. The moderately progressive artists among his circle of friends were free to exclude the academicians; yet their policies were not so liberal that anyone at all could exhibit. The plan thus tended to eliminate incompetents as well as undesirables. On the practical level, however, there were several major drawbacks. It was impossible for several groups to exhibit at the same time; the club's seventy-five-foot gallery was not spacious enough; and many artists disliked the semiprivate character of the club, preferring larger, well-established galleries distinctly associated with the art of painting.

THE ARMORY SHOW

Although the MacDowell Club plan represented the most complete realization of Henri's philosophy of exhibitions, another group of progressive artists —Jerome Myers, Elmer MacRae, Henry Fitch Taylor, and Walt Kuhn— launched a new, more ambitious organization in 1911. This was the American Painters and Sculptors (later incorporated as the Association of American Painters and Sculptors), whose major role was to stage the Armory Show of 1913. Walt Kuhn, earlier a member of Henri's entourage, took over the role of standard-bearer and power behind the scenes in the twenty-five–man society.

It would be an exaggeration to say that the A.P.S. was designed to oppose Henri's MacDowell Club scheme; but that group, unlike the Club, did believe in "exhibiting the works of progressive and live painters, both American *and foreign*." [1] The intrusion of the foreign element is the jarring note as far as Henri's philosophy is concerned; though he admired European art, he always feared that it might dominate American art. But Kuhn, at this point even more liberal than Henri, was willing to embrace "every kind of art, even that which I do not like." [2] Henri and his friends were invited to become members of the A.P.S., but grudgingly; as Kuhn admitted: "Henri and the rest will have to be let in—but not until things are chained up so that they can't do any monkey business." [3] It is clear that by taking Henri and "the soft boys" into the organization, Kuhn had no intention of awarding them major roles in determining policy. Regarded by the younger man as a well-meaning but *retardataire* group that had now been overshadowed as the real avant-garde of American painting, they were admitted belatedly and in a spirit of concession. Sloan recalled: "Henri and the rest of the group around him were rebuffed whenever they asked questions." [4]

Henri was not invited to any meetings of the A.P.S. until fifteen days after its founding. When he appeared at the meeting of January 2, 1912, he discovered that the officers had already been elected: as president, J. Alden Weir, a member of the Ten American Painters; as vice-president, the sculptor Gutzon Borglum, a well-known enemy of the policies of the National Academy; as treasurer, the Impressionist painter Elmer MacRae; and as secretary, Walt Kuhn. Although Arthur B. Davies had not yet become an officer of the association, Henri noted that he was "very active in it." [5] From the minutes of this meeting we know that Henri's only significant contribution was his motion to elect additional members. Thus it was that several of his associates —Bellows, Prendergast, Du Bois, Sloan, and Shinn—were proposed and voted in. Besides this, Henri's influence was limited both by his own lack of desire to participate and by the barriers erected by the inner circle who founded the association. There may be good reason for his reluctance to commit himself: even after the A.P.S. was established, he was convinced that the MacDowell Club scheme was a superior way to advance modern art.

So strongly did he believe in his own plan that he hoped that the A.P.S. would adopt his principle of self-judging groups. "Some there are," he wrote, "who would have it." [6] But in the power struggle that dominated the first month of the association's existence, Henri's plan was by-passed in favor of a constitution drafted by Davies, Borglum, and Mowbray-Clark. As a result, Henri grew rather skeptical about the merits of the A.P.S. Early in January, 1912, he wrote in his diary: "I [am] not interested in this Society except as it may be useful to check NAD [;] otherwise it is too much of the old thing— judging others and not working to the opportunity for others to exhibit and judge themselves." [7]

His limitation at this moment, in the light of our present historical perspective, was his undue preoccupation with the mechanics of arranging exhibitions; he seems to have lost sight of the formal and expressive significance of the works of art themselves, so involved had he become in guaranteeing a democratic method of selecting them. Perhaps it was this concern for procedure and his own recent successes with the MacDowell plan that allowed him to chide the association: "They are in slight prospect of doing anything. Not practical." [8] In these remarks, of course, he gravely underestimated Kuhn's and Davies' determination and great ability as organizers.

It may seem hard to believe, but Henri was approached by Gutzon Borglum early in January, 1912, to see if he would accept the presidency of the A.P.S., to replace J. Alden Weir, who had resigned after a brief tenure when he found the organization was thoroughly antiacademic. Henri declined, not wishing to be president of anything. But on the same day, MacRae telephoned him and asked whether he would vote for Arthur B. Davies for that office, and Henri gladly pledged support to his friend. There is good reason to believe that Kuhn and his associates meant to treat the president as a figurehead; but when Davies was elected, he astonished all but a few close confederates by becoming a phenomenally effective fund-raiser and administrator and an outspoken champion of avant-garde European art.

Henri, being outside the inner circle, was pessimistic about the future of the A.A.P.S. (now incorporated), especially in its formative months. But as a result of Kuhn's and Davies' energetic labors, a definite exhibition program was framed, which, with Pach's and Davies' active collaboration, led to the celebrated Armory Show of 1913. This, alone, was the Association's major achievement. The show was never repeated and the group disintegrated several years later. So in one sense Henri's reservations were justified: as an artists' society, it had failed. But the Armory Show changed the course of the history of American art in a way that he could never have anticipated in 1912.

The International Exhibition of Modern Art, as the Armory Show was officially called, attracted far more public attention than had any previous art exhibition held in the United States. It eclipsed the Exhibition of Independent Artists of 1910 in size, scope, and public appeal. While the Armory Show shared the antiacademic character of the earlier exhibition, it embraced advanced European as well as American art. As it turned out, the European entries stole the show, even though they occupied only one-third of the space. The foreign work also made it painfully clear that the majority of American artists were still rather provincial and retarded—even in their most advanced efforts.

While Glackens was put in charge of selecting the American entries, Henri, ironically enough, was appointed to the Committee on Foreign Exhibits, serving with Elmer MacRae (chairman), Borglum, Dabo, Davidson, Kuhn, Lie, Lawson, and Prendergast. We do not know exactly what role they played in assembling the foreign section of the show. But Henri, according to one newspaper account, refused to participate in the selection of the European examples while abroad unless given a free hand. Apparently working independently of this committee, three members of the inner circle actually selected the majority of the European entries. Kuhn, with Pach's help in Paris, traveled all over Europe, begging and borrowing modern works during the summer of 1912; and in November, Arthur B. Davies joined them in this task. By November 21 about 430 European examples had been secured, and on that day Davies and Kuhn sailed for home. As Milton Brown put it: "The time bomb had been set." [9]

The show opened almost three months later, on February 17, 1913, in the 69th Regiment Armory, which had been converted into a vast gallery to house about 1,300 works of art. As a public attraction, it was a tremendous success. Although the audience was shocked and stunned by what they saw, one thing was certain: American art would never be the same again.

What was the excitement about? There was a section devoted to the precursors of modern art, including Goya, Ingres, Delacroix, Redon, the Realists, and the Impressionists. Then there were the American Impressionists, who can be divided into two groups: Twachtman and Robinson, who tamely imitated French Impressionism; and Kuhn and Tucker, who employed a freer and more impulsive version of that style, reminiscent of early Van Gogh, as an inherently modern idiom. The Eight (minus Shinn), along with George Bellows, were heavily represented, though the style of Henri, Sloan, Luks, and Bellows suddenly appeared a generation behind the contemporary European entries.

Another group may loosely be termed Postimpressionist: Gauguin, Van Gogh, and the young Americans influenced by them, such as Charles Sheeler and Marsden Hartley. There were also works by Cézanne and his American followers, such as Bernard Karfiol, who emphasized structure and compositional order while remaining faithful to their sensations of nature. But the most radical examples in the show were by Kandinsky, Matisse, and the Cubists—work that generated confusion and laughter among the great majority of the audience who saw the show. True, the shock of America's artistic provincialism was mitigated to some small degree by the presence of work by Alfred Maurer, who was close to Matisse; John Marin, who fused the intense colors of the Fauves with the angular distortions of the Cubists; and the remarkable Italian-born artist Joseph Stella, who had been exposed to Futurism in Europe and whose work resembles that of Severini. Though these Americans were more up-to-date than the rest of their contemporaries, none of them had originated the artistic innovations they practiced; they owed almost everything to the European avant-garde.

The degree of the show's importance and its effect on American culture are questions still open to debate today. But two things are certain: it confused and exasperated a public that was almost completely unprepared for it, and many young American painters of progressive tendency realized how far behind they had fallen and tried their best to assimilate the latest artistic currents emanating from Europe. The show also had an inescapable effect, direct and indirect, upon Robert Henri.

Most of the witness accounts tell the same story: Henri's artistic beliefs and personal leadership were seriously challenged by the Armory Show. And, as things turned out, the rising generation of artists who matured in the 1920's and 1930's intently explored the new territory it opened up. Even Sloan accepted the implications of the show, viewing it as "a clarion call to freedom." [10] And Davies, Henri's old friend and associate, for a time imposed Cubist faceting over his nude female figures. Of the younger men, Bellows, Speicher, Kroll, and Davey rallied to Henri after 1913; but this was a hollow victory, for the mainstream of American art had shifted, for better or worse, to those who embraced European modernism.

If the new generation could detach themselves from the group around Henri, he, in turn, could secede from the organization that impelled young American artists toward modern European art. At an A.A.P.S. meeting held after the close of the Armory Show, several men in Henri's circle expressed justifiable curiosity about the financial management of the show. When no one would tell them where the money had come from, Du Bois, Henri, Bellows, Myers, Mahonri Young, and several others resigned on the spot and walked out. This discordant meeting marked the end of the Association as an effective body. Its major task accomplished—staging the Armory Show—it remained a paper organization for several years; then it died.

THE SOCIETY OF INDEPENDENT ARTISTS

The largest privately organized annual exhibition program in the United States, sponsored by the Society of Independent Artists, owed a real debt to Robert Henri's pioneering of nonacademic, jury-free shows in 1908 and 1910. Founded in 1916 after the example of the Société des Artistes-Indépendants in Paris (originated in 1884), the American Independents granted a showing to anyone who could produce a few dollars for annual dues; the constitution guaranteed that exhibitors could be "certain that whatever they send will be hung and that all will have an equal opportunity." [11] Their motto was that of the Paris Independents: "No jury, no prizes." Even the pictures were hung alphabetically, according to an equalitarian principle; and to overcome the inevitable favoritism of starting with A and ending with Z, the beginning letter was drawn by lot, thanks to a suggestion by Marcel Duchamp. In this way, the American Society of Independent Artists showed itself even more equalitarian than its French counterpart, which relied on a *comité de placement*.

The first of the annual exhibitions opened on the first floor of the Grand Central Palace on April 10, 1917, with 1,130 members displaying their work. In later years the shows drew large crowds to the top floor of the Waldorf-Astoria and the Fine Arts Society on West 57th Street. Although incompetents invariably participated, many talented artists who were, or became, well known also exhibited regularly.

Besides the French expatriates Villon, Duchamp, and Picabia, the chief founders of the organization included three men from Henri's circle: Pach, Glackens, and Prendergast. Henri belonged to the board of directors and the hanging committee for many years, but he was not directly involved in the formation of the Society, nor was he included on the board in the first year. As to his relation to the Society, Sloan observed: "He never had the real enthusiasm which he had for projects he had initiated and directed himself." [12] Two of his colleagues, however, found their way into its management: Glackens became the first president, serving for one year; he was succeeded by John Sloan, who was continually re-elected to that office during the life-span of the organization.

Henri was sympathetic to the principles of the Independents to the extent that they agreed with his idea of a year-round, jury-free open forum for the arts, "such as a free country should have, open alike to all movements, old or new, stimulating individuals presenting works in such way [*sic*] as to provoke active participation and judgment on the part of the public." He objected strenuously, however, to the alphabetical hanging, which resulted in "a disasterous hodge-podge" comparable to "eating in sequence mustard, ice cream, pickles, and pastry." [13] Although an alphabetical arrangement ruled out favoritism, he felt it damaged the work of many of the participating artists and hindered the public's appreciation of the show. A better solution, he thought, would have been to apply the MacDowell plan on a larger scale: exhibitors could form in groups of eight to twelve and serve as their own hanging committee using a series of equal-sized parcels of wall space for each group. In his private correspondence, Henri voiced further reservations about the Independents: "I do not care much for the plan of it for I am a very old fighter against the jury and prize system and through years of study have seen farther ahead than the 'Independent' salon which is of quite old date. We do not need big circuses of art. The *big show* has been a very bad thing as far as *art* is concerned all over the world—I do not refer in this to the occasional Exposition—but the annual salons, royal and other Academy shows. Pictures cannot be *seen* by the thousands, nor all at once (I might say that art evidences should be persistent not intermittent)—small homogeneous exhibitions continuing throughout the year in an agreeable sequence." [14]

The Society's annual exhibitions, if unwieldy in size and uneven in quality, did provide a much-needed opportunity for a number of little-known younger artists to obtain a wide audience and recognition from their peers. And it played a central role, as Sloan observed, as a bridge between the Armory Show and the general acceptance of the modern movement by dealers, collectors, and museums. After functioning successfully for twenty-eight years, the Society disbanded during World War II; it had served its purpose.

Later Teaching

THE INDEPENDENT SCHOOL

Having successfully operated the Henri School of Art for three years, Robert Henri turned it over to his associate, Homer Boss, who renamed it the Independent School. It is not surprising that, by 1912, Henri should wish to relinquish some of his teaching duties. He was undoubtedly taxed by the tremendous demands made upon his time by the MacDowell Club exhibitions, lecture engagements, and his research into the Maratta system of color, not to mention his own painting. Even so, he continued to give criticisms at the school until he was compelled to resign. Just as Henri's popularity as a teacher had earlier induced William Merritt Chase to leave the New York School of Art, so Homer Boss attracted so much student loyalty at the time of the Armory Show that the founder was obliged to withdraw from the school.

Two issues were at stake. The first was whether the students should be required to use the Maratta palette. Henri was totally committed to it at this time and strongly urged its adoption in his classes; Homer Boss, on the other hand, thought the Maratta system was too mechanical and that its use should be optional. The second issue was this: after the Armory Show, Henri's teachings seemed conservative by comparison to those of Boss, who unconditionally cast his lot with the latest trends from Europe. As a result, the younger man seemed to be in the vanguard and hence more relevant than

Henri. It was Boss, not Henri, who tried to guide the students along the paths opened up by the Armory Show. "Pretty soon," one member of the class recalled, "only examples of post-impressionism, cubism and futurism were being produced in the studio." [15] At this point, Henri severed his connection with the school.

Whatever his shortcomings might have been, the classes suffered from his absence. For a while, Boss directed the school with the help of A. S. Baylinson, another Henri student, who served as business manager and monitor. Attendance gradually dropped off, and ultimately Boss's interest in the school was bought out by some of the students. It continued to operate briefly under Baylinson's management as a workshop studio, where a group of students met for painting sessions without instruction, but it closed down during World War I after most of the students were called into the service. In the meantime, Henri had transferred his allegiance to the Ferrer School and the Art Students League. [16]

THE MODERN SCHOOL

Early in 1911, Henri became a devoted admirer of the anarchist Emma Goldman. It comes as no surprise, therefore, that he readily accepted her invitation to teach evening art classes at the Modern School of the Ferrer Center in New York. Founded in 1910, the Center was named in memory of Francisco Ferrer Guardia, a Spanish anarchist who had been court-martialed and executed in the preceding year after being falsely accused of leading an insurrection against the government. (Actually, his "crime" was undermining the power of the clergy by his network of progressive schools.) The Modern School was admittedly radical in its educational philosophy; it was patterned after the schools of the same name Ferrer had established in Spain. Among the founders of the New York school were two leading anarchists, Emma Goldman and Alexander Berkman.

Henri undoubtedly welcomed the opportunity to put into practice the libertarian educational principles for which he had already become well known. All reports indicate that his teaching at the Ferrer School, from 1911 to 1918, became even more progressive than it had been at his own art school. According to Emma Goldman, Henri (and Bellows, who replaced Henri on alternate weeks) "helped to create a spirit of freedom in the art class which probably did not exist anywhere else in New York at that time." [17] Although students drew the nude model, receiving comments when desired, they were also encouraged to bring in pictures they had done outside the class

173

to be criticized in detail by Henri or Bellows. Robert Brackman, a former pupil, recalled: "They tried to correct your sight, giving you a little help here and there." [18] However, he felt that Henri's comments were much too general and poetic. This is a criticism Henri may have deserved as a result of "his fervent belief," as another student reported, "that only freedom can bring out the best in the individual." [19] Moses Soyer, on the other hand, was so profoundly moved by Henri's ideas, on the basis of one session at the Ferrer Center, that the whole direction of his art was altered. Although Henri came to the school only two evenings a week, several artists who became well known benefited from his teaching: Man Ray, Niles Spencer, Harry Wickey, Robert Brackman, and Paul Rohland. By far his most celebrated student, however, was Leon Trotsky, who attended the classes during his brief exile in the United States, prior to returning to Russia in 1917 to play a decisive role in the Bolshevik revolution.

Henri and the Avant-Garde

Many stories have been told about how Henri was disturbed by the triumph of modern European art at the Armory Show. If we accept them uncritically, as Van Wyck Brooks has done, then Henri emerges as a foe of any artistic progress beyond the point reached by Georges Rouault; in fact, Brooks maintains that "Henri never had any interest either in Impressionism or in the new moderns except Rouault and a few Cézannes." [20] Henri may have been disgruntled by the Armory Show, but this was probably for art-political reasons rather than artistic ones. Violet Organ, his sister-in-law, recalled that he was far from indifferent to the advanced European trends represented in the show. He felt that the exhibition was noteworthy as a search for new insights, and he expressed much interest in the results of the ferment that would be definitely American. [21] We know that Henri counseled his students, several years before the Armory Show, to approach Matisse' work with an open mind; and Andrew Dasburg recalled that he frequently commented on Picasso, Braque, and Matisse in his classes. [22] As one of Henri's former pupils observed, apropos of the show: "It was only natural that we—having been students of the most progressive artist and teacher, Henri—now took to the new trends like ducks to water." [23] We know, too, that Henri made available to students his extensive gallery of photographic reproductions and postcards illustrating the work of Rodin, Degas, Manet, Van Gogh, Gauguin, Cézanne, Renoir, Daumier, Matisse, and early Picasso.

Henri had viewed the work of many of the progressive artists in Paris at the Salon d'Automne in 1908, 1910, and 1912. And a revealing letter, previously unknown, written by the collector Dr. Albert C. Barnes, indicates that he saw Picasso's and Matisse' work in or before 1912 at the Steins' apartment in Paris (it cannot be determined whether it was at Sarah and Michael Stein's or at Gertrude and Leo Stein's; both branches of the family were collecting Picasso and Matisse at the time).[24] Thus Henri entered the orbit, however briefly, of the most progressive American backers of modern art before the Armory Show.

In 1912, Henri also became a champion of the art of Max Weber, formerly a Matisse student—and, besides Arthur Dove, there was no painter in America more progressive than Weber at that time. Henri urged his pupils to study Weber's work on view in the Murray Hill Galleries, personally conducting them through the one-man exhibition. When Henri learned that the show was about to close, he convinced the owner of the gallery to grant a week's extension so it could be seen by a larger audience.

Henri's association with avant-garde art was little known by the large majority of artists and students in 1913, and when the Armory Show made his style of painting appear traditional by comparison to Picasso and Matisse, it was generally assumed that his entire mode of thinking was out of date. It would be more accurate to say that Henri hesitated to offer his unqualified acceptance to every modern current imported from Europe just because it was new and experimental. He encouraged innovation and experiment, that is certain; but he balked at purely formalistic exercises, just as a decade before he had rejected art for art's sake. In a 1911 letter he explained himself in this way: "Some of the 'ultra moderns' will tell you that design for design's sake is the thing. Beautiful design! But a great thing must be an organization of perfectly related parts and the result must itself be a unit. There must be an underlying motive to bring this about. In an Ibsen play there is always a philosophy, there are personages and events, but back of all this there is the still deeper Ibsen motive."[25] Formal integration—or "significant form," to use the term then in vogue—did not suffice by itself; the form of the work of art, for Henri, had to serve as a vehicle for some profound humanistic content transmitted through the artist's personal experience. As he said, "The big movement of the whole canvas should so possess one that the change from part to part, from flesh to collar to coat to shirt or trousers should be such that, however brilliant or sharp the change of color or texture might be in these [,] there would be no arrest in the observer's mind. He should be conscious of these changes, conscious of beauty in them, conscious that they are

175

right, but his sense should be of the life that flows beneath these superficial things." [26] He thus reveals himself as the heir of a long-standing humanistic tradition originating in the Renaissance and continuing to find expression in such artists as El Greco, Rembrandt, and Goya.

In these humanistic motivations, we can find the key to Henri's break with the "ultra moderns." He maintained an essentially "mimetic" approach to the arts, rather than a "musical" one, to use Meyer Schapiro's terms.[27] That is to say, he was sympathetic to works in which the content was communicated through the viewer's empathy with the postures and movements of the human figure—or groups of human figures—acting out their message against a more or less neutral background. This is undoubtedly why Henri was such an avid theater-goer and follower of the dance; and this is why he believed so thoroughly in studying the gesture of the human body.

The "musical" approach, on the other hand, requires the sum of the picture's integrated formal elements to express the desired content, as opposed to communicating strictly by association. Individual figures may be suppressed within an overall expressive scheme of color, tone, rhythm, and pattern, which affects the viewer's feelings in a more abstract, nonliteral way. It is the shift from the mimetic to the musical approach that characterized the advanced art of the early twentieth century. To the degree that Henri was incapable of transcending the norms of mimetic art, he was a nineteenth-century man, steeped in older humanistic modes of thought. That he could supplement this outlook by his own pseudo-scientific version of a musical approach to painting, under the strong influence of Hardesty Maratta's theories, is a testimony to his ability to grow under the influence of distinctly twentieth-century ideas.[28]

Henri and Eakins

The American artist with whom Robert Henri identified most closely was Thomas Eakins. His admiration for the Philadelphia painter, we recall, dated back to his student days, when he marveled at *The Gross Clinic* on view at Jefferson Medical College. Through the years, his appreciation of the master's genius grew. At the Chase School, the Henri School, the Art Students League, and the Pennsylvania Academy of the Fine Arts he lectured on Eakins' humanity and great integrity as an artist. To champion Eakins in the early years of the twentieth century was to fight for an unpopular cause, since the forthright honesty of his style and personality alienated him from academic circles; indeed, few artists and students in New York had any idea of what he had achieved. So when the Metropolitan Museum presented an Eakins Memorial Exhibition in 1917, Henri seized the opportunity to stir up interest in his work.

One of the most perceptive and moving tributes to Eakins' talent was Henri's open letter to the students of the Art Students League urging them to study the Memorial Exhibition. It is worth quoting at length.

Thomas Eakins was a man of great character. He was a man of iron will and his will was to paint and to carry out his life as he thought it should go. This he did. It cost him heavily but in his works we have the precious result of his independence, his generous heart and his big mind. Eakins was a deep student of life, and with a great love he studied humanity frankly. He was not afraid of what his study revealed to him.

In the matter of ways and means of expression, the science of technic, he studied most profoundly, as only a great master would have the will to study. His vision was not touched by fashion. He struggled to apprehend the constructive force in nature and to employ in his works the principles found. His quality was honesty. "Integrity" is the word which seems best to fit him.

Personally I consider him the greatest portrait painter America has produced. Being a great portrait painter he was as usual commissioned to paint only a very few. But he had friends and he painted his friends. Look at these portraits well. Forget for the moment your school; forget the fashion. Do not look for the expected and the chances are you will find yourself, through the works, in close contact with a man who was a man, strong, profound and honest, and above all one who had attained the reality of beauty in nature as is, who was in love with the great mysterious nature as manifested in man and things, one who had no need to falsify to make romantic or to sentimentalize over to make beautiful. Look if you will at the great Gross Clinic picture for the real stupendous romance in real life, and at the portrait of [Professor Leslie W.] Miller [Figure 28] for a man's feeling for a man. This is what I call a beautiful portrait, not a pretty, nor a swagger portrait, but an honest, respectful, appreciative man-to-man portrait. But I have no intention to specify. I simply ask you to look. I expect the pictures to tell you, if you can but see them from out of yourself, and I expect them to fill you with courage and hope. Eakins' pictures and his sculptures are the recordings of a man who lived and studied and loved with a strong heart.[29]

Henri appreciated Eakins as much for his personal courage and integrity as for his painting, and in this he tells us a good deal about himself. The best art,

Figure 28. Thomas Eakins, *Portrait of Professor Leslie W. Miller*, 1901. Oil on canvas, 88⅛ x 44″. Collection of the Philadelphia Museum of Art.

Henri believed, resulted from an honest transaction between the painter and the experience of life, without concern for public acclaim. Indeed, he must have seen much of his own career echoed in Eakins' struggle for acceptance. And it was clear that Eakins' example, in turn, could give young American students the courage to avoid the pitfalls of fashionable taste in art.

Henri voiced these ideas over the years in lectures, in articles, in *The Art Spirit*, and in letters to friends and collectors whose influence might help realize another major Eakins project: a permanent gallery of his work in his native city. In the late teens and twenties, several Philadelphians tried to stir up public interest in the gallery and, knowing of Henri's sympathy for Eakins, enlisted his aid as lecturer and propagandist. The essence of his arguments appears in a letter to the Pennsylvania Academy:

It would be a fine thing for Philadelphia, for America, for all of us and future generations if an Eakins gallery were to be established in Philadelphia. If they would only repeat the dimensions of that splendid room which held the Eakins exhibition at the Metropolitan here in New York. The room seemed to fit Eakins and there were many real artists—worth listening to—who regretted the passing of that wonderful unity. A city should recognize its own worth and a city's worth is in its personnel—and Eakins was a great man. Eakins himself needs no reward. He was one who had a wonderful life, his work proves it—but the work he did should be made safe—and kept as much as possible in a unit and available to the public, for the public can benefit much by it. . . . It is more important that a city preserve its own than it collect from outside—it may do both but it will do the former first—if it is a wise city.[30]

Although Henri continued to back the campaign for the gallery until the late 1920's, the Philadelphians failed to raise the money to honor the greatest painter the city produced in the late ninetenth century. Thus the indifference to his art that plagued Eakins throughout his life persisted even through Henri's lifetime. It was only in 1930 that the Philadelphia Museum of Art acquired and put on permanent display a large collection of Eakins' paintings, drawings, and sculptures. And these, for the most part, were given by his widow and Miss Mary A. Williams, not by public subscription.

Henri, Anarchism, and Socialism

Established political parties did not interest Henri seriously after his early voting years. Like most Southerners, his family was solidly Democratic, and in casting his first votes he followed the party line almost invariably. As a young man in Philadelphia, his humanitarian instincts were roused by the injustices of the Homestead Riots and the government's callous treatment of the American Indians. And his innate belief in the dignity and perfectibility of the individual man and in the evolution of an enlightened society through education paved the way for his acceptance of the theories of anarchism, which he embraced from the mid-nineties to his death in 1929. While he became skeptical of the value of political parties, he gladly accepted the philosophical and social doctrine of anarchism preached by Emma Goldman. The experience of meeting her and hearing her lecture was the catalyst that helped him translate his abstract belief in philosophical anarchism into a deeply felt personal creed.

When Henri encountered Emma Goldman in 1911, she had become nationally famous for her vocal support of anarchism. Born in Lithuania (then part of Russia), she emigrated to the United States in 1885 and four years later allied herself with the anarchist movement. From that point onward she became a vigorous spokeswoman for the cause, through writing, lecturing, and editing the anarchist magazine *Mother Earth*. Her lectures dealt more with theatre and the arts than anarchism per se, though her political radicalism unquestionably affected her views about the fine arts.

Henri was overwhelmed with admiration for Miss Goldman when, in 1911, he heard her lecture for the first time. In his diary he noted: "A woman of remarkable address, convincing presence. I never have heard so good a lecture. This is a very great woman." [31] Immediately thereafter, he read her recently published book, *Anarchism and Other Essays*, which he praised as "a great work by a great and noble woman." [32] For the remainder of the year, he became a faithful member of her lecture audiences in New York. Frustrated by viewing her at a distance, he finally mustered his courage and introduced himself after one of the lectures.

Henri and Emma Goldman immediately recognized each other as kindred spirits. Although they never became intimate friends, she did attend some of his Thursday evening receptions, where she found herself in sympathy with his libertarian ideas about education. We have already seen that Henri responded eagerly to her invitation to institute an art program at the anarchist Ferrer Center in New York, a school she had helped to establish. While some personal contacts between the two must have resulted from their association with the Center, Henri, in 1915, took the initiative in asking her to come to his studio to pose for a portrait. Three versions were executed during these sittings, hours that gave them a valuable opportunity to exchange views on art and the tenets of anarchism.

To Henri, Emma Goldman seemed to have found the answers to the pressing problems of society, particularly the evils of World War I, which he deplored: "Her arguments are for order and for human kindness; and they are undoubtedly destroying to all those institutions of our civilization which not only make possible, but bring about war, labor strife, all kinds of prostitution, and education which does not set the spirit free." [33] The close analogies between Emma Goldman's socio-political doctrines and Henri's own belief, derived from Whitman and Emerson, in individualism and freedom from institutional fetters hardly require elaboration.

While her expression of humanitarian ideals attracted Henri—no doubt because they corresponded so closely to his own views—he would not ally himself to anarchism as a political movement, particularly in its more violent aspects. By the same token, his belief in individualism made it difficult for him to embrace the political aims of the Socialist party. In 1908, John Sloan's socialist friend, Charles Wisner Barrell, tried to stimulate Henri's interest in Debs and involve the artist in the Socialist movement by inviting him to lecture about art before a meeting sponsored by the party. But Barrell's overtures did not bring the desired results; Henri was already too convinced a philosophical anarchist to be won over to the Socialist cause.[34]

Barrell, however, found a willing convert in Sloan. He called on the artist in 1907 and 1908 and early in the following year convinced him to accept the principles of the Socialist party. Sloan joined the party in 1910 and, with the energetic collaboration of his wife Dolly, worked for the Socialist cause until World War I. After espousing socialism, Sloan tried, in vain, to convince Henri to share his political views. While the younger man agreed with Henri that "all government is violence," he thought the abolition of government was a long-term goal that should not deflect people from the present struggle for "immediate social advance." [35] Thus Sloan had to chide Henri for being impractical, saying: "Idealistic anarchists are people who look at a ladder and want the top rung without working their way up." [36]

Despite their political differences, Henri was sympathetic enough to Sloan's ideas to contribute illustrations to the Socialist magazine the *Masses*. Founded in 1911 as the house organ of the writers' and artists' cooperatives, the *Masses* was reorganized in 1912 by Art Young and Charles Winter, who, with the help of Sloan, Maurice Becker, and a new editor, Max Eastman, converted it into a journal of social satire with a humorous slant, following the example of such magazines as *Jugend*, *Simplicissimus*, and *L'Assiette au beurre*. During the period of Sloan's greatest interest in the *Masses* (1912–1914), before it became an outlet for hard-line Socialist propaganda, about sixty artists sympathetic to him contributed drawings without pay. Many were Henri's friends and students: in addition to Sloan's contribution as artist and art editor, drawings were submitted by, among others, Bellows, Glackens, Luks, Davies, Stuart Davis, Glenn O. Coleman, Maurice Becker, and Henry J. Glintenkamp. Henri's own illustrations, which were few in number, stressed social satire rather than political propaganda. Those who were not Socialists, such as Henri and Glackens, contributed illustrations as they would to any other magazine, the political views of the editors counting less than the artists' friendship with Sloan and their common belief in humanitarian causes. There was another motive, too: while the artists were not paid, the *Masses* offered high-quality, full-page reproductions of their best work in a graphic format surpassing that of any other illustrated magazine of the period.

The Art Spirit

One of Henri's most influential and lasting contributions was his book *The Art Spirit*. First published in 1923, it has become a classic that remains in print to the present day (a paperback edition was also issued in 1960). This remarkable work gives us the essence of Henri's thought as expressed orally and in writing. Compiled by his student Margery Ryerson from letters, articles, notes, and talks, *The Art Spirit* draws upon the accumulated wisdom of forty years' involvement with the arts. It has had universal appeal because it addresses the audience on so many levels: as a painter's manual, a guide to aesthetic appreciation, a philosophy of art and life, and a spur to creative activity. *The Art Spirit* proves that Henri was as gifted with the pen as with the brush: thousands have been inspired by the advice he gave in his typically crisp, eloquent prose. His style sometimes recalls William Morris Hunt's well-known *Talks on Art* (Boston, 1880, 1883), which is said to have influenced his teaching,[37] and there are echoes, too, of Anshutz' tersely phrased precepts. But most of it is unadulterated Henri, expressing himself in what he called his "Southern brogue."[38]

How did the book evolve? Margery Ryerson, a Vassar graduate who had studied under Henri at the Art Students League for two years, initiated the idea by asking his permission to publish her class notes. He had turned down previous offers to write books, but he welcomed this proposal as a means of putting his thoughts into print with a minimum expenditure of time and energy. Working in concert with Miss Ryerson, he enlarged the scope of the book to include excerpts from articles, letters, lectures, and other writings, drawn chiefly from the 1900–1923 period.

He had kept carbon copies of most of his correspondence since 1900, which he selected and edited for use in the book. Many of the letters were filled with advice to pupils who had sent their work for criticism; others were his semipublic mimeographed "letters to the class" addressed to his students at the Art Students League. Additional fragments were drawn from sketchbooks and notebooks in which he jotted down thoughts on art and life. After making the selections, Henri had the material typed and handed it over to Miss Ryerson. She, in turn, contributed the notes she had taken from Henri's criticisms and class talks.

It was Miss Ryerson's task, as an experienced editor, to sift the material and put it in order. Cutting and fitting, she eventually had to eliminate about half the text to avoid duplication. At first, she grouped the material in chapters, according to subjects; but this did not seem right to Henri. The manuscript was then reorganized in its present form, which follows no logical sequence. Believing in freedom of thought, Henri did not want *The Art Spirit* to become a systematic handbook that could be followed by rote. And he excluded reproductions of his own work in the early editions because he did not wish to imply that "this is how to do it." [39] Thus even the format of the book reflected a kind of anarchist distrust of too rigid a code of rules. It was up to the individual to react to it in his own special way: "The opinions," he wrote in the foreword, "are presented more as paintings are hung on the wall, to be looked at at will and taken as rough sketches for what they are worth. If they have a suggestive value and stimulate to independent thought they will attain the object of their presentation." [40] In place of chapter headings, Henri prepared a comprehensive index; "he liked to do that kind of thing." [41]

Although he initially planned to call the book "Comments on Art," no one was impressed by that title, so Miss Ryerson drew up a list of six or seven potential titles, some selected from key phrases in the manuscript. Reading over the list, he immediately seized upon "The Art Spirit"; it rang true, so further discussion was unnecessary.

The book was successful from the moment it was published. Enthusiastic letters poured in from artists, writers, college professors, from high school students, and from people unrelated to the arts. Every generation, it seems, requires its artist's bible; the eager acceptance of *The Art Spirit* leaves no doubt that Henri satisfied this need. As one of Eakins' former pupils said: "It is the only book on art that artists like to read. As a matter of fact it is really the only book *on art*." [42]

It is difficult to gauge the full extent of the book's influence on American art and artists, but one major effect is certain: it has spread Henri's teachings to a vast audience, known and unknown, throughout the country. Since 1923, 76,000 copies of *The Art Spirit* have been sold.

The Science of Painting

There is a fascinating aspect of Henri's career that has received little notice: his deep involvement with the pseudo-scientific theories of color and composition promulgated by Hardesty Maratta and reinforced by the teachings of Jay Hambidge. Today, these theorists and their systems are out of fashion—not to say forgotten. Yet from the early teens to the early twenties of the present century their teachings attracted the attention of many serious artists in America, and their ideas later influenced art education as well. Henri, Bellows, Sloan, and Eugene Speicher became intrigued with the problem of discovering infallible methods of achieving harmony in color and pictorial design, and as a result of their study of Maratta's and Hambidge's theories, their methods of painting underwent a significant change. Needless to say, they were not influenced in the same direction or degree, but the influence is clearly discernible in each case.

THE MARATTA SYSTEM

The story begins with Hardesty Gillmore Maratta, an unsuccessful Chicago painter who, after years of study, developed a rationally ordered system of color harmony and marketed the pigments that were needed to make it work. In March, 1909, Henri interviewed Maratta, who visited the school to promote his Margo colors and to demonstrate his laws of color. Two months later he gave Henri a set of pigments to try, and at that time Henri executed the first of his little-known "color studies" or "color notes" based on experiments with the Maratta system. Further essays in color derived from figure and landscape motifs followed in July. In these small pictures, often on canvas paper, he abandoned realistic details in favor of the broadest possible relationships of color; but in these the subject matter was still discernible. Such sketches, however, were the forerunners of his remarkable abstract color notes dating from 1911 to about 1916, which were done ostensibly to demonstrate Maratta's principles, but which stand as highly significant abstract compositions in their own right.

When the Henri School of Art reopened in September, 1909, Maratta appeared again; but the responsibilities of the school, work for the Independent Exhibition, and a summer abroad prevented Henri from indulging in further experiments with the Maratta colors until the fall of 1910. At that time he began to work directly under Maratta, who often came to the studio to spend hours demonstrating his theories of color relationships and schemes of compositional harmony. Maratta had become involved with geometric systems of proportion, too, and revealed the secrets of his discoveries, which he embodied in transparent celluloid overlays, or "webs," crisscrossed with geometric figures to guide the artist in creating harmonious patterns. Henri became a diligent student of these methods, devoting much of the winter of 1910–1911 to study and experimentation. Sloan, too, maintained a lively interest in Maratta's theories and attempted to apply them in his painting. Sloan's diary provides an accurate record of his own and Henri's progress in these investigations. In November, 1910, Sloan visited Henri and "found him busy 'triangulating,' working at the geometric theory of Maratta," [43] and in the following month observed that Henri was working with a triangular arrangement of the primary colors on his palette.

These experiments continued well into 1911, with Henri becoming more actively involved with Maratta and his theories. As Sloan reported in his diary:

He is deep with Maratta in the geometrical problem of rhythm in construction and design of pictures and form. There is a great deal he is sure and so am I. Maratta claims that it was well understood by the ancient Greeks and Egyptians, etc. . . . He [Henri] goes into the thing with his usual thoroughness. He has a large full length shape black board cloth on canvas stretcher ruled with scratches in the geometric triangulations, dividers, compasses, T-squares, etc. I am the one let in to the secret he says as I am in belief with the idea.[44]

Maratta seems to have been working perpetually on a definitive treatise that would elucidate his theories of color and proportion. Unfortunately, except for a few articles, there were only two tangible products of his researches.[45] The first, copyrighted in 1914, was a small octagonal diagram printed on cardboard called "A Chart for Finding 'Triads and Chords' in Sounds and Colors," in which the twelve notes of the diatonic scale were matched to twelve color equivalents; red was paired to the note C, red-orange to C-sharp, and so on around the chromatic circle. The second item was more ambitious, though the accompanying text was minimal: a thin portfolio, published in New York in 1915, entitled *The Web of Equilateral Triangles: An Instrument for the Use of Draughtsmen and Designers.* The essential elements were a celluloid sheet imprinted with the "web" and a number of loose pages, each containing a complex network of intersecting rectangles, triangles, and hexagons. The role of this "web" was to determine harmony in directions, measures, and shapes. The instrument would not only permit artists and designers to analyze the canons of design in the art of the past, but also—and more important—could guide their present creative efforts by providing "a consistency and unity obtainable in no other way." [46]

Although Maratta introduced him to these mysteries, Henri's diary indicates that, beginning in 1911, he and some of his friends advised and collaborated with Maratta in the preparation of the manuscript of a book. Henri, Bellows, Sloan, Randall Davey, Charles Winter, and A. F. Levinson spent many an evening experimenting with Maratta's system, making diagrams, and developing musical analogies. Just as with scientists working on a joint research project, it is difficult to ascribe the final manuscript to a single author. Maratta, of course, deserves the majority of credit as the originator of the scheme. But it was through Henri's belief in the absolute value of these investigations that they were pursued so exhaustively. The manuscript is the sole surviving monument to Maratta's theories of color; today it remains an unpublished manual illustrated with elaborate colored diagrams executed in oil by Henri. It thus stands as a collective record of the evolution of the Maratta system from 1913 to 1920, as amplified and articulated by Henri and his friends.

The system of color relationships devised by Maratta and utilized by Henri and his friends is based on the division of the chromatic circle into twelve equal parts, in the manner of a clock face. Each color on the circumference of the circle thus corresponds to a point on the prismatic spectrum; and the three primary colors (red, yellow, and blue) are placed equidistant from each other. The equality of the intervals between the colors of the spectrum, which Maratta compared to the exactness of musical intervals, made the system unique in American art. Sloan observed, "This instrument was like having a tuned piano." [47]

In addition to Maratta's twelve basic "colors," there was another set of pigments closely related to them, called "hues," which were manufactured by taking each of the pure "colors" and reducing them in saturation by adding a carefully prescribed proportion of black. In other words, a second set of grayish tones, keyed to the "colors," was fabricated for the purpose of systematically representing shadows, aerial perspective, and so on. Later in the development of the system a third set of partly neutralized tones, called "bi-colors," was introduced between the "colors" and the 'hues."

Maratta's schematic method of arranging colors allowed Henri and his friends not only to visualize color harmonies conveniently, but also to take the next important step in the system: to assign to these colors equivalent notes on the musical scale. This musical analogy, in turn, enabled the painters to produce color harmonies as they would create musical harmonies, drawing an analogy between the abstract relationships of musical notes, chords, and keys, and the painter's language of hue, value, and intensity. The theory dictated that there should be a color to match every musical tone; this system, however, was not absolute, but relative, shifting according to the key signature and whether the harmony was in the major or minor mode. Working by this method, Henri and his friends (particularly Sloan and Bellows) began systematically to plot their color relationships well in advance of painting their pictures.

The device that facilitated this rational planning was the "set palette." With the Maratta pigments in hand, the painter had only to determine which harmonies he wished to employ and then set up the palette with the appropriate colors. (If the artist desired hues more subtle than those provided by the pigments Maratta supplied, they could easily be produced by mixtures of these pigments.) Using three ranks of forty-eight colors, a total of 144 possible mixtures could be prepared in advance. As a result, Henri had to construct an elaborate palette containing 144 individual pans to hold the paint! Mixtures were made on a large sheet of glass laid on a table top. For outdoor painting, he devised a large palette equipped with an array of small aluminum trays to hold 120 colors, which was mounted in a frame and supported by a four-legged stand.

There were two methods of notation. The first, established by Charles Winter in 1915, was a rectangular diagram divided into equal-sized squares, forming a grid of horizontal and vertical lines (Figure 29). The hues were plotted in horizontal bands, while the values were placed on a vertical scale. A wide variety of "set palettes" could thus be created by selecting those com-

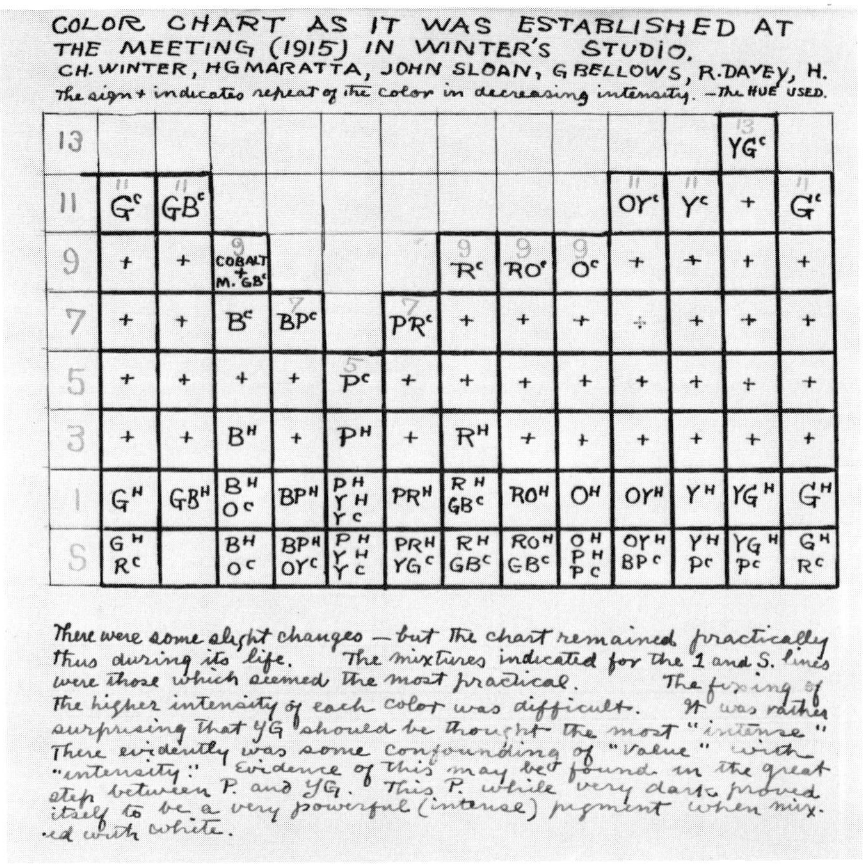

COLOR CHART AS IT WAS ESTABLISHED AT THE MEETING (1915) IN WINTER'S STUDIO.
CH. WINTER, HG MARATTA, JOHN SLOAN, G BELLOWS, R. DAVEY, H.
The sign + indicates repeat of the color in decreasing intensity. — The HUE USED.

13												YG^c	
11	G^c	GB^c								OY^c	Y^c	+	G^c
9	+	+	COBALT M. GB^c				R^c	RO^c	O^c	+	+	+	+
7	+	+	B^c	BP^c		PR^c	+	+	+	+	+	+	+
5	+	+	+	+	P^c	+	+	+	+	+	+	+	+
3	+	+	B^H	+	P^H	+	R^H	+	+	+	+	+	+
1	G^H	GB^H	B^H O^c	BP^H	P^H Y^H Y^c	PR^H	R^H GB^c	RO^H	O^H	OY^H	Y^H	YG^H	G^H
S	G^H R^c		B^H O^c	BP^H OY^c	P^H Y^H Y^c	PR^H YG^c	R^H GB^c	RO^H GB^c	O^H P^H P^c	OY^H BP^c	Y^H P^c	YG^H P^c	G^H R^c

There were some slight changes — but the chart remained practically thus during its life. The mixtures indicated for the 1 and S. lines were those which seemed the most practical. The fixing of the higher intensity of each color was difficult. It was rather surprising that YG should be thought the most "intense" There evidently was some confounding of "value" with "intensity." Evidence of this may be found in the great step between P. and YG. This P. while very dark proved itself to be a very powerful (intense) pigment when mixed with white.

Figure 29. Robert Henri, *Color Chart*, 1915. Beinecke Rare Book and Manuscript Library, Yale University.

binations deemed harmonious on the basis of the diagram. For his own use and for teaching, Henri made (and had his students make) sets of tiles painted with the full range of Maratta colors and their derivatives.

The second means of notation was a triangular color diagram Winter developed on the basis of one by a Frenchman named Dudeen, which Sloan introduced to Henri in 1919 (Figure 30). The three primaries (red, yellow, and blue) were placed at the three outside points of the triangle, while the secondary colors were arranged at equal intervals along the three sides; within these boundaries there was a second, smaller triangle for the "bicolors" (semineutrals) and within this was a still smaller one designating the almost neutral "hues." "Blank" diagrams were available, which enabled the painters to plot their color harmonies by pasting sample colored patches as a guide to the arrangement of their palette. In both methods of color notation, the resulting diagram served as a permanent record of the palette, or scheme of color harmony, used for any given painting.[48]

This system demanded that Henri and his friends follow a creative process different from that they had used before their contact with Maratta. Instead of working by instinct, they now determined their color harmonies on an abstract basis before starting the picture. We know from Henri's notes that a specific set of color-tones was assigned to each major area of the subject—the flesh and its shadows, the hair, the drapery, the background, and so on (Figure 31). With these decisions made in advance, the artist was free to concentrate on other important problems that confronted him in painting the picture, particularly the matter of drawing. Sloan said about the Maratta system: "It made possible setting a palette of selected color notes which could be used to draw with, as though working with colored chalks."[49]

This rationalized approach, however, called for a practiced eye and an intuitive feeling for color; it goes without saying that the Maratta system could not provide a flawless mathematical formula for good painting. Some of the work of George Bellows, along with that of Henri's less talented students, conclusively proves this point. Even Henri refused to be a slave to the system; as he explained, tongue in cheek, in demonstrating his procedures: "You have to use your head a little."[50]

HAMBIDGE AND DYNAMIC SYMMETRY

Something should be said, too, about Jay Hambidge, whose researches into mathematical systems of composition paralleled Maratta's and also influenced the Henri group. A native of Canada, Hambidge earned his living as a re-

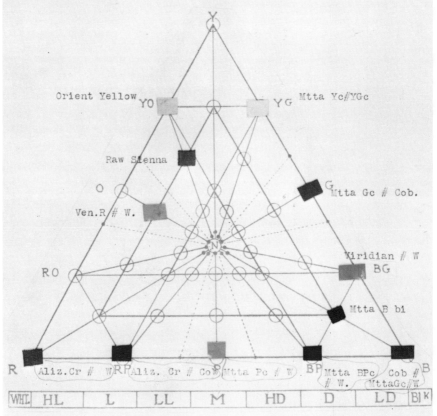

Figure 30. Triangle Palette (Charles Winter "Universal" Palette), 1919. Beinecke Rare Book and Manuscript Library, Yale University.

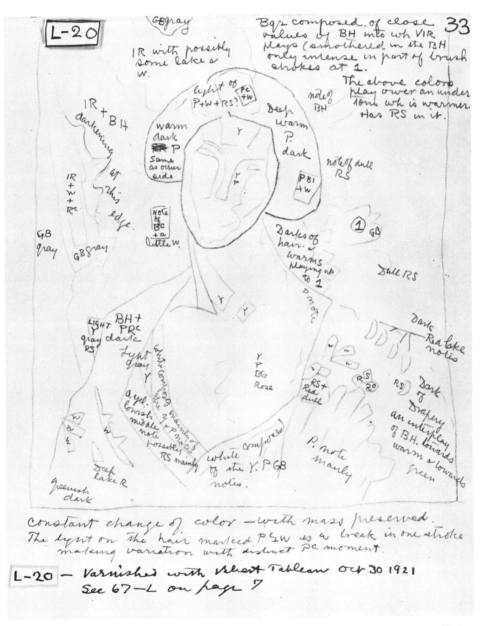

Figure 31. Robert Henri, *Diagram of Color Notations for Portrait of Helen Geary*, 1919. Beinecke Rare Book and Manuscript Library, Yale University.

porter before studying at the Art Students League and working as an illustrator for *McClure's* and the *Century Magazine*. Artists first heard his theories presented in his informal discourses at a Tenth Street bar; beginning in 1916 or 1917 he gave several lecture courses in New York under private auspices which further stimulated the interest of young painters and designers in his doctrines. Bellows, Henri, Leon Kroll, and Alfred Maurer are among the better-known painters who heard Hambidge's lectures. He received the stamp of approval from the academic world when he was invited to teach at Harvard and Yale after World War I. Essentially a writer-theorist in later years, Hambidge, unlike Maratta, succeeded in circulating his ideas widely through his books *Dynamic Symmetry* (1919) and *Dynamic Symmetry in Composition* (1923) and his magazine the *Diagonal* (1919–1920).

It is well known that George Bellows became a staunch advocate of the doctrine of dynamic symmetry. In 1917 he discovered the weekly classes in which Hambidge proclaimed "the coming of a new understanding and the key to the Greek mysteries." [51] Full of enthusiasm, Bellows announced his new find to Henri.[52] Since Hambidge's researches had not yet been published, the author having recalled his manuscript to revise it, Henri was prompted to write out a manuscript based on Hambidge's geometric systems of proportion and composition, probably as an aid to his own teaching. As far as we know, Henri's manuscript was never printed.

The chief subject of the Henri-Hambidge text was the "whirling square" rectangle and the division of its proportions into smaller squares according to the ratio of .618 to 1,000. Henri cited Hambidge's belief that the Greeks and Egyptians used just such a system of proportion, a theory that was also enunciated by Maratta in his studies of the same subject. Henri, unlike Hambidge, was not dogmatic in asserting that the architects and painters of the ancient world and the Renaissance consistently followed some mathematical system of proportion. He was satisfied to believe that artists consciously or unconsciously gravitated toward a harmonious geometrical framework in their work. Nonetheless, he felt that a knowledge of the whirling square rectangle and its subdivisions would be a valuable aid to painters by helping them place their subject harmoniously on a canvas divided into "structural lines." [53]

It is hard to isolate any single motive behind Henri's search for the laws of harmony and order in art. Although he consistently advocated personal, subjective interpretation on the artist's part, he also believed that discipline and order should inform the craft of painting. We must understand, too, that he was a product of his time in responding to the lure of mathematics and geometry, following a course parallel to that of Juan Gris, Albert Gleizes, and Le Corbusier in France. These artists, along with Henri, became deeply involved in a search for artistic structure and order during the second decade of the twentieth century, and each in his own way drew upon scientific and pseudo-scientific methods to solve their problems. Scientific color theory, too, was essential to the art of Delaunay and the Orphists, not to mention the closely related American Synchromist movement also flourishing in France.

Viewed in historical perspective, Henri emerges as the American heir to a long European tradition in which artists have applied scientific and mathematical laws in their work. Indeed, much of Maratta's color theory and Hambidge's doctrine of dynamic symmetry can be traced to such artists and theorists as Seurat, Signac, and Sérusier, who delved into nineteenth-century scientific theories of color and methods of composition based on mathematical principles that were employed in ancient Greece, during the Italian Renaissance, and in the French Academy in the seventeenth century.

In the late nineteenth and early twentieth centuries mathematical and geometrical systems of harmony were not the sole province of the fine arts. There was widespread curiosity about the ramifications of these systems for religion, architecture, and society at large. For example, Paul Sérusier, a member of the Synthetist group, ascribed ideas of God, the Trinity, and so on, to simple geometric relationships; thus, in his mind, geometric figures could be conceived as echoes of divine knowledge. Related interests were evidenced both within and outside the Synthetist group by the Theosophists, who likewise sought to construct outward forms embodying numerical ratios upon which the order of the universe is based. To mention an American example, Claude Bragdon, the architect and Theosophist, wrote at length about how these geometrical systems of harmony, applied to architecture, would have an enlightening effect upon humanity.

More important for our purposes are the implications of these interests on the social plane. As a philosophical anarchist, Henri (and Bellows, too) might be thought to disdain the imposition of rigid systems of control upon any realm of activity. But actually just the opposite was the case when it came to art and design. As Professor Donald D. Egbert has pointed out, social radicals repeatedly tend "to apply reason to human problems in a way thought to be completely scientific, and to praise those arts, especially the art of music, which best exemplify harmony created by human beings."[54] Egbert's observation also sheds considerable light on Henri's and Bellows' concern, inspired by Maratta, with musical analogies to the art of painting. Appropriately, it was Manuel Komroff, secretary of the anarchist Modern School, who in 1915 fabricated and presented to Henri and Bellows proportional compasses that would enable them to construct the golden section and other harmonious proportions in their paintings.

For a few years, a scientific approach to harmony in art appeared to social radicals and Theosophists as the most effective means of leading mankind to a new vision of intellectual order. The belief in these methods was especially strong during and just after World War I, when many felt a need for an antidote to the disintegration of social, moral, and religious values for which the war seemed to be responsible. Thus a renewed world order would, they hoped, be fostered by surrounding man with products designed according to immutable rules of harmony. That Henri believed in this principle is confirmed repeatedly in his published and unpublished writings, such as the following:

It is disorder in the mind of man that produces chaos of the kind that brings about such a war as we are today overwhelmed with. It is the failure to see the various phases of life in their ultimate relation that brings about militarism, slavery, the longing of one nation to conquer another, the willingness to destroy for selfish, unhuman purposes. . . . The revolutionary parties that break away from old institutions, from dead organizations are always headed by men with a vision of order, with men who realize that there must be a balance in life, so much of what is good for each man, so much to test the sinews of his soul, so much to stimulate his joy.[55]

Science could therefore aid in the creation of a new world order, but it should not dominate the artist. Like Delacroix and Seurat, Henri believed in science as a means of rectifying human sensibility, not as an alternative to it. Repeatedly he tells us in *The Art Spirit* that intuition and logic must balance each other: "In the past every step of human progress has been directed by art and science. These two are inseparable, and cannot exist in their pure sense, the one without the other. Theirs has been the effort to apprehend from nature the principles by which we must live if we are to extricate ourselves from the uncertainties and misunderstandings in which we now find ourselves." [56]

11

Recollections of
the Later Years

Life in New York

HENRI's LATER life in New York followed a year-in-year-out pattern—lectures at the Art Students League, portrait commissions, and writing, plus the customary talk fests in the studio at 10 Gramercy Park. Preoccupied with a variety of routine chores and unable to afford assistants, he was compelled to report in 1919:

I am at one time my own businessman, secretary, laborer, canvas stretcher, errand boy. I attend to shipments of pictures, framing, glass cleaning, necessary social functions, necessary official businesses relative to art movements. I must respond to the demands and enquiries of some students who come to me in the spirit of student to master—for years I have come very close to working 18 hours a day at my job.[1]

To relax, he often played pool with George Bellows at the National Arts Club or attended prize fights with him, activities usually followed by a leisurely walk along the avenues to admire the crowds and the rush of traffic and to make frequent stops for Henri to admire "the clear cut integrity"[2] of the tools in hardware store windows. After he returned on these occasions, he would make drawings of street scenes or caricatures of the prize fights, himself, and George Bellows, or, when settled in his Morris chair, browse through a newly purchased art book. If he professed little fondness for poetry, he enjoyed the cadences of fine prose and liked to read George Moore's novels aloud to Marjorie, who shared his literary and musical tastes.

Marjorie and Emma Bellows seldom accompanied their husbands to the fights, but the theatre was another matter. A week rarely went by without the Henris attending one production or another, usually with friends. Through the years, he enthusiastically recommended to students and friends the plays of Eugene O'Neill at the Greenwich Village Theatre and those of Chekhov at the Cherry Lane. Despite having to put up with hard benches and indifferent ventilation, he and Marjorie hardly ever missed a performance or withheld the comments that were so often asked of him to stimulate attendance.

He was also a great appreciator of the "gesture" of the dance, ranging from the ecstatic, full-bodied movements of Isadora Duncan and the fiery spirit of the Duncan Girls to the abandoned gyrations of the hula-hula damsels. On behalf of this art he urged his friend Frank Crowninshield, editor of *Vanity Fair* and a fellow dance enthusiast, to "suggest a mighty propaganda for some sort of a theatre in New York for such great artists as Ruth St. Denis and the beautiful girl we saw the other afternoon—Roshanara, to give their best in, instead of being hampered by vaudevillians and sandwiched between imitations of George Cohan and only seen at that at rare intervals. . . . Can't you inspire some backers to action? The Dance must come. It is too great an art for us through our inertia to miss. . . . Let's have the Theatre of the Dance." [3]

Early in his career Henri was considered "an artist's artist" for the uncompromising quality of his work. This could be said with wider significance in later years, thanks to the vigor with which he used his reputation in bringing notice to painters who had been overlooked or assisting young students suffering from financial difficulties. For deserving aspirants to a career in the arts, whether graphic, literary, or musical, he obtained scholarships from such wealthy philanthropists as Mrs. Ben Ali Haggin, Adolph Lewisohn, Otto Kahn, and Bradley Martin. Whenever the struggles of budding small theatre groups or the ventures of "little magazines" were brought to his attention, he invariably gave them his support. Requests for recognition of all kinds of creative work were rarely declined; he enjoyed giving what he called "a boost" to innovators and experimenters in the arts. Among the efforts he encouraged were such small publications as Max Weber's *Cubist Poems* and the *Glebe*, a monthly edited by Alfred Kreymborg devoted to the writings of known and unknown authors chosen for their merit alone, irrespective of any commercial value. Another pocket-sized effort he sponsored was the *Pagan*, "a magazine for eudaemonists," which featured short stories by Knut Hamsun, one-act plays translated from foreign publications, and drawings by vanguard artists.

While Henri regarded the young "ultra moderns" (as he liked to call them) with kindly tolerance during the 1920's, his closest associates among the artists were George Bellows, Eugene Speicher, Leon Kroll, Richard Lahey, and others who congregated in the New Society of Artists—A. Stirling Calder, Hayley Lever, Albert Sterner, Gifford Beal, Henry L. McFee, and Paul Dougherty.[4] This was a middle-of-the-road group, neither too advanced in style nor academically conservative. By the twenties, their styles appeared tame by comparison, say, to Dove's or Weber's at the same time. For the most part, they were artists who had reaped the rewards of Henri's battle to defeat academic taste; they had won the public acceptance that had been denied to Henri's circle in the period before the Armory Show.

The Henris spent many memorable evenings at the Glackenses' home on West Ninth Street, where Ernest Lawson told droll stories with quiet humor, Everett Shinn wise-cracked about the millionaires with whom he so often consorted, and John Sloan indulged in diatribes against capitalism or, if in a genial mood, sang his inimitable "I've Got Sixpence" or "Show Me the Way to Go Home." There were also spirited parties at Bill and Mary Roberts' apartment at Eighteenth Street near Third Avenue, where many celebrities—Mary was keen on celebrities—gathered regularly for lavish dinners. Talk centered about such subjects as the subtle grace of Kimura, the Japanese dancer who performed at the Neighborhood Playhouse, meetings with Gertrude Atherton at Petitpas, Emma Goldman's lectures on Tolstoi, or Isadora Duncan's solo dances, with full orchestra, at Carnegie Hall.

Henri wrote appreciatively of those evenings in his diary, as he did about his many visits with the Sloans. In addition to a complete catalogue of his paintings, he kept a sentimental scrapbook of theatre programs—even from his early Paris days—and special notebooks recording the pigments he used in his paintings, with critical comments on their quality, their application indoors and out, and notes on the media used with them. Sloan made a satirical drawing of Henri—at an advanced age Henri never reached—showing his stooped figure bent over a file of records in a studio overflowing with notebooks diligently compiled during a lifetime of painting (Figure 32).

While Henri continued to see most of his old friends from the Eight after 1913, the Armory Show unquestionably disrupted the solidarity of the group. John Sloan, for example, shook off his dependence on Henri's aesthetic, believing that his mentor was incapable of adapting himself to the latest developments revealed by the show. An ideological rift had already begun to develop between Sloan and Henri about 1909 over the respective virtues of socialism and anarchism; with the advent of the Armory Show, the

Figure 32. John Sloan, *Studio of Robert Henri, A.D. 1950*, 1904. Crayon on paper, 15 x 11″. Collection of Mr. and Mrs. Julian Foss, Verona, New Jersey.

rupture became even more serious. Sloan did not move completely out of Henri's orbit, by any means, but the relations between the two men were not as cordial as before. Only in the mid-1920's was their close friendship reinstated.

For a decade, it was George Bellows, more than Sloan, who represented the fullest embodiment of Henri's ideas. Bellows had entered the New York School of Art in 1904 as a wide-eyed Ohioan, a semiprofessional baseball player richly endowed with an illustrator's talent. His optimistic, healthy realism, his immense facility with the brush, and his devotion to characteristically American subjects made him a perfect candidate for many (but not all) of Henri's teachings. At the school, Bellows absorbed the master's style and quickly equaled him in technical brilliance. (See, for example, Bellows' *Kids*, 1906 [Figure 33].) Henri's prize pupil, in turn, became his intimate friend and continually benefited from his advice. This close personal relationship between teacher and pupil, unspoiled by jealousy, flourished until Bellows' untimely death in 1925. His passing was a severe blow to Henri that brought to an end what had become almost a father-and-son relationship.

Through the years, Marjorie presided at the Thursday evenings in the Henri studio, whether the occasion was a poker game or a session to discuss the arts. Not being a card player herself, when the Bellowses, the Speichers, the Sloans, and the Robertses gathered for play, she would make sketches of them or retire to the Morris chair with her perennial favorite, George Moore, or whatever new books had arrived from Brentano's. Whenever the men went into a huddle over Hambidge's theories, the wives would retreat to the couch to discuss the magic of Nijinsky's performance in "L'Après-midi d'un faune" or, in another vein, the hobble skirt vogue, the newest formula for bathtub gin, or who among them would be the first to bob her hair. To make her points, Marjorie would often draw unflattering sketches of herself in bobbed hair and hobble skirt, rarely stopping before inserting similar portrayals of Emma Bellows, Elsie Speicher, and Dolly Sloan.

These evenings were often prefaced, as in earlier days, by dining at Petitpas, where John Butler Yeats presided, genially dismissing conversation that smacked of argument in favor of more gracious give-and-take: "Arguments killed the fine art of conversation," he maintained.[5] Yeats often found occasion to chide Marjorie for not making enough of her own fine talent or taking it as seriously as she did Henri's art and well-being. By temperament she was neither assertive nor egotistical, though she had a mind of her own. She once was heard to remark that the extra grain of ego she needed might have spoiled

Figure 33. George Bellows, *Kids*, 1906. Oil on canvas, 32 x 42″. The Rita and Daniel Fraad Collection, New York.

her understanding disposition. She freely admitted that she worked only when the spirit or the subject moved her, or when exhibition time approached; then sketches casually jotted down were redrawn with care. Many withering pen-and-ink cartoons against Prohibition, published as comic strips, brought her notice and applause.

Unlike Henri, who maintained a detailed catalogue of his paintings and drawings, often working after midnight to keep it up to date, Marjorie rarely did anything about her sketches other than consign them to a portfolio to await further consideration. Managing a household, arranging the model's pose when necessary, and providing Victrola music did not help her concentrate on her own work. But she was philosophical about it and most of the time considered Henri's art more important than her own. Were it not for his care of her drawings and water colors—he usually matted and filed her sketches when she left them lying about—they might not have survived as evidence of her power of characterization.

By contrast, "The Boss," as Marjorie usually called Henri, had a forceful, aggressive personality. While usually restrained in his criticisms of people, he did not compromise with anyone whose opinions on art, teaching, and life differed sharply from his. They were welcome to their point of view, while he held strongly to his, acknowledging candidly that he was always an egotist in being true to himself. As Guy Pène du Bois, one of his former students, observed: "He is man enough to have a great many enemies." [6] As man or artist Henri was not given to hail-fellow-well-met friendships; but the friends he cultivated, and they were many, were bound by close ties of mutual trust and admiration.

When the occasion warranted it, he could be "insufferably crude," as a lady journalist described him after she appeared one summer morning for an unannounced interview on the subject of "woman's most beautiful age." In a quiet moment after breakfast Henri was tending some nasturtiums growing on a trellis against the porch of his summer cottage. On the trellis some daddy-long-legs were dallying. He acknowledged her ebullient greeting—"She just happened to be in the neighborhood and thought . . . etc."—and went on with his work without replying to her question. Not to be rebuffed, the journalist genially exclaimed as she pointed to the daddy-long-legs: "What an interesting insect—looks like a species of the daddy-long-legs family." "You are wrong," said Henri coldly. "The insects are merely daddy-long-legs propagating." [7]

In classes, he was rarely tactful about sloppy palettes and dirty brushes or

201

about photographic literalness lacking in spirit and personal quality. Several sensitive women students at the Art Students League are said to have packed up and left when he criticized them roundly for their artistic blindness; having advised them in vain, he decided to ignore them completely. If he could not speak appreciatively of an artist's work, he usually kept silent. As he once remarked to Sloan: "One should be so busy proclaiming his delight in what he likes that he would have no time to mention at all what he dislikes." [8]

Summers: Santa Fe and Achill Island

Robert and Marjorie Henri left New York almost every year to make summer painting trips to various sites in the United States and Europe. To counterbalance the routine management of art affairs of the winter months, he depended on the summers as a time to concentrate on his own painting. For practical reasons, too, he required uninterrupted periods of work to amass the necessary canvases for the exhibitions that would yield the sales that provided much of his income.

Because he wished to encounter a wide variety of human types, Henri demanded frequent changes of environment for his summer work. He would sample one locale after another, sometimes returning for several seasons, as at Santa Fe, or, in the case of La Jolla and Ogunquit, would abandon the site after a summer's trial. When he became saturated with the character of the people in any given region and had produced enough successful pictures to satisfy himself, he would grow restless and search elsewhere for fresh new subjects. Only Achill Island, Ireland, seems to have satisfied him, for he purchased a house and returned there for five consecutive seasons.

Except for Ireland, Henri spent more time in Santa Fe, New Mexico, than at any other summer painting site. While visiting San Diego in 1914, he was introduced briefly to the culture of the Southwest Indians by Dr. Edgar L. Hewett, ethnologist and director of the School of American Archaeology in Santa Fe, who had been called to California to prepare the Indian exhibits for the Panama-Pacific Exhibition. Dr. Hewett's enthusiasm was one factor that influenced Henri to spend the summers of 1916, 1917, and 1922 in Santa Fe. Another attraction was the presence of so much that reminded him of Spain: the clear, sun-drenched atmosphere, the blazing blue skies, and the nightly singing of the Mexican workmen as they sauntered by his rambling adobe house on Palace Avenue.

As was his habit, Henri followed a regular daily routine in Santa Fe: performing household chores and preparing for work in the morning, then painting until evening. His favorite models were picturesque types chosen from the local Indian and Mexican populace; but after he purchased a Model T Ford, he and George Bellows made frequent excursions to sketch landscapes in the rugged mountains surrounding Santa Fe. As a rule, the Henris showed little interest in the social life of the well-to-do residents of the city. After a period of receiving visitors every Wednesday, traditionally the calling day on Palace Avenue, they escaped the ritual and the teas that followed in its wake by devoting Wednesdays to picnics in the wooded country behind the house. Equipped with a well-filled lunch basket, drawing pads, and books, Marjorie would read aloud while Henri made sketches of the fuzzy burros that grazed so amiably on thistles.

In his first year at Santa Fe, Henri worked in a studio in the Palace of the Governors, which Dr. Hewett had remodeled and generously placed at his disposal. A man of rare artistic sensibilities, Dr. Hewett possessed vast knowledge of Indian lore. Through him Henri was introduced to the Indians of Tesuque, San Ildefonso, Santa Clara, and Santo Domingo. Driving in their Model T, "Henrietta," Henri, Marjorie, and their friends visited the ceremonial dances at Taos and Acoma, where the Indians re-enacted their forefathers' tribal invocations to the Great Spirit for rain, good crops, and favorable hunting.

While the rituals impressed him, he was moved even more deeply by his passage through the wild, mountainous landscape on his way to and from pueblos of Taos and Laguna. For Henri, the pueblos and their Indian inhabitants represented the last vestiges of a noble and mysterious primitive civilization which he eagerly tried to capture in his Santa Fe paintings. Of his work in Santa Fe he wrote Mary and Bill Roberts:

I have painted some landscapes and water colors of the pueblos and ceremonial dances as well as some portraits. Among the portraits that of the Tesuque drummer chief Diegito [Figure 34] pleases me as well as some portraits of Indian girls in ceremonial attire and one of Maria of Tesuque and her baby.

I have painted them as I felt without regard to fashions old or new. I feel myself a decided modern though not of the modernistic school and am egotist enough to give all my thought to what interests me. If it is art, all right. If it is not art, all right. If it is liked I am overjoyed, if it is not I can't help it. I am having a wonderful time in my life. Human faces are incentives to clairvoyance. The picture is the trace of the adventure and to me that is the only reason for valuing

Figure 34. Robert Henri, *Diegito Roybal (Po-Tse-Nu-Tsa)*, 1916. Oil on canvas, 65 x 40¼″. Museum of New Mexico, Santa Fe.

a portrait or of its being of interest in any way to others.

The painting of the drummer chief Diegito gave so much pleasure to the old warrior that when I presented it to the Museum he would sit by it for hours every day enjoying without a smile or a sense of awareness the attention of the visitors in the Gallery.[9]

Whether the Indians lived on the pueblos or practiced their crafts in Santa Fe, their tragic history and proud spirit impressed him, and in many cases his appreciation of their artistry developed into warm friendship. Manuel of Tesuque, whose ceremonial dances he admired, would often sit on the lawn of Henri's Santa Fe home and amuse the artist's mother by singing Indian songs, while she, in turn, enjoyed telling him of the Indians she knew during her youth in the South and later on the Nebraska frontier. She even claimed there was Indian blood in her family, a claim never proved.

If the culture of the New Mexico Indians affected Henri's painting, his presence, in turn, influenced the course of contemporary art in Santa Fe and, to a lesser extent, in Taos as well. For three summers the force of his style and personality was felt in the art colony at Santa Fe, an effect readily acknowledged by the reviewers of the regional exhibitions at the Museum of New Mexico, Santa Fe. The program of the Museum, too, came under Henri's influence, since it was he who advised the director, Dr. Hewett, to adopt a unique democratic open-door policy, beginning in 1918, which allowed any artist in the state to engage exhibition space without going before a jury.

Henri's national prominence as an artist and his glowing descriptions of Santa Fe also helped to attract other major painters to the growing art colony. Bellows was the first of Henri's circle to taste the new environment, visiting his mentor in the summer of 1917, to be joined later in that year by Leon Kroll. John Sloan and Randall Davey followed suit in the summer of 1919. They liked Santa Fe so well that Davey bought a house three miles from town and became a permanent resident, while Sloan was to spend four months of the year there for over thirty years.

The Henris made their first trip to Ireland during the summer following the Armory Show, traveling a roundabout route through the country to search for a painting ground that would provide a fuller outdoor life as well as interesting new subjects. John Butler Yeats, whose portrait Henri painted that spring, had often spoken of the special qualities of Ireland, praising the country like a minstrel far from home by quoting his son's poetry. Henri once remarked that reading certain poetry—Browning and free verse in particular—made him feel like a horse on roller skates, but the poetry of William

Butler Yeats, as chanted by the poet's father at Petitpas, infused warmth, wonder, and vision into the inspired lines.

On their rambling journey from Cobh to the northwestern counties the travelers sampled the pleasures of the sidecar in all sorts of showers, as well as donkey rides through the beautiful Killarney lake country. They reached their goal in the primitive mountains of Achill Island, off the western coast of Ireland, a site inhabited by a poor but hospitable populace who eked out a living by fishing and farming. Henri was convinced that the island had inspired J. M. Synge: "It's all just like the *Playboy* [*of the Western World*] and like nothing else." [10]

Fortunately, they found a house for rent, built about sixty years before by Captain Charles Cunningham Boycott, the land agent who was ostracized and driven back to England by the impoverished residents of County Mayo, whom he had ruthlessly tried to oppress. The rambling thirteen-room house, called "Corrymore," was nestled high on the side of a heather-covered hill and offered a commanding view of Keel Bay and the ancient village of Dooagh two miles below. Henri and Marjorie immediately fell in love with the people of Achill Island, whose witty, whimsical tales and innate poetic sense fascinated them. To Henri, the islanders were a special breed who were markedly superior to city dwellers: "Folk who live in remote places, and especially those who live on islands, are thrown on their own responsibility for amusement, and, in the general life, each one has to develop the power to entertain others and himself, and so they become exceptional people. There is a lot of detail of life in great communities which they do not know, but they become possessed, through the force of necessity, of facts of life which it would be desirable for any city man to know." [11]

Marjorie did most of the letter-writing and instructed Mary O'Donnell and her husband Pat, the caretakers attached to the house, in certain domestic rites. Pat tackled the heavy chores and faithfully accompanied Henri on fishing trips, while Mary usually found time between duties to regale Marjorie with local history and tales of the County Mayo spinsters who had occupied the house for the past two summers.

Their first season at Achill proved a happy and fruitful one. Henri made many paintings of the people, the whitewashed cabins with their geranium-lined windows and blue half-doors, and the mist-shrouded Minaun Cliffs rising across Keel Bay. Following an afternoon of painting in the studio, Henri and Marjorie would climb into a hired sidecar for a drive down the stony road to the village, Henri to make informal sketches by twilight, Marjorie to play the role of keen observer. On their way they enjoyed the friendly greetings of the villagers and chatted with local fishermen, who, in response to Henri's questions, were only too happy to reveal the haunts of trout in the glistening streams while wondering why a man in his right mind should waste good time trying to catch the tiny things when fine fat mackerel and herring could easily be taken from the sea close by.

Henri was greatly impressed with the innocence and unconventional beauty of the children who stood shyly by the half-doors or hid in the folds of their mothers' skirts when he and Marjorie passed by on evening sketching trips. He was drawn to them out of a deep inner conviction: "If one has a love of children as human beings, and realizes the greatness that is in them, no better subjects for painting can be found. The majority of people patronize children, look down on them rather than up to them, think they are 'cute,' 'sweet,' when in reality it is the children that have not yet been buried under the masses of little habits, conventions and details which burden most grownups." [12] In time, the children conquered some of their shyness and came up to pose for Henri, no doubt attracted by the bread and jam Marjorie fed them during rest periods and the entertaining songs she made come out of "a box"—the Victrola. "They are generally in a state of speechless embarrassment when they pose," he observed. "It's impossible to break the ice with some of them—and those who can be induced to open their mouths generally do it in whispers." [13]

In the spring of 1924, after an eleven-month stay in Spain, the Henris decided to return to Achill Island, attracted by cherished memories of the lush, heathered hills, the prospect of trout-fishing, and an outdoor life impossible in Madrid. They inquired whether "Corrymore," the Boycott house, would be for rent again, but after a long wait for a reply were told the government had put it up for sale and that it could not be rented under any circumstances. "Buying was of course out of the question," Henri wrote a friend, "we being near the end of our string—so we bought it." [14] Actually, the price of £200 —then equivalent to $870—was more than reasonable for the house and fifteen acres, not to mention the magnificent views and access to the well-stocked trout streams half a mile away. Henri delighted in pointing out to his friends in New York that, by virtue of its location at the extreme western tip of Ireland, "Corrymore" was the nearest inhabited house to America.

The remaining summers of Henri's life were spent at Achill, where, in addition to painting, he became an ardent trout fisherman who soon learned to be as indifferent to wind and rain as any native. Following an afternoon of painting children, he would trudge up the boggy slopes to Corrymore or Keel Lake and there fish with Pat O'Donnell until the long twilight ended at 10:00 or 10:30. Frequently, dawn—it broke about 2:30 in early summer—found Henri entering the evening's fishing score in his diary, along with notes on accompanying weather conditions and detailed descriptions of the most effective flies. Just as often, however, he was too tired from the day's exertions to do anything but smoke and listen to Marjorie's accounts of the latest happenings up and down the road, as told by the postman or Mary the housekeeper. Dinner was rarely over before midnight, after which they read by the turf fire, indulged in the Mah Jong craze, or reminisced about the people with whom they had spoken on their drives.

Henri could not have been more satisfied with his existence at his Irish retreat: "There is nothing to equal this way of working," he wrote his dealer. "No telephone, no visitors, I don't even read the newspapers. . . . Half the day is in the studio and the other half is in the open, rain or shine, on the lake—and a lot of climbing over the rough bog." [15] In the last five years of his life, he indulged in the pleasures he had denied himself during forty years of diligent hard work as a student, artist, and public figure. While he never purposely shirked his responsibilities, friends and associates could not get at him in Ireland and even his letters went unanswered for months. Trout-fishing, his new avocation, kept him out of doors and active—a welcome antidote to the circumscribed life of the New York city-dweller. In a sense, this was Henri's version of retirement, though he probably did not regard it as that. For while he painted almost every day, he did not embark on any new formal adventures, being content to paint the same kind of subjects over and over again.

Last Days

Henri's last days in Ireland were in mid-October, 1928. On a fishing trip the day before he left for home, he received a thorough drenching, presumably the cause of an ailment diagnosed during the trip back to the United States as a painfully inflamed sciatic nerve. When he arrived in New York, he entered St. Luke's Hospital for treatment, confident that he would soon recover and go off on a trout-fishing expedition. While he was indeed troubled by sciatica, he purposely was not told that he was suffering from an inoperable case of cancer of the pelvic bone, a diagnosis known only to the doctors and his wife.

Throughout the winter and spring of 1929, Marjorie remained by his bedside from early morning until closing time, reading aloud and keeping him abreast of world affairs. Henri's friends and former students rallied to him, too, in an effort to relieve the boredom of his enforced confinement in the hospital. At appointed times, many of them brought in recent work for comment and criticism. "One of his [Henri's] canvases was propped on a chair at the foot of his bed so that he might study and contemplate it," Ira Glackens recalled. "And there were fishing rods in the room, and catalogues of piscatorial equipment lying on the bed," [16] all testifying to his belief that, once he recovered, he would carry on just as before.

He remained alert and in good spirits until early in July, when he suddenly became weaker and slipped into a coma, from which he never awakened. The end came during the night of July 12, 1929. "He died most beautifully," Marjorie wrote Edith Glackens, "never a sound, or death rattle, or movement, or anything—just a drifting. . . . Bob just went out without knowing a thing, and this was what I was praying for, as I didn't think I could stand it, if he woke up, and realized he was going and would never paint, or see any of us again." [17]

He had requested that, at his death, things be kept simple and dignified, and so they were. The funeral was private; his body was cremated; and the ashes were interred in the family's vault in Philadelphia.

The news of Robert Henri's death at sixty-four came as a surprise to the public at large. Few beside his artist friends had known of his illness, and those who did had no idea of how serious it was. The profound impact he made on the American consciousness was attested by the many long obituaries that appeared in major newspapers and art magazines, not to mention the flood of letters of consolation that came to his widow from devoted friends and former students. Typical are the remarks of Forbes Watson, editor of *The Arts:*

For me Henri, quite aside from his extraordinary personal charm, was an epoch-making man in the development of American art. I have known, literally, hundreds of his students who adored him and every one of them received from him a terrific push toward the spiritual, as directly opposed to the material, view of life. I don't think any finer influence could be recorded of any man and when you realize that students who had not seen Henri for fifteen years still acknowledged that their greatest indebtedness for a finer life was to him, who could help being proud to have known him? [18]

To Marjorie, life without Henri must have been unthinkable. She could not bring herself to negotiate with dealers who asked for his pictures; since she had enough money, it was not really necessary to sell them. The paintings, she told Margery Ryerson, were all she had left of Henri, and so she kept them about her. As it happened, little time remained for Marjorie to reflect on the memory of Robert Henri. She died less than a year later.

12

The Art of Robert Henri,

1892-1928

Style, 1892–1899

IMPRESSIONISM was the first style that Henri practiced when he embarked on a career as an independent artist after three years of study in France. In the early nineties it was still considered a daring idiom, particularly in the hands of an American painter. For Henri, however, Impressionism represented progress away from the stale academic ideals that had been imposed upon him in Philadelphia and Paris. To view him as a full-fledged Impressionist follower of Monet, Sisley, or Pissarro would be misleading, because certain academic and realistic conventions remain in his work during the early nineties. In his treatment of color and light, however, he definitely belongs in the Impressionist camp.

Typical of this phase of his early work is a group of paintings executed on the New Jersey shore in 1892 and 1893. His little-known *Figures on Boardwalk* (1892) (Figure 35) shows how thoroughly he understood the Impressionists' goal of capturing a brief moment in the passing spectacle of life—in this case several clusters of figures promenading on the boardwalk at Atlantic City. The picture was undoubtedly executed directly from nature, rather than in the studio: the shape and gestures of the figures are suggested in the most summary fashion by rapidly brushed, loose touches of paint, perhaps applied with the aid of the palette knife (we know he used this implement in other paintings of the same type). Because Henri introduced broad, uniform tones of reduced color in the beach, water, and sky, but used broken color in the figures, the painting may be likened to a cross between a late Whistler and a Monet of the mid-1870's, perhaps recalling, too, something of the spirit of Boudin's beach scenes. This youthful sketch does not rank with the work

Figure 35. Robert Henri, *Figures on Boardwalk*, 1892. Oil on canvas, 12 x 18″.
Collection of Mr. Henry Sears, New York.

of the above-named masters, but Henri is already beginning to reveal his authority in handling the brush, capturing quickly the essentials of the scene with a minimum of well-chosen strokes.

More studied in execution, but equally revealing of his liaison with Impressionism, is a painting of the following year, *Girl Seated by the Sea* (1893) (Plate I), produced while he was teaching at Avalon. Here, under the full light of the sun, a young woman in white sits among the dunes and casts her glance toward the sea. The suggestive theme of the isolated figure looking seaward (there is also the familiar sailboat on the horizon) was a popular one during the nineteenth century, but Henri's interest is clearly not in the story but in the effects of sunlight falling upon the figure and the landscape. These he views in almost purely Impressionist terms—that is, in the vein of Monet in the early and mid-1870's—representing the surface of the figure and the grass on the dunes by a multitude of highly colored touches of pigment. With the technique of divided color, Henri successfully conveys the scintillating quality of bright sunlight striking the figure, whose shadows are appropriately tinted blue. But elsewhere in the picture the Impressionist effect is not so pronounced: hints of the lingering tradition of the Barbizon school still remain in the Corot-like treatment of the distant landscape. By the same token, Henri has not become a thoroughgoing Impressionist because he continues to treat the human figure as a distinct entity that refuses to be dissolved in light and color; in this, his approach is close to his contemporaries Vonnoh and Robinson. Indeed, this fidelity to the tangible identity of the subject is characteristic of most American Impressionists. What distinguishes Henri from the growing academic trend in American Impressionism, as evidenced by Weir and Vonnoh, is his fresh and vigorous transaction with nature, in which there is little place for sentimentality.

Despite Henri's competence in handling the Impressionist idiom, he abandoned it around 1895; why he did so remains an unanswered question. Whatever its drawbacks might have been, his affiliation with Impressionism drew him to the contemporary world of everyday events as the source of his subject matter. And this mode demanded rapid and accurate perception of that world, along with the manual dexterity to convert these perceptions into a pictorial image. Thus Henri's rapid method of working and his belief in decisive, immediate brushwork may be traced, in part, to his Impressionist experience.

For Henri the mid-nineties were a period of exploration and experiment in which he tried to find his proper *métier*. He had by no means settled upon regional and racial "types" as his primary subject matter, though he worked on these subjects, along with portraits and landscapes, at this time. And before he left Philadelphia in 1895 to live in Paris for a second time, Henri briefly tried his hand at painting scenes from the ballet in which he employed compositional devices that almost certainly reflect the influence of Degas. While he never followed the stylistic possibilities evidenced in these few small works, they adumbrate his future interest in the female dancer as a major subject type after 1900.

It was in France, from 1895 to 1899, that Henri finally established a consistent direction in style and subject matter. As a result of his growing interest in Whistler, Millet, Courbet, and the pre-Impressionist work of Manet, reinforced by a knowledge of Velázquez, the bright colors of Impressionism disappeared from his palette rather suddenly in favor of somber tans, grays, blues, and dark greens. Henri, in short, became a tonal painter rather than a colorist. Accordingly, his means of expression came to be the full range of values from light to dark, though most often, as we shall see, he favored low-keyed tonalities during this period. Between 1895 and 1899, we can watch him progressively becoming a more accomplished artist, thanks to sustained, intensive work at his painting. If his efforts about 1895 were sometimes rather stiff and quasi-academic, his production at the end of the decade is that of a mature artist with a highly developed personal style.

During the first phase of this period, 1895-1897—the time of his second prolonged stay in Paris—Henri established himself as a painter of peasants and peasant life (both urban and rural), Parisian cityscapes, studio portraits, and figure studies—in that order of importance. His pictures representing peasant life are by far the least successful of these types, probably because Henri did not paint them with the same conviction as his landscapes and portraits. *A Normandie Fireplace* (1897) (Figure 36), for example, shows that Henri had not completely detached himself from the conventional mode of the Salon picture—in this case the acceptable academic type, based on the idiom of the Barbizon school, that glorified the picturesque peasant. It is possible, but not probable, that he felt the subject deeply; more than likely he was painting in the manner of the Barbizon school as the accepted way to make "pictures," in other words, to show that he could do what, in the 1890's, was expected of a professional artist.

This same lack of deep involvement with the subject also flaws such half-

PLATE I. Robert Henri, *Girl Seated by the Sea*, 1893. Oil on canvas, 17¾ x 23¾".
Collection of Mr. and Mrs. Raymond J. Horowitz, New York.

Figure 36. Robert Henri, *A Normandie Fireplace*, 1897. Oil on canvas. Present location unknown; from a newspaper reproduction.

length figure pieces as *A Profile* (1895) (Figure 37) and the *Boy with Carafe* (c. 1897). These are cast in the mold of the typical studio picture: figure holding object—cup or bottle—posed in an "interesting" manner. Evidence of the art student's limitations emerges in the rather wooden treatment of the figure, which, in both canvases, seems incapable of organic movement as a result of its bolt upright position. That Henri later destroyed most of these works is sufficient evidence of his low opinion of them.

His essays in painting cityscapes did not go through these growing pains, undoubtedly because he could respond much more directly to specific visual data before his eyes. During the periods 1895–1897 and 1898–1899, he painted more than sixty cityscapes in Paris and its suburbs which, taken together, stand as sensitively conceived records of the city's varied moods. In these he managed to sidestep the temptation to make pictures that looked like "art"; while some of his stylistic vocabulary may be traced to the work of other painters, the final product is Henri's own.

The majority of his street scenes of 1896–1897, such as *A Boulevard, Paris* (c. 1896–1897) (Figure 38), followed a standard compositional pattern in which deep space in the center is established by perspective diagonals flanked by architecture at the left and right. These open vistas are invariably populated by city-dwellers going about their daily activities—strolling, shopping, driving carts and carriages. Henri, however, does not treat men and women as specific individuals; his method of painting is too broad for that. Rather, the figures are generalized types whose individuality, as in Camille Pissarro's Impressionist scenes of Paris in the 1890's, is subordinated to a broad overall effect of color and tone.

In these cityscapes, the comparison to Pissarro applies to the general conception, not the color, for Henri almost invariably continues to use a low-keyed palette dominated by grays, blues, blue-greens, and olive greens, highlighted occasionally by spots of red, as was Corot's practice. Mention of Corot suggests one of the sources of his color-range: the Barbizon school. Whistler's influence is evident too, along with that of Manet and possibly Courbet. In his brushstroke, however, Henri follows no specific precedent; we can simply say that in his loose and fairly rapid application of pigment he recalls Manet and the early phases of Impressionism.

As he gained experience in painting city scenes in the late 1890's, he became a master of suggesting moods—particularly evening and night effects. Whistler's well-known remark that the artist's work could commence at the moment the artificial lights are turned on applies justly to Henri in a painting

Figure 37. Robert Henri, *A Profile*, 1895. Oil on canvas. Destroyed; from a newspaper reproduction.

Figure 38. Robert Henri, *A Boulevard, Paris*, c. 1896–1897. Oil on canvas, 26 x 32″. Collection of Mr. Richard J. Marlitt, Portland, Oregon.

Figure 39. Robert Henri, *Fourteenth of July—Boulevard Saint-Michel,* 1898.
Oil on canvas, 15¼ x 19¾". Collection of Mr. Brock Arms, Glencoe, Illinois.

such as *Fourteenth of July—Boulevard Saint-Michel* (1898) (Figure 39).
Here we feel that he started with a dark canvas and introduced only those
accents of light needed to convey the general impression of the scene. Thus
the lights that illuminate the street become a galaxy of dancing spots, which,
like the men and women promenading in the foreground, emerge from the
mysterious darkness that dominates the picture. Undoubtedly he had learned
from Whistler that the evocative mood of night in the city could be en-
hanced by working within a limited range of the deepest tones on the palette.
This method of painting, with its mysterious shadows engulfing the substance
of things, allows the artist to work by suggestion rather than direct statement, so that his subjective experience of the scene will be effectively registered in the work.

If expression of mood through the totality of pictorial effect was Henri's
chief goal in a painting such as *Fourteenth of July—Boulevard Saint-Michel*,
it is still no less decorative as a work of art. His instinctive sense of pattern
emerges in a group of canvases executed from 1897 to 1899 which represent
café scenes and popular entertainment. Among the most decorative examples
of this type is *Fourteenth of July—"La Place"* (c. 1897) (Figure 40), a
street at night jammed with crowds celebrating the anniversary of Bastille
Day. This work demonstrates Henri's little-known kinship with the international Symbolist-Nabi idiom of the nineties, the decade when Bonnard and
Vuillard rose to prominence as the leading painters of the Nabi group. Bonnard's *Le Moulin Rouge* (or *Place Blanche*) of 1896 (Figure 41) and Vuillard's *At the Pastry Cook's* (c. 1898) (Figure 42), to select two typical
works, exemplify the idiom that Henri found so attractive for a brief period
in the late nineties. His *Fourteenth of July—"La Place"* borrows the conventions of the Bonnard-Vuillard style: the surface of the canvas is respected as a
flat, inherently decorative entity, the result of being divided by horizontals
and verticals rather than by space-creating diagonals; figures and architecture
are stacked vertically, according to the convention, inspired by Japanese art,
that "above means behind" (again, a means of denying the illusion of deep
space); and the people who inhabit the picture are treated not in terms of
mass but as areas of nearly flat pattern in a carefully considered decorative
relationship to each other. Henri's style can be distinguished from the
Bonnard-Vuillard tradition only by his rather stiff, motionless figures; in this
example and others like it, he reveals one of his shortcomings at this time: the
inability to endow the human form with convincing movement.

In *Fourteenth of July—"La Place"* and related pictures, Henri comes as

Figure 40. Robert Henri, *Fourteenth of July—"La Place,"* c. 1897. Oil on canvas, 32 x 25¾". Collection of the Nebraska Art Association, Lincoln.

Figure 41. Pierre Bonnard, *Le Moulin Rouge (Place Blanche)*, 1896. Oil on canvas, 24 x 15¾″. Collection of Mr. Wright Ludington, Santa Barbara, California. Permission A.D.A.G.P. 1969 by French Reproduction Rights, Inc.

Figure 42. Edouard Vuillard, *At the Pastry Cook's*, c. 1898. Oil on canvas. Present location unknown; from Claude Roger-Marx, *Vuillard, His Life and Work* (London, 1946), following p. 24. Permission S.P.A.D.E.M. 1969 by French Reproduction Rights, Inc.

close as he ever will to practicing a decorative style (a style, incidentally, that he later urged his students to reject). Even while he was producing city scenes like this one, we can find him working in quite a different manner as a figure painter, witness *Woman in Manteau* (1898) (Figure 11). While the color scheme remains subdued, the figure is modeled so substantially in three dimensions that it emerges as a tangible entity from its neutral background. The *Woman* still retains the aura of a studio painting; she is more than just an ordinary subject picked at random from the streets. Henri has made her a "picturesque," romantic figure by draping a great cloak over her shoulders and underlining the doleful expression on her face. This is one of the rare instances in which he borrowed from a specific prototype: in this case, as Adolph Karl has shown, the pose is loosely adapted from Rubens' *La Pelisse* (*Helena Fourment*).[1] To quote, but not copy exactly, a recognized old master in this way was perfectly legitimate—indeed encouraged—within the French academic tradition.

While there are romantic overtones in *Woman in Manteau*, the terms of Henri's stylistic vocabulary in *The Man Who Posed as Richelieu* (1898) (Figure 43) stem primarily from mid–nineteenth-century realism and its seventeenth-century sources. *Richelieu* effectively reveals how he could integrate elements from Manet and Courbet, and, indirectly, Rembrandt and Velázquez, to create a style for portraits that served him well into the 1900's. As in the *Woman in Manteau*, there is something of a seventeenth-century "old master" aspect about the *Richelieu* in the conventional placement of the figure on the canvas and the extremely dark background. Specifically, Velázquez is called to mind in the glance of the subject's eyes, peering directly and intently at the spectator. But in many other respects, this is unmistakably a nineteenth-century painting that combines Manet's flat, frontal lighting and sketchy brushwork (*Portrait of Roudier*, c. 1860) (Figure 44) with Courbet's sense of material substance in the treatment of the head and figure (*Portrait of Max Buchon*, 1854) (Figure 45). The result is also remarkably close to certain early paintings by Cézanne—the *Portrait of Valabrègue* (1866), for example—but we have no reason to believe that Henri knew the Frenchman's work at this time. The relationship is probably coincidental, the result of both artists' drawing upon similar sources.

By the end of his third period in France (1898–1899), Henri had become a mature artist—a maturity that was recognized by the French government by their purchase of his *La Neige* (Figure 12). In these two years he finally purged himself of many of the lingering habits of the art student to achieve a

Figure 43. Robert Henri, *The Man Who Posed as Richelieu*, 1898.
Oil on canvas, 32 x 26″. The Brooklyn Museum.

Figure 44. Edouard Manet, *Portrait of Roudier*, c. 1860. Oil on canvas, 24 x 19¾″. Rijkmuseum Kröller-Müller, Otterlo, Netherlands.

Figure 45. Gustave Courbet, *Portrait of Max Buchon,* 1854. Oil on canvas, 77½ x 43¾″. Musée des Beaux-Arts, Vevey, Switzerland.

command of technique and an ability to construct paintings that places him on a level with, or even above, such better-known contemporaries as William Merritt Chase and Frank Duveneck. And there are a few moments when, in this writer's opinion, Henri's work of the late nineties begins to approach Whistler and Sargent in quality. Like the four American painters just cited, he shaped a large part of his style from intensive study of works of art in the Louvre and other European museums; however, the subject matter he chose and the resulting content of his work placed him in a rather unpopular position. While in the nineties he was glad to exhibit at the Salon, the forthright honesty of his cityscapes and portraits alienated prospective buyers instead of inviting popular success. Henri's was an advanced style at this time, and it is to his credit that he did not compromise and abandon it, for this was to be the foundation for some of the finest paintings of his career executed in America in the early 1900's.

Style, 1900–1912

When Henri settled permanently in New York in the fall of 1900, he planned to establish himself as a painter and to teach only as a means of supplementing his income. Accordingly, between 1900 and 1904 he produced an unparalleled number of works of high quality and originality. This is a period when we can sense his intense concentration on the art of painting, virtually excluding other interests. It is not surprising, therefore, to find much of his best work within this span of years; after 1904 he became more deeply involved in teaching, and in the latter part of the decade the exhibitions of the Eight and the Independents drained much of his creative energy. Of course, he continued to paint in the face of these distractions. But we cannot help feeling that, by the mid-1900's, he began to realize himself just as much by helping others create and exhibit as in producing art himself.

During the period from 1900 to 1912, Henri gradually abandoned landscapes and cityscapes (though these subjects occasionally reappear after 1912). Just why this happened is hard to explain; whatever the reasons were, his declining interest in landscape is regrettable, for in this genre we find some of the finest canvases of his career. Although his reputation was based to a large extent on portraits and figures, the little-known landscapes and city scenes of this period exerted a strong influence on the course of American art.

LANDSCAPES AND CITYSCAPES, 1900–1903

The style of Henri's early New York cityscapes originated in his Parisian work of the late nineties. While the Parisian pictures are perfectly competent performances, the style gains greater appeal when applied to New York subjects. This is probably a result of his growing fondness for his native country —a Whitmanesque appreciation of America that is reflected in his enthusiasm in depicting it. We can sense, too, much greater congruity between Henri's essentially realistic style of the early 1900's and the urban cityscape of New York; the city was relatively new, often architecturally disorganized and tasteless, free of the inevitable picturesque associations of Paris. Of course, Henri managed to find poetry in the New York scene, just as he had in Paris; this is what makes *Cumulus Clouds—East River* (1901–1902) (Figure 46) and *Derricks on the North River* (1902) (Figure 47) memorable evocations of a lost era in the life of the city.

Just as the color scheme of his Parisian pictures is usually restricted to ochres, greens, grays, and blacks, so these are tonal paintings in which the image is presented in terms of broadly conceived areas of dark and light. By exaggerating value contrasts, as he does in the early 1900's, he transcends a merely literal recording of visual data to stress the dramatic quality implicit in the scene—a quality that is heightened by his enthusiastic response to New York as something alive with a special personality uniquely its own. The dramatic element is particularly strong in *Derricks on the North River*, where the towering derricks stand out as giant silhouettes against a threatening sky. This glorification of an industrial apparatus reveals Henri as an "ashcan" painter in the sense that he, like Van Gogh and the Neoimpressionists during the 1880's, could turn to the less genteel aspects of city life as suitable and valid subjects for painting. It is worth observing that the *Derricks*, along with paintings such as *The Coal Breaker* (1902),[2] forecasts by more than thirty years Charles Burchfield's fascination with the sombre poetry of industry and the machine in *Black Iron* (1935).

Henri could respond just as vigorously to the mountainous landscape of northeastern Pennsylvania and the primitive rockbound coast of Maine. His summer trips away from the city took him to Black Walnut, Pennsylvania, and to Boothbay Harbor and Monhegan Island, Maine, in 1903; it was in or near these three sites that he created a series of superb small paintings of landscapes. The oil sketches in this group, as distinct from his larger finished canvases, demonstrate his phenomenal ability to observe the landscape and ab-

Figure 46. Robert Henri, *Cumulus Clouds—East River*, 1901–1902. Oil on canvas, 25½ x 32″. The Rita and Daniel Fraad Collection, New York.

Figure 47. Robert Henri, *Derricks on the North River*, 1902. Oil on canvas, 26 x 32″. Andrew Crispo Collection, New York.

stract its essential masses without being encumbered by unnecessary detail. Furthermore, the agitated brushstrokes in a small panel such as *Landscape at Black Walnut, Pa.* (1902) (Figure 48) testify to his high state of excitement in capturing a passing effect in nature in a type of painting that might be called "tonal impressionism"—tonal because it is conceived in terms of value relationships, not color vibration, and impressionist because a brief moment in the changing spectacle of nature is seized. That Henri was conscious of the advantages of the tonal method in recording his impressions is attested by the following remarks. Justifying his method by citing Manet's example, he stated: "I am not of the opinion that the spot-broken color or broken mass method is the best for presenting the idea of vibration—I think big flat (or practically flat) masses of form or color may render [a] sense of light and vibration—air—if the realization of value and color are right." [3]

Evidence from the brushwork alone reveals his swiftness in capturing the momentary impression; but more than this, the activated stroke reflects the immediacy of his response to the scene as something vital and alive. And the quality of motor excitement in his brushstroke can, I believe, be compared favorably to that found in the action painters of the New York school some fifty years later. The latter group, of course, frequently painted without indicating recognizable subject matter. While Henri never produced an abstract action painting, the philosophy behind his creative process in works such as *Landscape at Black Walnut* is not as far removed from action painting as we might suppose.

For different reasons, the more carefully finished landscapes of Black Walnut and Monhegan are just as impressive. *The Rain Storm—Wyoming Valley* (1902) (Plate II) reveals Henri's mastery in capturing effects of the weather—here an approaching rainstorm and a mass of threatening gray clouds moving slowly toward the sun-streaked plain in the foreground. The painting stands as a record of his immediate experience of the subject, possibly being executed entirely at the site. There is a freshness, too, about the color and design that makes it superior to many of his earlier landscapes in which traditional compositional formulas were all too evident. The qualities of freshness and immediacy Henri achieved in recording the changing effects of the weather cannot help but call to mind the attitude toward nature of the great English landscape painter John Constable, who likewise immersed himself in nature to capture its varied moods. We know from Henri's unpublished lectures that he admired Constable's work, so it is not surprising to find Constable's influence echoed here, albeit by a lesser artist.

PLATE II. Robert Henri, *The Rain Storm—Wyoming Valley*, 1902. Oil on canvas, 26 x 32″. Collection of Bernice and Joseph Tanenbaum, Bayside, New York.

Figure 48. Robert Henri, *Landscape at Black Walnut, Pa.*, 1902. Oil on panel, 5 ¾ x 8″. Present location unknown.

Figure 49. Robert Henri, *Maine Coast*, 1903, repainted 1908. Oil on canvas, 26 x 32". Present location unknown.

Henri's view of nature as a living force which interacts with man finds even more potent expression in the Monhegan seascapes. One of the finest of this group, *Maine Coast* (1903, repainted 1908) (Figure 49), illustrates even better than *Landscape at Black Walnut* how, through brushwork, he could empathize with the thrusts, the push-and-pull, of forces within the landscape. The opposition of the huge, jagged rocks to the ocean rushing against them gave Henri an opportunity to activate the pigment as a visual and tactile vehicle to convey the swirling energy of the water, He was, of course, not the first artist to work in this manner. Van Gogh and Monet (in his Belle Ile seascapes) employed pigment in a similar way, predicting, as does Henri himself, the tormented brushwork of such twentieth-century Expressionists as Soutine and Kokoschka.

His deep involvement with nature as a dynamic force suggests an obvious debt to a major American artist of the preceding generation, Winslow Homer, who in 1903 was still alive and painting at Prout's Neck, Maine. Specific analogies may be drawn between the color scheme and composition of many of Homer's and Henri's seascapes, undoubtedly the result of the influence of the older artist on the younger. In Henri's *Maine Coast* and related oil sketches of the sea, he seems to have been freed, through Homer's influence, from any preordained compositional format. One novel design after another —particularly close-ups of the turbulent sea—were invented under the pressure of seizing the immediately perceived effect in nature. It is as if Henri did not have time to worry about constructing works that looked like pictures.

It is curious that Henri should have executed side by side with these landscapes a set of much more conservative ones such as *Old Brittany Farmhouses* (1902) (Figure 50), which are handled in the traditional manner of the Barbizon school. These paintings, executed from memory or from earlier sketches, lack the fresh authenticity of the Pennsylvania and Maine landscapes; they are carefully fabricated studio-pieces in the tradition of Corot and Millet that were painted with the knowledge that they would appeal to the taste of an American audience. They represent his "public" image, while the landscapes done from nature in the early 1900s—particularly the oil sketches—reveal the real Henri painting to satisfy himself.

He did not cease painting landscapes in 1903, though this was the last year he produced them in large numbers. On his summer trips to Spain and Holland, a landscape motif would occasionally attract his attention; but from 1904 onward he became primarily a painter of portraits and figures to the virtual exclusion of other subjects.

Figure 50. Robert Henri, *Old Brittany Farmhouses*, 1902. Oil on canvas, 26 x 32″. Chapellier Galleries, New York.

PORTRAITS, 1900–1912

Henri spent the first few years after 1900 recording the physiognomy of his friends and relatives. Too little known at that time to survive exclusively on portrait commissions, he gained experience by painting models he knew well—and who would pose without cost. In this period we find a whole gallery of his friends among the artists, writers, and newspapermen: Sloan, Luks, Glackens, Sadakichi Hartmann, Byron Stephenson, and Edward W. Davis, just to mention a few.

If anything characterizes this group of portraits, it is Henri's effort to communicate each individual's unique character by carefully determining the pose, costume, and background of the painted image. The differences in personality between his *Portrait of George Luks* (1904) (Figure 16) and that of his wife Linda in *Lady in Black* (1904) (Figure 10) are examples of his methods of heightening personal characteristics. The broad mass of Luks's body is turned to face the spectator squarely, while Henri clothes him in a huge rumpled dressing gown—both devices designed to emphasize Luks's open, easygoing, and thoroughly masculine character. The *Lady in Black*, on the other hand, is pictorially more reserved. Where Luks's head is set at an angle and his hand rests easily on the top of the fireplace, Linda stands erect and alert, her figure describing a long unbroken vertical relieved only by the horizontal line at waist height. The design is thus more severe and restrained, as is appropriate to her personality.

Any number of such comparisons could be made to demonstrate Henri's sympathetic understanding of his subjects and his ability to embody their personal qualities in the painted image. Rather than repeat a formula from one sitter to the next, as so many of his contemporaries did, Henri made each portrait a new and individual entity. Of course his portrait style was not simply a result of recording what he saw before him; as in his landscapes, previous masters of portraiture helped to shape his vocabulary. If we recall those portrait painters Henri most admired—Velázquez, Hals, and Rembrandt—it will not be difficult to find these influences echoed in his portraits of the early 1900's. To be sure, he refrained from close copying of the work of any one of these seventeenth-century masters, but because he studied them so intently, their impact on his style is revealed in a variety of ways. Typically (though not always) we can trace the dignified full-length pose to Velázquez; the rapid, summary brushwork to Hals; and the use of strong, direct illumination, with accompanying dark shadows, to Rembrandt.

To see these influences at work in a single painting we have only to consider Henri's *Portrait of W. J. Glackens* (1904) (Figure 51). The subject, himself an artist, assumes a formal pose typical of countless members of Habsburg royalty painted by Velázquez: the full-length figure in three-quarter view, one hand on the hip with the other slightly extended at waist height (in this case grasping a cane), and the eyes peering intently at the spectator. The tone of seriousness is underlined both by the quiet immobility of the pose and the grays and blacks that dominate the canvas—both elements again recalling Velázquez. The influence of Rembrandt, however, is found in the treatment of the head as a solid mass revealed by strong, direct light from the left; the resulting shadow, as in many of Rembrandt's portraits, is so dark that the features are almost totally obscured. More than in most portraits by Velázquez, Henri employs contrasts of light and dark to sharpen the features of the face and ultimately to reveal the sitter's character as honestly as possible. As to Hals, Henri's interest in that painter's virtuoso brushwork is present, though not obviously so, in the broad, loosely applied strokes of pigment in the subject's vest.

Merely to enumerate these sources is, of course, to do Henri an injustice, because his paintings of this period represent much more than just a composite of influences. It is through his knowledge of these seventeenth-century masters that he forged a personal style, much as his older contemporaries Chase, Sargent, and Duveneck had done a few decades before. Indeed, these three American painters, along with Whistler, in a subtle way may also have influenced Henri's portrait style, though he would have been loath to admit it. Whether he was conscious of it or not, he was clearly working in a tradition analogous to theirs.

FIGURES AND HEADS, 1900–1912

In the past few pages our subject has been Henri as a painter of portraits of specific individuals; closely related in style to the portraits are his studies of heads and costumed figures posed by professional or amateur models, a group which includes some of his most famous canvases. There are models in contemporary dress such as Eugenie Stein (known as Zenka of Bohemia), the subject of *Young Woman in White* (1904) (Figure 52), or Jesseca Penn, portrayed in *Young Woman in Black* (1902), who posed in the studio to give Henri an opportunity to demonstrate his skill as a figure painter on a large scale. The results were destined for the major national exhibitions, particularly

Figure 51. Robert Henri, *Portrait of W. J. Glackens,* 1904. Oil on canvas, 77 x 37″. Chapellier Galleries, New York.

Figure 52. Robert Henri, *Young Woman in White*, 1904. Oil on canvas, 78¼ x 38⅛″. National Gallery of Art, Washington, D.C., Gift of Miss Violet Organ.

those of the National Academy of Design and the Society of American Artists.

To a second, less formal group belong the smaller canvases representing anonymous common people—often children—picked off the streets, such as *Eva Green* (1907) (Figure 22), painted in New York, *The Working Man* (1910) (Figure 53), from Holland, or *Segovia Girl, Half-Length* (1912) (Figure 54) from Spain. In addition, this was the period when Henri embarked on a continuing cycle of more ambitious costume pieces representing Spanish subjects—dancers, bullfighters, and gypsies. This interest gets underway in a series of full-length paintings of Anna Maria Bustamente in the dress of a Spanish dancer painted in his New York studio two years before his first concentrated painting expedition to Spain in 1906. During that summer in Spain and in successive trips in 1908, 1910, and 1912, he nurtured this interest at the source, so to speak, producing such authentic Spanish canvases as *Gitano* (1906), *Antonio Banos (Calero)*, *Picador* (1908) (Figure 56), and *Segovia Girl, Half-Length* (1912). Because his activities as a teacher and organizer of exhibitions severely restricted his output during a large part of each year between 1906 and 1912, his summers abroad were the only time he could concentrate on his own painting. As a result, Dutch and Spanish subjects comprise a large majority of his *oeuvre*, besides portraits, during this period.

In Holland, Henri responded to the stimulus of Frans Hals's work, which he saw in the museums of Haarlem and Amsterdam. Hals had previously counted as one of several major influences upon Henri, but now, for a few summers, Henri yielded completely to the Dutch master, producing many canvases distinctly in his idiom, such as *Cori Looking over Back of Chair* (1907) (Figure 20), *Martsche in White Apron* (1907) (Figure 21), and *The Working Man* (1910) (Figure 53). Hals also appears to have been the catalyst that thoroughly liberated Henri's brushwork. From the mid-1890's his strokes tended to be free, in the manner of Sargent and Chase; but now, under the influence of Hals, the movement of Henri's hand becomes frenetic at times, applying the paint in quick, choppy strokes, though without all of Hals's masterful control. Henri's Dutch canvases of 1907 and 1910 mark the beginning of his capacity to make the activity of the pigment on the surface of the painting serve as a vehicle for his feelings about the human being who stood before him, an aspect of his style that we will find in full force in most of his informal portraits of Irish subjects painted after 1912.

We sense that Henri was exploring the common people of Holland and Spain because they fascinated him as human beings, not because they were

Figure 53. Robert Henri, *The Working Man*, 1910. Oil on canvas, 24 x 20″. Private collection.

Figure 54. Robert Henri, *Segovia Girl, Half-Length*, 1912. Oil on canvas, 40½ x 33″. Collection of Mr. and Mrs. Robert J. Cooper, Hubbard Woods, Illinois.

quaint, picturesque subjects that would attract American buyers. It is here that his endless search for vital, unspoiled humanity began—a quest that pre-occupied him for the rest of his life. This search led him to those types who could stand as an antidote to a materialistic, overly cultivated society that ignored the natural, instinctive virtues of man, the individual. Holding this romantic outlook, which may be traced to Rousseau and Emerson, among others, Henri seized upon a variety of types remote from, or unspoiled by, the evils of contemporary society: children and young people in their teens, preferably from the lower classes; Negroes; gypsies; and performers of popular music and the dance.

If he was periodically attracted to the laboring classes, as in *The Working Man* (1910) and *The Fish Market Man* (1910), he did not caricature them as downtrodden masses exploited by the capitalist system. Rather, he emphasized their dignity, their worth as individuals who, though only workers, were endowed with as much human value as wealthy, socially prominent businessmen. Indeed, the working classes were somehow more "real" to Henri as a result of their integrity and genuine lack of affectation.

Such qualities he also found in the common people of Spain, who figure in much of his summer work in 1906, 1908, 1910, and 1912. Like Manet in the 1860's, Henri became a convinced Hispanophile; and it was Manet, in works such as *Torero Saluting* (1866) (Figure 55), who set an example for the American to follow in articulating full-length Spanish figure paintings such as *Antonio Banos (Calero), Picador* (Figure 56). The young man, holding a lance on his shoulder, is dressed in the full regalia of the bull ring, and as in Manet's paintings of similar themes, he is shown at an arrested moment in his action. Yet he appears capable of moving, thanks to a slightly raised foot and the fragmentation of the lance—a device that suggests a continuous spatial environment to the left and right of the figure. It would be appropriate to say that Henri's painting echoes but does not imitate Manet in its neutral, undefined background and the tendency of the bulk of the figure to dominate the picture space. As Henri's Spanish style developed, however, he tried to slough off such stylistic reminiscences.

Segovia Girl, Half-Length (Figure 54) illustrates how he transcended influences from other artists to arrive at his own personal style. By forcing analogies, one could point to Rembrandt's impact on his heavily loaded brushstroke dragged across the bodice of the dress or the Manet-like effort to simplify the planes of the face. But just as Henri's contemporary, the architect Louis Sullivan, ultimately broke away from eclectic combinations of

244

Figure 55. Edouard Manet, *Torero Saluting*, 1866. Oil on canvas, 67⅜ x 44½″. The Metropolitan Museum of Art, The H. O. Havemeyer Collection, Bequest of Mrs. H. O. Havemeyer, 1928.

Figure 56. Robert Henri, *Antonio Banos (Calero),
Picador,* 1908. Oil on canvas, 87 x 37″. Chapellier Galleries, New York.

various historical sources to achieve a personal statement of a functional aesthetic in architecture, so Henri in this and later canvases shows that he could transcend traditional styles to paint pictures that looked only like Henris.

Style, 1913–1929

The year 1913 is the logical point at which to begin a discussion of the third and final period in Henri's artistic development. It was the year of the Armory Show, an event that radically altered the subsequent course of American art and indirectly contributed to Henri's decline as the foremost exponent of artistic progress in the United States. For at least fifteen years he had fought for the right of artists to develop as individuals outside the accepted academic channels and to exhibit freely without restraints imposed by juries. By 1913 he had won a large part of this battle, and we cannot help feeling that, at forty-eight, he was glad enough to turn over some of his responsibilities as crusader to the younger generation so that he could concentrate on his own artistic development.

At this stage Henri had arrived; there was no question about his being one of the country's foremost artists. As such, he no longer felt compelled to paint for the large national exhibitions. While he continued to enter his work in these shows and was given several important museum exhibitions during this period, one feels that he now painted largely as he pleased.[4] Furthermore, the experience of the Armory Show induced him to reassess his knowledge of pictorial structure, especially in the light of what that exhibition revealed of the art of Postimpressionism, Cubism, and Fauvism. After 1913, then, Henri embarked on a program of renewed study and experiment: "I continue the study of art," he wrote a friend, "make a thing which I think is a picture now and then as a sort of offput—landmark of my progress."[5] For an artist of Henri's age and experience to continue to learn is a most unusual trait—a quality often overlooked by certain hostile critics who view his later work as a facile, mechanical repetition of his style before 1913.

His first trip to Ireland in 1913 served as a catalyst that led him to a fresh approach to painting. Here he discovered a galaxy of new subjects virtually made to order for his tastes: ancient villages, serene landscapes, and countless Irish "characters" and children—all radiating a quality of quiet innocence that he found absorbing. Landscapes such as *Menaune Cliffs* (1913) (Figure 57) comprised about one-third of his production during his initial Irish so-

Figure 57. Robert Henri, *Menaune Cliffs*, 1913. Oil on canvas, 26¼ x 32″. Collection of Mrs. J. Murray Mitchell, Lismore, Ireland.

journ. In this and related paintings he revived aspects of his style of the early 1900's but now approached the canvas with even greater sensitivity to compositional refinement. Practically nothing remains of the "old master" look; the painting reveals a stunningly fresh vision of a pristine landscape, unscathed by man's presence. Although *Menaune Cliffs* brings to mind the work of John Constable, it is enough of an optical record of a particular scene to rule out direct influence from Constable at this stage.

His newly discovered enthusiasm for Ireland and the Irish also gave rise to the best-known paintings of his entire career: the pair of portraits of Johnny Cummings and his wife entitled *Himself* (1913) (Figure 58) and *Herself* (1913) (Figure 59). His remarks about the subjects at the time of painting them are worth recording:

Yesterday I painted an old lady . . . very fat and with a jovial red round face—she is over 75 but still has perfectly black hair and a sturdy stride. . . . She tells you she is of a quality superior to the natives here—she came about 55 years ago from a miserable little town on the mainland—called Westport—a great city no doubt to these people—she was a runaway match—her folks objected—his folks objected. So they run away—that is I suppose they "took up" and so the mighty families had to agree and they were married—13 children resulted and for the 55 years they have been in a state of admiration and fondness for each other punctuated at close intervals with quarrels that have been for the 55 years the interest and amusement of Dooagh. I have a painting of him, too. . . . He fishes, wears a coat turned wrong side out—a brown vest and has under his long and broad upper lip an antique clay pipe and a brush of yellow red whiskers.[6]

It is easy to see why these became popular favorites with the American public: the subjects were common people—"characters," one might say—treated with dignity and respect. In his attitude toward the sitters and in his selective realism, Henri recalls something of the spirit of Frans Hals. At the same time, this pair of portraits shares some of the universal appeal (but not necessarily the influence) of Rembrandt's late character studies of the inhabitants of the poorer quarters of Amsterdam.

More typical of Henri's Irish subjects are the hundreds of children he painted in the summer of 1913 and during subsequent visits every year from 1924 to 1928. They usually range from ten to sixteen years of age, a period of precious innocence and naïveté that Henri glorified as an antidote to the evils of oversophistication that stifled man when he reached adulthood. To select a few representative examples from such a large number of canvases is always

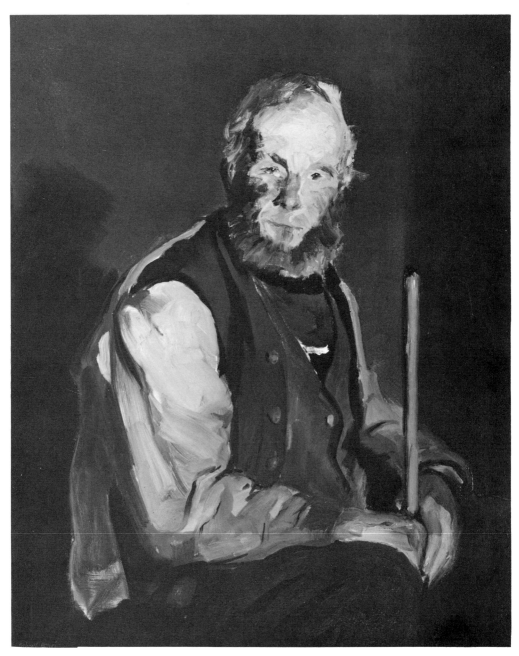

Figure 58. Robert Henri, *Himself*, 1913. Oil on canvas, 32¼ x 26⅛″. Courtesy of The Art Institute of Chicago, Walter H. Schultze Memorial Collection.

Figure 59. Robert Henri, *Herself*, 1913. Oil on canvas, 32 x 26″. Courtesy of The Art Institute of Chicago, Walter H. Schultze Memorial Collection.

difficult; but *Patrick* (1913) (Figure 60) and *Blonde Bridget Lavelle* (1928) (Plate III) may stand as proxy for their countless Irish brothers and sisters. Both are informed with that distinctive quality of "life" that became ever more precious in Henri's eyes. These are not the slouching urchins of the type popularized in J. G. Brown's paintings, but are vital creatures, who, if they do not actually move before us, seem charged with the ability to do so at any moment. In *Patrick*, the earlier of the two paintings, the spirit of vitality emanates not so much from the brushwork but through the alert glance of the eyes peering intently at the spectator—one of Henri's favorite devices for establishing the subject as a living, communicating being. In *Blonde Bridget Lavelle*, the eyes are turned to the right, but the same intensity of glance remains; she, like *Patrick*, is alive, alert, and involved. The tilt of the shoulders and torso, too, contributes to her potential for action. Above all, Henri's swiftly moving, summary brushwork serves as a direct index of his vision of the subject as a vital creature.

In Henri's view, these are ideal young people—healthy, optimistic types, rich in human dignity and thoroughly natural and unaffected. These same qualities, as we suggested earlier, attracted him in a wide variety of international types. Although he did not travel to Africa or China, he sought out Negroes and Chinese-Americans, along with Mexicans, Indians, and gypsies in the United States. They constitute what he termed "my people":

The people I like to paint are "my people," whoever they may be, wherever they may exist, the people through whom dignity of life is manifest, that is, who are in some way expressing themselves naturally along the lines Nature intended for them. My people may be old or young, rich or poor, I may speak their language or I may communicate with them only by gestures. But wherever I find them, the Indian at work in the white man's way, the Spanish gypsy moving back to the freedom of the hills, the little boy quiet and reticent before the stranger, my interest is awakened and my impulse immediately is to tell about them through my own language—drawing and painting in color.[7]

Henri's outlook was clearly international, as evidenced by the diversity of races and nationalities represented by his subjects. His repeated painting of these types seems to have been his own antidote to the evils of nationalism and "patriotism" that impelled mankind through four years of tragic self-destruction during World War I. Typically, Henri's testament was a vivid individual statement, a personal crusade; he refused, as was his custom, to fight

PLATE III. Robert Henri, *Blonde Bridget Lavelle*, 1928. Oil on canvas, 28 x 20″. Collection of Mr. and Mrs. W. J. Bowen, Winter Park, Florida.

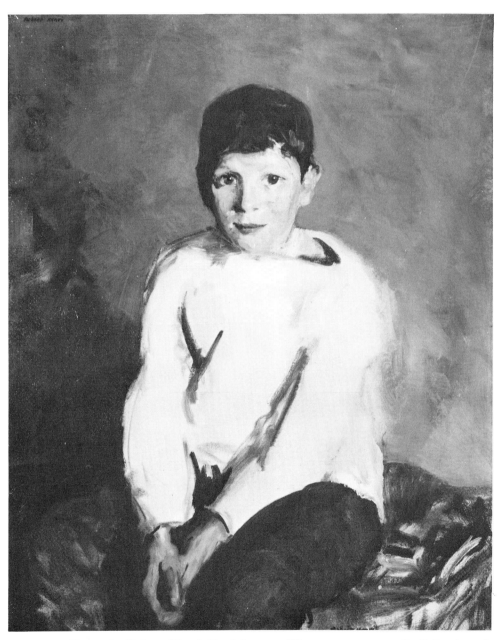

Figure 60. Robert Henri, *Patrick*, 1913. Oil on canvas, 32 x 26″. Collection of Mr. and Mrs. Louis Sosland, Shawnee Mission, Kansas.

the iniquities brought about by organized institutions by founding or joining one himself. As he said: "No blind, intense devotion for an institution that
has stiffened in chains of its own making. My love of mankind is individual,
not national, and always I find the race expressed in the individual." [8]

To discover and paint these individuals. Henri made periodic summer ex-
peditions to the West and Southwest, beginning in 1914. In the latter part of
that year, he made his home in La Jolla, California, and there and in nearby
San Diego he chose his subjects from the Mexican, Chinese-American, and
Indian population. Just as in his Irish work, girls outnumbered boys among
his subjects, though he did find Sylvester, a Negro newsboy, a particularly
intriguing subject worth painting again and again. For these pictures, Henri
would select a few typical models that appealed to him, such as the Chinese
girl *Chow Choy* (1914) (Figure 61) and Jim Lee, an old Chinese vegetable
man, and depict them repeatedly in different poses, as if to provide a cine-
matic account of every aspect of their personality. His aim, of course, was
not to produce factual documents but, as in the Irish pictures, to seize the
qualities of dignity and vitality in the individual subjects.

Summer trips to Santa Fe in 1916, 1917, and 1922 provided further opportunities to study different national and racial "types," particularly Mexicans
and Indians. Once again he employed the series method to capture the various
facets of his favorite models—*Julianita* (1917) (Figure 62), Gregorita, and
Diegito (1916) (Figure 34). In his Indian paintings he made a greater effort
than ever before to provide a documentary record of the subject's costume;
personal "character," of course, still prevailed, but it was reinforced by the
distinctive appurtenances of the Indians' mode of life. There is a long tradition for this type of portrait, stemming back ultimately to the nineteenth-
century American painter George Catlin; and by the second decade of the
twentieth century, Santa Fe had spawned an artists' colony whose chief subject matter was the life and physiognomy of the American Indian. Henri
probably would have been attracted to these subjects in any event, but the
presence of an established tradition undoubtedly stimulated his production of
Indian paintings.

Just as Henri appreciated the marginal elements of society, so too he discovered admirable personal qualities in fellow artists working in forms different from his—particularly dancers and actresses. Since his early twenties, he
had been drawn to the theatre and dance as media suggesting significant parallels to his own art. With his growing interest in gesture, particularly after
1910, it follows that he should study the great dancers of his time. We have

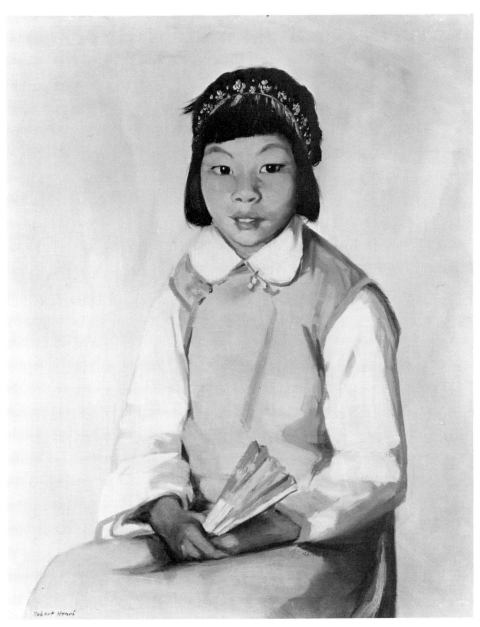

Figure 61. Robert Henri, *Chow Choy*, 1914. Oil on canvas, 32 x 26″. Present location unknown.

Figure 62. Robert Henri, *Julianita*, 1917. Oil on canvas, 32 x 26″. Courtesy of Kennedy Galleries Inc., New York.

seen that he was devoted to Isadora Duncan, whose movements he sketched in pencil and oil; but his full-scale celebration of the dancer as a modern heroine was reserved for Ruth St. Denis, Betalo Rubino, and Roshanara (Olive Craddock), each of whom posed for canvases of monumental size in the late teens. These were not commissioned works, as their large dimensions might suggest, but were painted in homage to the subjects' creative genius.

The best-known work of this group is his life-size portrayal of *Ruth St. Denis in the Peacock Dance* (1919) (Figure 63). The dancer, shown in full costume, had become famous for her dance illustrating the legend of an Egyptian princess whose spirit was confined in the body of a peacock. Like sculptures of athletes from fifth-century Greece, she is not shown in a pose of dynamic motion, but at a point just prior to, or following, a moment of action. Yet the figure is still endowed with a subtle movement because it follows the pattern of a slowly undulating S-curve from head to toe. It is this pictorial rhythm, rather than the imitation of actual bodily motion, that gives life to this image of one of America's most celebrated interpretive dancers.

Henri also demonstrated his interest in the gesture of the human body in a group of little-known paintings of nudes which were produced chiefly from the mid-teens to the early twenties. The most famous example of this type is *Figure in Motion* (1913) (Figure 64), executed shortly before the Armory Show of 1913 and destined to appear in that exhibition. It is hard to determine why Henri painted this large canvas of a nude at this time; it is exceptional as a subject in his early work. Very possibly he considered it a visual manifesto of his artistic tenets at the time of the Armory Show: the relatively unidealized treatment of the figure testifies to his frankness in accepting "nature" as it is. And the completely open expression of nudity—or nakedness—in a realistic painting must have had a predictable shock value for the American public of 1913, in much the same way that Manet's *Olympia* scandalized Paris when it was shown at the Salon of 1865. That the subject is a nude in motion invites parallels with Marcel Duchamp's celebrated *Nude Descending a Staircase*. Could Henri have seen this foreign entry to the Armory Show, or heard about it from Davies or Kuhn, before he painted the *Figure in Motion* in January, 1913? It is quite possible, though difficult to prove. But if he did know about the *Nude Descending a Staircase*, it would not have been beyond him to paint a definitive picture to "rival" Duchamp's canvas.

For him, the *Figure in Motion* is exceptional in being a painting of a nude submitted to a major art exhibition. Most of Henri's subsequent paintings of nudes were executed simply as a means of studying the figure and were rarely

Figure 63. Robert Henri, *Ruth St. Denis in the Peacock Dance,* 1919.
Oil on canvas, 85 x 49″. Collection of Mr. and Mrs. John C. Le Clair,
Glen Gardner, New Jersey, and New York.

Figure 64. Robert Henri, *Figure in Motion,* 1913. Oil
on canvas, 77 x 37″. Collection of Mr. and Mrs. John C.
Le Clair, Glen Gardner, New Jersey, and New York.

shown before the public. They were posed by professional models, for the most part, suggesting that he was not involved with the subjects as individual personages but rather as vehicles of more abstract qualities of rhythm and relationship. In a painting such as *Edna Smith* (1915) (Figure 65) he does not attempt to evoke associational values or use her facial expression to establish rapport with the spectator. Henri's interest here is primarily in the over-all harmony of color and the relationship of the parts of the body to each other. We know from his private records that he usually applied the Maratta system in painting nudes, subjects that served better than portraits or clothed figures as something suitably "abstract" which would afford the necessary freedom to explore formal relationships of rhythm, volume, and color.

Mention of Henri's interest in the abstract, formal construction of the work of art brings us to an aspect of his style that is practically unknown: the production of completely nonobjective "color studies" or "color notes" before and after the Armory Show of 1913. As a result of his discovery of the Maratta system of color in 1909, Henri in that year began to paint a series of small vertical panels which translated figures, still lifes, and landscapes into extremely simple areas of flat color. It was the last of these types that provided the necessary breakthrough to pure abstraction: by reducing landscapes or seascapes to a series of parallel bands of color, stacked one above the other, Henri, as early as 1909, occasionally succeeded in eliminating all representational elements. And the titles he gave many of these panels confirm his move toward abstraction: in 1909 and 1910, he simply called them "color notes," and in 1911 used the terms "study of areas" and "color and form study." By 1911 and 1912, completely nonobjective color sketches appear frequently in his *oeuvre*.[9]

Although Henri certainly never thought of these color experiments as paintings to exhibit, they are much more than just diagrams: they illustrate his remarkable sensitivity to the relationship of variously colored areas in a situation where the need to "experiment" liberated him from fidelity to subject matter in the external world. The resulting geometric and curvilinear abstractions of 1915 and 1916 (see Plate IV), his most inventive period in this genre, recall Delaunay and Klee and, without stretching the point, may be considered unintentional precursors of the nonobjective work of Motherwell, Rothko, and De Staël. Henri's understanding of the abstract valence of color and his skill in pictorial design revealed in these small studies also help us to understand why he liked to consider himself an abstractionist in his later years. When his work was grouped with the "Realists" at an exhibition of the

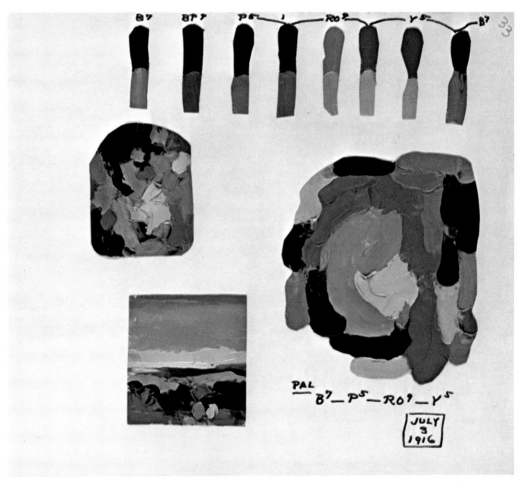

PLATE IV. Robert Henri, *Color Notes*, July 3, 1916. Oil on paper. Beinecke Rare Book and Manuscript Library, Yale University.

Figure 65. Robert Henri, *Edna Smith*, 1915. Oil on canvas, 41 x 33″. Collection of Professor Gian L. Campanile, Chicago.

Society of Independent Artists, he protested loudly: "My work is not realistic. My work is pure abstraction. I abstract from what I see—men, rivers, lights, women—the ideas of those things, and that's what I paint. I refuse to be grouped with people who paint mere things." [10]

Keeping in mind Henri's abstract work just discussed, one cannot help speculating on the role he might have played in stimulating the invention of Synchromism, the first movement in abstract painting founded by American artists (in this case, by Americans living in France). One of the cofounders of the movement in 1912, with Stanton Macdonald-Wright, was Morgan Russell, a former Henri student, who was joined in this enterprise by Patrick Henry Bruce and Arthur B. Frost, likewise products of Henri's atelier. From their letters, we know that all three felt that Henri was a major influence on their lives as artists. Russell probably spoke for Bruce and Frost, as well as himself, when he confessed to his former teacher:

You are the man who had more to do with the tempering of my character (if indeed it is tempered!) than any other. . . . From a general point of view, the more lasting and valuable influence was yours because it was first of all moral in the large classic sense—and then all you ever taught or said was so intelligent and undogmatic, the accent you put on it was so true that it is applicable to the practice of any art or any direction a given art may take and so serves always. You gave us also your own heat and inspired us with what I like to call the habit of creative spunk.[11]

We have surveyed various facets of Henri's art in the 1913–1929 period, but it is impossible to speak of a "linear" evolution in his style because, like Picasso in the late teens and early twenties, Henri kept several different styles going side by side. In Henri's case, the type of subject matter often suggested the style appropriate to it. Thus landscapes would be handled differently from portraits, nudes in an idiom distinct from his abstract "color notes."

While it is fashionable to discount the influence of the Armory Show on Henri, two major changes in his style took place in 1913. First, his color range opened up tremendously, and he became capable of working with the full gamut of hues from the most intense reds and oranges to deep, rich blues and violets. From some of the artists we know he admired in the period following the Armory Show, we can find some clues to the sources of his new interest in color: Turner, Delacroix, Renoir, Gauguin, Signac, and Henri-Edmond Cross.[12] But it is the Maratta system, as we observed earlier, that forced Henri to adopt the full range of spectral colors. And, as a result of Maratta's influence, Henri conceived of color harmony and relationship abstractly, prior to painting the picture, so that almost all his later canvases embody "musical" harmonies of color. These harmonies, Sloan observed, were never repeated from one picture to the next. Thus, in his later work, Henri's inventiveness is found not so much in drawing or composition, but in the creation of continually changing color relationships. In this writer's view, this is one of the most successful and satisfying aspects of his work in the years after the Armory Show.

After 1913, he also revised his approach to composition. Whereas he had previously subscribed to the traditional mimetic practice of stressing the figure as an expressive vehicle, while allowing the background to remain neutral, after the Armory Show the figure and ground became more and more integrated as a unified whole. Thus he abandoned a strictly mimetic approach to the human figure (always the essential element in his art) by establishing a close relationship of the background to it for purposes of harmony and expression. This new direction in his work is particularly evident in his studies of Indians executed at Santa Fe, as in *Julianita* (Figure 62), where the richly figured backdrop of an Indian blanket creates a positive design valence that is played off against the figure. We also know that the art of Cézanne and the writings of Clive Bell, the English critic, took on increasing significance in Henri's thinking at this time, so we may assume that his growing awareness of "plastic integration" in painting was stimulated by these sources.[13] Henri's brushwork, too, undergoes a significant change after 1913: it becomes ever more rapid and summary, to the point that, in the late twenties, he could seize the expression of a child in a half-hour. In the act of painting, the speed and vitality of his stroke serve a visual equivalent to the life-energy he experienced in the subject. Therefore, late in his career, Henri came to believe that a picture should be finished as quickly as possible. He said:

Work quickly. Don't stop for anything but the essential. (A dilatory worker has too much time to see things of little importance.) Make the draperies move, don't let them stop. Keep the flow going. Don't have islands of "things." The "things [,]" however wonderfully done, are just what bring a picture down to the commonplace. I never really had any ambition to paint "things." It's the spirit of the thing that counts.[14]

Often a by-product of this technique is a summary kind of drawing in which the solid structure of the head and body seems to disintegrate under the flourishes of the brush. Some critics have regarded this merely as a sign of superficiality, evidence of what is thought to be an inevitable tendency among artists to resort to a formula once the initial creative impulse has cooled. In Henri's case, the heat was always present; but it would be skirting the issue not to admit his increasing independence on shorthand devices to represent the eyes, nose, and mouth. These we must accept as an inevitable result of his emphasis on rapidity of execution as a key element in his aesthetic.

There are several important reasons underlying Henri's impulse to complete his pictures as quickly as possible. In later years, he increasingly came to believe that the work of art represented the imprint of the painter's state of being—an elevated state of functioning of the mind and body that occurred only at brief moments in man's existence. Therefore, he tells us: "Paint like a fiend when the idea possesses you." [15] This creative process was chronicled by Mary Fanton Roberts in a rare eye-witness account of Henri painting at Woodstock in 1921. Apropos of *Summer Storm* (1921) (Figure 66), she wrote:

He had been painting quietly in his studio when suddenly a terrific storm roared and flashed up over the top of the mountain and blew down, wild and sweet, over the hillside. . . . As the fury of the storm broke, he painted like mad the tumbling white and gray clouds, the shadowed valley, the tumult of the wind in the trees. The great volume of the storm seemed to pour through his very spirit out on to the canvas. He appeared a part of this sudden rush of furious power that was sweeping over the earth. For the moment he had withdrawn from the world of people and was immersed in the mighty, terrifying spectacle that nature had flung forth.[16]

A better description would be hard to find; it illustrates how he was caught up in the spirit of the moment— in this case, one of nature's rare moods that moved him deeply. Henri's empathy with the storm suggests a distant ancestry in Turner's seascapes, which likewise resulted from the artist's ability to channel the dynamic forces of nature through his own personality, committing these energies to canvas in freely brushed strokes. Van Gogh, too, must come to mind as one of Henri's sources, though the latter's strokes in *Summer Storm* are more spontaneous than most of Van Gogh's, thus placing the American squarely in the tradition of twentieth-century Expressionism, transplanted to American soil.

As we have indicated, Henri's method could be applied equally to landscapes, portraits, or figures. It was not the picture that counted, he thought, but the artist's "attainment of a state of being, a state of high functioning, a more than ordinary moment of existence." [17] The work of art was valid in-

Figure 66. Robert Henri, *Summer Storm*, 1921. Oil on canvas, 26 x 32″. Collection of Mr. Charles J. Malmed, Great Neck, New York.

sofar as it was "a by-product of the state, a trace, the footprint of the state." [18] In practicing this kind of painting himself, he realized that the work might not come off successfully every time, so he developed the habit of keeping several unused canvases close at hand. "When things went wrong," his friend Sloan recalled, "he started a fresh canvas. That was his way." [19] Sloan tells us that, in later years, Henri mustered his forces for a brief period every afternoon in which he concentrated his energies on the act of painting for a half-hour to an hour. [20] In this short span of time, if all went well, the painting could be realized, but not "finished," for Henri did not believe in the conventional tying up of loose ends, in "disguising unfinish, smoothing down faults which remain nevertheless." [21]

Many aspects of Henri's creative process invite comparison to the American action painters who matured in New York after World War II. It would be fruitless to make a case for Henri's being a dominant influence on their aesthetic, for it can be easily traced to Surrealism and automatism practiced in the twenties and thirties, among other sources. What Henri promoted in his teaching and writing was a freedom of artistic expression in America, the country that nurtured the rise of Abstract-Expressionism in the early 1940's. The action painters associated with this current in American art may or may not have read Henri's *The Art Spirit;* if they did, they could have found some of the principles of action painting expounded in its pages. Where Henri parts company with the Abstract-Expressionists is in his allegiance to recognizable subject matter; although he painted nonobjective studies, they were done to explore color relationships, not the potential of the expressive brushstroke. Yet there is a definite link between Henri and one member of the Abstract-Expressionist group who was frequently an action painter: this is Adolph Gottlieb, once his pupil at the Art Students League.

Henri's quest for the expression of vitality and the fast pace of his brushwork frequently forced him to sacrifice solidity and rigorous compositional order in his late work. Given the terms of his creative process, it is inevitable that many of his paintings of the 1920's should appear repetitious in form and conception. These apparent shortcomings have therefore led critics to regard his late work as falling below the standards of excellence he established in the early 1900's. While these criticisms are valid if his work of the third decade of the twentieth century is compared to that of the first, we must realize that Henri's artistic aims underwent significant changes when he reached his late fifties and early sixties. At this time he consciously shifted his emphasis to a more immediate, spontaneous execution, foreshadowing action painting, and concentrated on ever more inventive combinations of color. A greater artist might have succeeded in keeping all these factors simultaneously in balance; for Henri, it was enough to explore new possiblities of form and color while sacrificing some of his former interests.

Robert Henri, in his formative years, responded to a wide range of influences from earlier and contemporary art. With the help of these sources, he created a significant personal style of his own. Henri sought originality in his own work and in his students'; but originality, he believed, should be built on a foundation of artistic principles drawn from the work of established masters. His view of "tradition" differed from that of the Academy in that he adopted a vocabulary from a wide variety of European and American sources, including many that were too realistic or too avant-garde for the academic mind to embrace.

When he is compared to such European masters as Velázquez, Rembrandt, Courbet, and Manet, Henri appears as an artist of lesser magnitude who inevitably suffered from America's cultural provincialism. Henri and his circle belonged to a generation that preceded America's ascendance, after World War II, as an artistic power of the first rank on the international scene. Viewed in relation to American artists contemporary with him, Henri emerges as one of the most able and talented painters of his time. In his more conservative mode he was capable of equaling or surpassing Chase and Duveneck. As a painter of city scenes and personalities from the late nineties to about 1908, his closest parallels are found in the art of Sloan, Glackens, Luks, and Shinn, who owed much to Henri's inspiration but whose work sometimes overshadows his in quality and depth of feeling.

Robert Henri was an amazingly productive, but somewhat uneven, painter. Certain of his pictures, it must be admitted, fall below the high standards he advocated in his teachings and writings. But there were numerous instances at every point in his career when he produced work of real distinction within the broad framework of America's provincial artistic environment. His reputation as a painter, combined with his great contribution to the growth of art in his native country, helped to eradicate this provincialism—a necessary step for America's recent emergence as a world leader in the fine arts.

13

Epilogue

WHEN THE news of Henri's death reached Santa Fe, John Sloan responded immediately by launching a movement there and throughout the country to raise a two-million-dollar endowment for a Robert Henri Memorial Gallery in New York to fulfill Henri's dream of an open forum for artists.[1] As Sloan wrote: "The great emancipator of the artists of America has stepped into the place in history for which he was made and *another* great name, *Robert Henri*, has been made and grandly made. Now we who remain must see to it that these United States take note." [2] When Marjorie Henri was notified of the movement, she withheld her consent with deep regret, knowing that her husband would never have agreed to asking artists to give time, thought, or money for a project of that kind. He had made his views clear on such matters when he was promoting an Eakins Gallery in Philadelphia. Marjorie, it goes without saying, deeply appreciated Sloan's efforts, which were motivated by the esteem born of a lifelong friendship. Her decision was guided only by what she thought Henri's will in the matter would have been—to her the only will that counted.

Sloan, however, was instrumental in assembling a memorial exhibition of Henri's paintings for the Metropolitan Museum in 1931. Working with the curator Bryson Burroughs, Sloan, Eugene Speicher, and Violet Organ carefully selected seventy-eight paintings from museums, private collections, and the estate to represent every phase of his style from 1898 to 1928.[3] In addition to paying tribute to one of America's leading artists, the exhibition played an important role in reshaping Henri's public image. By drawing attention to his early work, particularly the landscapes and cityscapes painted around the turn of the century, the exhibition committee counteracted the popular notion that Henri was only interested in painting portraits and figure studies in a dashing, colorful style.

268

If the memorial exhibition was a successful retrospective summary of his career, it came too late to change the direction of American painting in any significant way. This is not to take any credit from Henri, for those who early benefited from the example of his style—Sloan, Luks, Bellows, and Speicher, to mention only a few names—had long since reached maturity. His teaching and private encouragement of young artists, many of whom did not follow his style, also bore fruit long before 1931. The exhibition, then, may be regarded as a posthumous tribute to an elder statesman who had already achieved his goal of influencing American art and artists from the late 1890's to the early 1920's.

While several major artists received their initial impulse from Henri's style, a much larger number were inspired by his teaching. More often than not, they evolved their own personal styles, just as he had urged them to do. "Don't paint like me" was his constant warning. He gave his students, not a style (though some imitated him), but an attitude, an approach, which has been documented in the pages of this volume and in his own book, *The Art Spirit*. It is safe to say—and it is saying a great deal—that he was the single most important teacher and force for artistic change in his generation. The effects of his crusade are still being felt today.

$\mathcal{N}otes$

Chapter 2. *The Early Years, 1865–1886*

1. The information in this chapter concerning the history of Henri's family has been derived from the records kept by his mother, Theresa Gatewood Cozad; from "Cozad Family Record," a manuscript by H. S. Clark in the New-York Historical Society; and from *Genealogy and Brief History of the Descendants of Job and Hannah (Winmans) Cozad of Branchville, Sussex County, New Jersey* (Ohio, 1900).

2. William Allen was a fiery lawyer-politician, congressman, senator, and supporter of President Buchanan. Henry Cozad was the first merchant in Allensville and became the postmaster when a post office was established there in 1839.

3. Most of our data about the life of John Jackson Cozad come from recollections of those who knew him published in the booklet *Early History of Cozad and Surrounding Community*, ed. Frank Johnson (Cozad, Neb., 1955). Additional material appears in his wife's diaries and in Dr. Robert H. Gatewood, "His Son, Robert, Became a World Famous Artist," Cozad *Local*, Nov. 27, 1956, sec. 2, pp. 1–2, and in the same author's unpublished manuscript, "Who Was Robert Henri?," Sept. 20, 1932, 18 pp.

4. John Sloan notes, on deposit in the Delaware Art Center, Wilmington, Delaware. Sloan's second wife, Helen Farr Sloan, encouraged him in his later years to reminisce about his personal life and his career as an artist; a 355-page typescript is the result of these informal interviews. It is a priceless art-historical document for the period in question.

5. Sloan notes.

6. These were William Early, died Feb. 9, 1867; Plunket, died July 19, 1870; and Alexander, died Feb. 6, 1873.

7. Cozaddale, situated in Hamilton Township, Warren County, Ohio, is still on the map today, though it is hardly more than a crossroads. An early

county history reports: "Mr. Cozad spent money very liberally in putting up buildings and improving the place, hoping to make a permanent manufacturing town, but his hopes were not fully realized, as evidenced by the many tenantless houses. There are now in the village two stores and one shoe shop" (*The History of Warren County, Ohio* [Chicago, 1882], p. 618).

8. An extensive account of the founding and growth of the city of Cozad appears in Johnson, *Early History of Cozad*. Additional information may be found in Gatewood, "His Son, Robert" and "Who Was Robert Henri?" and in Mari Sandoz, *Son of the Gamblin' Man: The Youth of an Artist* (New York, 1960), a novel based on the lives of John Jackson Cozad and Robert Henri in the period before 1883. Miss Sandoz informed me that the historical incidents and dates mentioned in her book are based on actual facts established by extensive archival research; portions of the narrative and dialogue are, of necessity, fictional.

9. *Hundredth Meridian*, Nov. 28, 1876.

10. Henri scrapbook, *c.* 1879.

11. Henri letter to Thelma Anthony, March 3, 1926.

12. *Ibid.*

13. *Ibid.*

14. *Ibid.*

15. Henri letter to George B. Zug, Aug. 14, 1919.

16. A description of Robert Henri's early pictures may be found in Sandoz, *Son of the Gamblin' Man*. Miss Sandoz

informed me that she studied some of the boy's works that had been saved by a cowboy who had been employed in Cozad but who later moved to the Sand Hills region of Nebraska. The present location of these pictures is unknown. When the Cozad family left the town of Cozad in 1882, many of the artist's drawings and illustrations were left behind in the hands of Mrs. Cozad's family. Unfortunately, this material was destroyed by fire (information courtesy of Dr. Robert H. Gatewood, letter to the author, Aug. 1, 1964).

17. Henri diary, Sept. 21, 1880.

18. Sept. 13–19, 1880.

19. Aug. 15, 1881.

20. A clue to the family's belief in their French origins may be found in the brief statement that Robert's brother John wrote about himself in the former's scrapbook: "J. A. Cozad, December 24th 1878, an American by birth a Frenchman by descent." In his letters of 1886, Robert signed himself "R. Earl Henri." He registered under this name at the Pennsylvania Academy of the Fine Arts. He consistently signed his name "Robert Henri" beginning in 1891.

21. Philadelphia, 1923, p. 239. Citations will be made to the page numbers of the hard cover, rather than the paperback edition.

22. "The Significance of the Frontier in American History," reprinted in *The Turner Thesis*, ed. George Rogers Taylor (Boston, 1956), pp. 17–18.

23. Fortunately Henri kept complete records of his own paintings, in which

he usually listed the subject, date, and size of the work, and often accompanied this data by a small sketch of the picture. This catalogue has been used by the present writer as the chief source of information about Henri's work.

24. Henri diary, Feb. 23, 1887.

25. Letter, Oct. 2, 1886. Letters by Henri to his parents, Mr. and Mrs. Richard H. Lee (usually addressed as "Missus and Boss" or "Folks at Home"), have received no designation other than "Henri letter" or "letter." After December 15, 1906, the date of his father's death, the "Henri letter" designation refers to letters from Henri to his mother. The recipients of all other letters are identified by name.

Chapter 3. *An Art Student in Philadelphia, 1886–1888*

1. W. C. Brownell, "The Art Schools of Philadelphia," *Scribner's Monthly*, XVIII (Sept. 1879), 741.

2. Charles Bregler, "Thomas Eakins as a Teacher," *Arts*, XVII (March, 1931), 385.

3. Brownell, "The Art Schools," p. 745.

4. *Ibid.*, pp. 744–745.

5. Fairman Rogers, "The Schools of the Pennsylvania Academy of the Fine Arts," *Penn Monthly*, XII (June, 1881).

6. Quoted in Lloyd Goodrich, *Thomas Eakins, His Life and Work* (New York, 1933), p. 30.

7. James P. Kelly *et al.*, letter to the Board of Directors, Pennsylvania Academy of the Fine Arts, March 12, 1886.

8. *The Art Spirit* (Philadelphia, 1923), p. 87.

9. Letter to George B. Zug, Aug. 14, 1919.

10. Helen W. Henderson, in *One Hundred and Fiftieth Anniversary Exhibition* (exhibition catalogue; Pennsylvania Academy of the Fine Arts, Philadelphia, Jan. 15–March 13, 1955), p. 106.

11. Diary, Oct. 4, 1886.

12. Nov. 16.

13. *Ibid.*, Nov. 17.

14. *Ibid.*, Nov. 29.

15. *Ibid.*, Dec. 11.

16. *Ibid.*, Feb. 3, 1887.

17. *Ibid.*

18. *Ibid.*, Dec 17, 1886.

19. *Ibid.*, Jan. 8, 1887.

20. *Ibid.*, Dec. 1, 1886.

21. *Ibid.*, Oct. 18.

22. *Ibid.*, Nov.22.

23. *Ibid.*, Mar. 22, 1887.

24. *Ibid.*, Dec. 28, 1886.

25. *Ibid.*, April 9, 1887.

26. *Ibid.*

27. *Ibid.*, April 18.

28. *Ibid.*

29. *Ibid.*, April 19–May.

30. *Ibid.*

31. *Ibid.*, Dec. 8, 1886.

32. *Ibid.*, April 7, 1887.

33. *Ibid.*, April 13.

34. *Ibid.*, March 11.

35. *Ibid.*, Jan. 14, 1927. (In his entry of Feb. 17, 1887, his comment on the picture was simply: "masterly work.")

36. *Ibid.*, Jan. 25, 1887.

37. *Ibid.*, Dec. 28, 1886.

38. *Ibid.*, March 3, 1887.

39. Dec. 18, 1887.

40. *Ibid.*, March 21, 1888.

41. *Ibid.*

42. Henri diary, May 8, 1888.

43. *Ibid.*, May 3.

44. Letter, n.d. [1886–1888].

45. Henri diary, Oct.–Dec., 1887.

Chapter 4. *Study in Paris, 1888–1891*

1. Diary, Oct. [Sept.] 15, 1888.

2. *Ibid.*, Sept. 20.

3. *Ibid.*

4. *Ibid.*

5. *Ibid.*, Sept. 22.

6. *Ibid.*, Sept. 27.

7. *Ibid.*

8. *Ibid.*

9. Letter, Oct. 6, 1888.

10. *Ibid.*, Jan. 25, 1890.

11. *Ibid.*

12. *Impressions and Opinions* (New York, 1891), pp. 199–200.

13. Letter, Oct. 6, 1888.

14. *Ibid.*, Nov. 3.

15. *Ibid.*, Oct. 12.

16. *Ibid.*, Nov. 6.

17. Diary, Sept. 25, 1888.

18. Letter, Oct. 6, 1888.

19. Nov. 29.

20. *Ibid.*, June 9, 1889.

21. *Ibid.*, March 11.

22. *Human Intercourse* (Boston, 1885), pp. 5–6.

23. Henri letter, Dec. 16, 1888.

24. *Ibid.*, Jan. 19, 1889.

25. *Ibid.*, Sept. 8.

26. *Robert Henri, His Life and Works* (New York, 1921), pp. 22–23. Mr. Bouché has informed me that the incidents and events recorded in his book were based on numerous interviews with the artist.

27. Henri letter, Sept. 16, 1889.

28. *Ibid.*

29. *Ibid.*, Feb. 1, 1890.

30. *Ibid.*, Feb. 11.

31. Diary, March 11, 1890.

32. *Ibid.*, May 3.

33. Letter, April 6, 1890.

34. *Ibid.*, Jan. 11.

35. Diary, May 23, 1890.

36. Henri letter, May 2, 1890.

37. At the "old" Salon Henri's favorite picture was Benjamin Constant's *Beethoven*—"a thing well thought out in a big poetic way, full of music" (Henri letter, May 2, 1890). Next to that, he liked Lefebvre's *Lady Godiva* —"it is most carefully studied—strongly drawn—is nice in color" (*ibid.*). The juxtaposition of the two paintings gave Henri an opportunity to voice his preference for personal interpretation over merely correct drawing from nature. Thus, about Constant's *Beethoven* he wrote, "The *artist* impressed me more than the *painter*" (*ibid.*). In the Salon he also noticed a portrait by Eakins, but had little to say about it except that it was untypical of his work. Eakins' teacher, Gérôme, however, command-

ed more of his attention; though Henri disliked some of his work, he wrote, "Gérôme feels and generally gets a big-noble sentiment" (Henri letter, May 29, 1890).

38. In his comments on the exhibition, he termed John Singer Sargent's *Ellen Terry as Lady Macbeth* and small portraits by Courtois "great," and about Carolus-Duran's *Mlle. S. in Gray* he wrote, "One of the best I've seen by him" (Henri diary, May 27, 1890). He also admired works by Dagnan-Bouveret, found Puvis de Chavannes "very agreeable and deco[rative] in his style," and saw "something in all of Alf[red] Stevens" (*ibid.*).

39. Henri letter, March 29, 1890.
40. *Ibid.*
41. *Ibid.*
42. Henri diary, July 15, 1890.
43. *Ibid.*, July 8.
44. Henri letter, Oct. 25, 1890.
45. *Ibid.*, Jan. 19, 1891.
46. *Ibid.*
47. *Ibid.*
48. *Ibid.*, Jan. 26.
49. *Ibid.*
50. *Ibid.*
51. *Ibid.*
52. *Ibid.*, Feb. 5.
53. *Ibid.*, Jan. 26.
54. *Ibid.*, Feb. 5.
55. *Ibid.*, Feb. 20.

56. *Ibid.*, Feb. 25.
57. *Ibid.*
58. *Ibid.*, March 29.
59. *Ibid.*
60. *Ibid.*, April 11.
61. Henri diary, Jan. 18, 1891.
62. *Ibid.*, April 1.
63. *Ibid.*
64. Henri letter, April 27, 1891.
65. *Ibid.*
66. Henri diary, Jan. 20, 1891.
67. *Ibid.*, Feb. 28.
68. Henri letter, Feb. 23, 1891.
69. Henri diary, March 9, 1891.
70. Henri letter, June 29, 1891.
71. Henri diary, March 19, 1891.
72. *Ibid.*, April 2.
73. *Ibid.*, Feb. 27.
74. Henri letter, May 11, 1891.
75. *Ibid.*, June (no day indicated).
76. *Ibid.*, May 30.
77. *Ibid.*, Aug. 31.
78. Diary, April 24, 1890.
79. *Ibid.*, March 5, 1891.
80. Letter, Nov. 24, 1889.
81. *Ibid.*, June 1.
82. Feb. 11, 1890.
83. *Ibid.*, June 11.
84. *Ibid.*, Sept. 14.
85. *Ibid.*, May 12.
86. Diary, March 15, 1891.
87. Letter, Jan. 11, 1890.
88. *Ibid.*, May 11, 1891.
89. *Ibid.*, April 20.

Chapter 5. *Life and Work in Philadelphia, 1891–1895*

1. Letter, Dec. 1891 (no day indicated).
2. *Ibid.*, Dec. 2.
3. *Ibid.*, Jan. 23, 1892.

4. Philadelphia *Times*, Jan. 21, 1892.
5. Henri letter, Jan. 31, 1892.
6. *Ibid.*
7. Philadelphia *Times*, May 31, 1894.

8. Philadelphia *Inquirer*, undated clipping (Henri scrapbook, *c.* 1893).

9. M. M. Piggott, "Glimpses of a Philadelphia Art Student's Life," *Arts*, May, 1895. Charcoal was the chief medium employed by Henri's pupils—a medium that allowed more generalization and breadth in handling values than was possible in the crayon method used at the Académie Julian. Most of his classes worked only in charcoal; the study of drawing thus served as a foundation for painting. Henri's approach to teaching at this time seems more conservative than that of Eakins, who permitted qualified students to move directly into the painting class after the briefest apprenticeship in drawing, believing that one should paint and draw simultaneously. Henri's allegiance to the academic view that stressed skill in drawing as a prerequisite for painting may be traced to his own training under Hovenden and Bouguereau, though he probably also took into account the relative inexperience of his pupils. Unlike Julian's academy, the transition from drawing to painting in Henri's classes must have been effected easily and naturally.

10. Philadelphia *Times*, April 25, 1893.

11. Unidentified clipping [May 31, 1894], Henri scrapbook.

12. April 8, 1893.

13. Among the members were William Glackens, F. R. Gruger, Vernon H. Bailey, J. Horace Rudy, and Albert Adolph.

14. Henri letter, 1893 (no day indicated).

15. Letter to Charles R. Harley, April 8, 1894.

16. *Ibid.*

17. Sloan notes.

18. *Ibid.*

19. *Ibid.*

20. "Robert Henri and the Emerson-Whitman Tradition," *PMLA*, LXXI, Pt. I (Sept. 1956), 617–636. We do not know precisely when Henri began to read Whitman, but the American poet was discussed in Paris by Henri and his circle as early as March, 1891. Shortly after returning from Paris, Henri engaged Sloan in a discussion of Whitman, after which Sloan gave him a better edition of *Leaves of Grass* than the one he owned.

21. Sloan notes.

22. *Ibid.*

23. *Ibid.*

24. *Ibid.*

25. *Ibid.*

26. *Ibid.*

27. In a letter to his parents (March 13, 1890) Henri mentioned Ingersoll as being one of America's greatest orators, an indication that he knew of the man before returning to Philadelphia in 1891.

28. Sloan notes.

29. *Ibid.*

30. *The Eight* (exhibition catalogue; Brooklyn Museum of Art, Brooklyn, Nov. 24, 1943–Jan. 16, 1944), p. 20.

31. Everett Shinn, "Artists of the Philadelphia Press," *Philadelphia Museum Bulletin*, XLI (Nov., 1945), 9.

32. *Ibid.*, p. 12.

33. Sloan notes.

34. *Ibid.*

35. *Ibid.*
36. *Ibid.*
37. *Ibid.*
38. Lecture delivered by Sloan at Hill and Canyon School, July, 1949.
39. The only definite connection that can be established between Henri and the American literary realists in the 1890's is his mention, in a letter to his family of Aug. 16, 1891, of his knowledge of William Dean Howells' writings.

Chapter 6. *Paris and Philadelphia, 1895–1900*

1. June 16, 1895.
2. *Ibid.*
3. *Ibid.*, July 10.
4. *Ibid.*, Feb. 18, 1897.
5. Letter to Henri, Nov. 14, 1897.
6. Diary, Jan. 25, 1897.
7. Nov. 15, 1897.
8. *Ibid.*, March 7, 1898.
9. *Ibid.*, Dec. 1, 1897.
10. *Ibid.*, April 30, 1898.
11. Diary, Dec. 25, 1898.
12. Letter, Oct. 22, 1898.
13. *Ibid.*, Sept. 11.
14. *Ibid.*, Jan. 13, 1899.
15. *Ibid.*, Jan. 5.
16. *Ibid.*, Feb. 20.
17. He enjoyed good reviews in the French press—for example, the remarks about his *L'Echarpe rouge* by Paul Adam, art critic of the *Petit Bleu* (May 8, 1899): " 'L'Echarpe rouge' décore d'un ton central le portrait d'une femme en brun, au visage net, âprement brossé. De la sincérité éclaire cette figure ovale aux sourcils arques; et que des bandeaux de cheveux encadrent sous l'ombre du chapeau à plumes. Souplement campée avec une expression de rude, d'intangible naïveté. Tout un esprit instinctif, orgueilleux, qui se sépare, est manifeste en elle. C'est un des belles choses exposées." In addition, Henri was asked by the Art Institute of Chicago and the Carnegie Institute of Pittsburgh to exhibit his portraits and was invited by an art dealer to show his work in Berlin, Cologne, and Düsseldorf. He accepted the American invitations, but declined the German offer, believing that it would be better in the long run for him to exhibit in the United States.

18. Letter, Jan. 24, 1899.
19. Apparently *La Neige* was not hung in the Luxembourg until 1902. It is now in the Musée National d'Art Moderne, Paris.
20. Letter, July 10, 1899.
21. Henri's father had engaged in a prolonged conflict with the authorities of Atlantic City, who wanted to drive a new boardwalk through his land, thus rendering it valueless. Lee (Cozad) was the last holdout and defended his pier and amusement pavilion by barricading it and personally defending his property rights, shotgun in hand. The city finally gave in and bought his property, which had been nicknamed "Fort Lee," at a just price.
22. Henri letter, Dec. 19, 1899.

Chapter 7. *Maturity and Public Recognition, 1900–1906*

1. Letter to Emilia Cimino, n.d.
2. April 3, 1902.
3. F. Newlin Price, *Ernest Lawson. Canadian-American* (New York, 1930), n.p.
4. April 6, 1901.
5. *Ibid.*
6. *Ibid.*
7. Diary, Jan. 2, 1902.
8. Henri letter, April 3, 1902.
9. *Exhibition of Pictures by Robert Henri* (exhibition catalogue; Macbeth Galleries, New York, April 1–12, 1902), n.p.
10. The lecture was published in the Philadelphia *Sunday Press*, May 12, 1901, and in revised form, in *The Art Spirit* (Philadelphia, 1923), pp. 78–87.
11. *Art Spirit*, p. 80.
12. *Ibid.*, pp. 82–83.
13. Letter, March 20, 1902.
14. *Ibid.*, April 7.
15. April 8, 1902.
16. "The Gilder," April 3, 1902.
17. Henri letter, April 7, 1902.
18. Henri's students at the New York School of Art included George Bellows, Rockwell Kent, Guy Pène du Bois, Glenn O. Coleman, Homer Boss, Julius Golz, Carl Sprinchorn, A. E. Cedarquist, Gifford Beal, Walter Pach, C. K. Chatterton, John Koopman, Arnold Friedman, Vachel Lindsay, Patrick Henry Bruce, and Josephine Nivison (Mrs. Edward Hopper).
19. Henri diary, Sept. 25, 1902.
20. *Evening Sun*, Dec. 27, 1902.
21. Henri noted in his diary that Thomas Eakins served with him on a jury at the Pennsylvania Academy, concrete evidence that the two painters met.
22. Letter, July 12, 1903.
23. He made his first etching, *Street Scene in Paris*, under Sloan's guidance in 1904. This was only an experiment; he did not pursue the medium further.
24. *Commercial Advertiser*, Jan. 20, 1904.
25. *Mail and Express*, June 25, 1904.
26. *Evening Sun*, Jan. 23, 1904.
27. July 20, 1904.
28. Dec. 4, 1904.
29. Henri diary, Dec. 6, 1904.
30. Sadakichi Hartmann, "Studio Talk," *International Studio*, XXX (Dec. 1906), 183.
31. The following remarks by Nathaniel Pousette-Dart, one of the few who studied under both men, represent a valuable witness account of Anshutz' personality and teaching methods; the similarity to Henri's approach is evident: "Thomas Anshutz was a simple, sincere and direct man. What he said you felt to be true—there was no bunk about him. His methods of teaching were very similar to those of Henri and he always gave his criticisms and talked to the whole class *after* the model had stopped posing. He liked to bring out his ideas, singling out the work of some particular student and discussing it in relation to the work of other students,

and to the work of great masters. He made everything very clear with his keen analysis and his remarks were always appreciative and stimulating. They carried convictions [*sic*] because of his obviously sincere approach. One never felt that he was trying to make a clever impression. . . . What Anshutz said about the work of the great artists of the past was most inspiring. He clarified the fundamental principle of creative art and stirred the aspirations of each student, by making him conscious of all the great creative art of the past. It was always the fundamental principle of art that he stressed—never clever technical tricks" (letter to the author, July 19, 1964). In the same letter Mr. Pousette-Dart recounted his experience upon entering Anshutz' life class in Philadelphia in 1903, having studied under Henri the year before: "Toward the end of the class, I heard a man enter the back of the classroom and when he started speaking, I said to myself, 'I didn't know that Henri was teaching here.' It was Anshutz, of course, but their voices were identical." John Cournos, who knew both men, believed

"Henri's art is probably the most perfect flower of the ideas Mr. Anshutz has so long taught and represented" ("What Is Art? Answered by Henri, Art 'Insurgent,'" Philadelphia *Record,* Dec. 25, 1910).

32. John Sloan diary, March 8, 1906. Sloan's diaries are on deposit in the Delaware Art Center, Wilmington. Large portions of the 1906–1913 diaries were published in *John Sloan's New York Scene* (New York, 1965).

33. May 3, 1906.

34. Edward Simmons, *From Seven to Seventy* (New York, 1922), p. 222.

35. J. Alden Weir, in Dorothy Weir Young, *The Life and Letters of J. Alden Weir* (New Haven, 1960), p. 198.

36. Florence N. Levy, ed., *American Art Annual, 1898* (New York, 1899), p. 295.

37. To Sloan, n.d. [1906].

38. To Helen Niles, Nov. 12, 1906.

39. Henri letter, Aug. 7, 1906.

40. *Ibid.,* Sept. 23.

41. *Ibid.,* Aug. 13.

42. *Ibid.*

Chapter 8. *Henri and the Independent Movement, 1906–1910*

1. Henri letter to Helen Niles, Nov. 16, 1906.

2. After selling their property in Atlantic City, Mr. and Mrs. Lee had lived in retirement since 1901, first in Far Rockaway and then in an apartment in Manhattan.

3. In 1920 she came back to New

York to live in an apartment below Henri's studio at 10 Gramercy Park. She died there in 1923. Neither of John and Theresa Cozad's sons had any children who survived them. We know that Linda had a miscarriage in Paris, and that a daughter, Jennie, born to Frank and Jennie Southrn in 1892, died in early adulthood. No children resulted from Henri's marriage to Marjorie Organ.

4. Sloan diary, April 30, 1907.

5. New York *Post*, March 13, 1907.

6. March 24, 1907. He was quoted by the New York *Sun* as saying: "I don't care for the wall, I only care for the men" (March 16, 1907).

7. Letter, March 14, 1907.

8. *Ibid.*, April 6.

9. *Ibid.*, April 12.

10. New York *Mail*, April 11, 1907.

11. New York *Herald*, April 12, 1907.

12. Henri letter, April 12, 1907.

13. *Ibid.*, May 14.

14. Feb. 15, 1927.

15. New York *Sun*, May 15, 1907.

16. Sloan notes.

17. Henri diary, Feb. 15, 1927.

18. This popular label was not invented by the painters nor was it used at the time of the exhibition of the Eight at the Macbeth Galleries. Indeed, a search of the art literature published during Henri's lifetime does not reveal any use of the phrase "the Ashcan school." It was popularized only in the mid-1930's, probably first used in Holger Cahill and Alfred H. Barr Jr.'s widely circulated *Art in America in Modern Times* (New York, 1934; reprinted, with additions, as *Art in America: A Complete Survey* [New York, 1939]). Referring to the Eight, Cahill wrote: "When they first showed as a group in 1908 they were anathematized as 'The Ashcan School' and 'The Revolutionary Black Gang'" (1st ed., p. 31). Cahill probably seized upon the expression during his association with

John Sloan, who pointed out that it derived from an argument between the cartoonist Art Young and himself when they were both working for the *Masses* in 1916. Young, a doctrinaire Socialist, was dissatisfied with the lack of propaganda value in the satirical, human-interest drawings that Sloan and his friends published in the *Masses* and reprimanded them because the only way they attempted to achieve revolutionary content was, he claimed, to introduce ashcans in their drawings. Sloan's widow, Helen Farr Sloan, recalled in conversation with the author that Sloan thought Cahill used the phrase to make a distinction between the older group (the Eight) and the "social-consciousness painters" of the 1930's. The term "Ashcan school" was probably voiced among artists and critics in New York in the late twenties and early thirties; Forbes Watson picked up something close to it when, in 1929, he referred to what Henri's enemies called "the garbage can school of painting" ("Robert Henri," *Arts*, XVI [Sept. 1929], 3). Referring to the Henri group, Helen Appleton Read, a former Henri student, used the term "Ashcan school" in the introduction of *New York Realists, 1900–1914* (exhibition catalogue; Whitney Museum of American Art, New York, February 9–March 5, 1937), p. 8. This exhibition and its accompanying reviews were undoubtedly responsible for spreading the use of the term. Some of the work of George Bellows (who is often mistakenly considered a member of the Eight) also may have inspired the use of the ashcan or garbage-can label. Several of his widely circulated lithographs of slum subjects feature ashcans, notably, *Disappoints of the Ash Can* and *Hungry Dogs*. The fact is that very few paintings of the so-called "Ashcan school" include ash-cans. For an earlier discussion of the "ashcan" label, see Lloyd Goodrich, *John Sloan, 1871–1951* (New York, 1952), pp. 35, 47.

19. New York *Evening Sun*, May 15, 1907.

20. *Ibid.*

21. Draft of letter to David H. Dodge, Dec. 29, 1907.

22. New York *Sun*, May 15, 1907.

23. *Ibid.*

24. This point is made by Robert G. McIntyre in "The Eight," *1963 Festival of the Arts* (Southern Vermont Art Center, Manchester, summer, 1963), n.p.

25. New York *World*, Nov. 21, 1907.

26. Letter to Joseph Edgar Chamberlin, May, 1908 (no day indicated).

27. Letter, May 24, 1907.

28. *Ibid.*, July 28.

29. *Ibid.*

30. Henri letter to Helen Niles, Nov. 12, 1907.

31. Sloan diary, Feb. 2, 1908.

32. Letter to Hartman K. Harris, Feb. 4, 1908.

33. These were Davies' *Redwoods* and *Autumn River;* Henri's *Laughing Child* and *Coast of Maine;* Shinn's *Blue Girl;* Luks's *Old Woman and Goose;* and Lawson's *Floating Ice*.

34. Sloan diary, Feb. 17, 1908. According to a letter from William Glackens to his wife, Feb. 25, 1908, Macbeth claimed that if it had not been

such a bad year, he could have sold $25,000 worth of pictures (quoted in Vincent J. de Gregorio, "The Life and Art of William J. Glackens," Vol. II [unpublished Ph.D. diss., Ohio State University, 1955], p. 335.

35. *William Glackens and the Ash Can Group; The Emergence of Realism in American Art* (New York, 1957), p. 89.

36. Unidentified clipping, Macbeth Galleries scrapbook, 1908, Archives of American Art, Detroit, Mich.

37. *Ibid.*

38. *Town Topics*, Feb. 6, 1908.

39. Unidentified clipping, Macbeth Galleries scrapbook, 1908.

40. New York *Sun*, Feb. 9, 1908.

41. *Ibid.*

42. Feb. 9, 1908.

43. Giles Edgerton [Mary Fanton Roberts], "The Younger American Painters: Are They Creating a National Art?," *Craftsman*, XIII (Feb. 1908), 523, 524, 531.

44. Charles Wisner Barrell, "Robert Henri—'Revolutionary,'" *Independent*, LXIV (June 25, 1908), 1429.

45. Sloan diary, March 28, 1908.

46. Looking back on the show, years later, Sloan was more cautious than he had been in 1908 about their degree of success: "Don't think for a moment that our work became successful. We didn't begin selling or having more exhibitions. There was no demand for us. A sure sign that we were not successful: we didn't have a wave of imitators" (Sloan notes).

47. Oct. 5, 1908.

48. Sloan diary, Nov. 2, 1908.

49. He paid a second visit to the

Salon d'Automne in 1910 and while in Paris called on Patrick Henry Bruce, who at that time worked in a style close to Cézanne and Matisse. Along with a few other American artists living in Paris, Bruce had absorbed the most recent avant-garde currents in French painting (three years later he allied himself with the Synchromist movement). In view of Henri's curiosity about revolutionary movements in art, it would be surprising if he had not discussed these currents with Bruce. While we do not know Henri's response to the works of art he saw at the Salon d'Automne in 1910, he did discuss the Matisse movement with his friends shortly after returning to the United States. He saw the Salon for the third time in 1912.

50. The following is a list of the more important pupils who attended the Henri School of Art (compiled from his diary and other sources): A. S. Baylinson, Henry J. Glintenkamp, Florence Dreyfous, Amy Londoner, F. Middleton Manigault, Prosper Invernizzi, Harry Daugherty, Homer Boss, Guy Pène du Bois, P. Scott Stafford, Hilda Ward, George Bellows, Maurice Becker, Stuart Davis, Paul Manship, Helen Appleton Read, Morgan Russell, Paul Rohland, Eugene Speicher, Joseph Laub, Andrew Dasburg, Bernard Karfiol, Rex Slinkard, Carl Walters, and Randall Davey.

51. "'I Paint My People' Is Henri's Art Key," Brooklyn *Eagle*, Feb. 12, 1916.

52. *Robert Henri: A Commemorative Exhibition* (exhibition catalogue; Hirschl and Adler Galleries, New York, March 31–April 30, 1954), n.p.

53. Henri noted: "Macbeth said he would be sorry to see 8 any place else. There will probably be no 8 show therefore—this winter in N.Y." (Henri diary, Dec. 14, 1908).

54. Sloan diary, April 20, 1909.

55. *Ibid.*, Dec. 21.

56. Early in January, Henri proposed to form a limited society, the Independent American Artists, which would sponsor a continuing cycle of year-round exhibitions. Meeting on January 10, 1910, Sloan, Myers, Von Gottschalk, Shinn, Henri, Pach, and Luks discussed Henri's "plan of organizing about twenty artists[,] then going to people with money and getting some— giving pictures in return, to be selected during the exhibition period" (Sloan diary, Jan. 10, 1910). Ullman and Sloan, in the meantime, moved ahead with a design for another kind of exhibition to be called the Associated American Artists, similar to the one Sloan had discussed with Henri in December—but they intended to inform their associates about it only when it was well under way.

57. John Sloan hoped the backers would be repaid by means of collecting a fee from each exhibitor. After the show, he managed to pay back 33⅘ cents on the dollar to the "special contributors."

58. $10 for one picture, $18 for two, $25 for three, and $30 for four.

59. A news article by Guy Pène du Bois, one of Henri's former students, indicates that the exhibition committee

had recognized, as early as 1910, the American followers of the latest developments in modern European painting. He wrote: "There will be represented in the exhibition paintings by the realists, the impressionists, the men who, with Matisse, followed the theories of Cézanne, the followers of the geometrical art of Picasso [cubism] and by men whose art, purely personal, is directly connected with no concerted movement" (New York *American*, March 17, 1910).

60. Henri, as quoted in the New York *Evening Sun*, March 16, 1910. Many years later, Sloan recalled the rationale behind the committee's selections: "[We] invited anyone whom we thought was doing worthwhile and interesting work. It was not anti-academy, but just looking for alive progressive work and especially wanted to exhibit work that could not get a hearing elsewhere" (Sloan notes).

61. March 23, 1910.

62. What effect did these plans have on Alfred Stieglitz and his circle, the only other artistically liberal group in the United States at the time, oriented toward European modernism? Sloan noted: "[Pach] tells me that Stieglitz of Photo Secession is hot under the collar about our show. The whole curious bunch of 'Matisses' seem to hang about him and I imagine he thinks we have stolen his thunder in exhibiting 'independent' artists" (Sloan diary, March 22, 1910). (The term "Matisses" undoubtedly stems from the exhibitions of Matisse' work Stieglitz staged in 1908 and 1910.)

63. Sloan diary, March 25, 1910.

64. *Ibid.*, April 1.

65. This sales report is based on notations in Henri's diary. According to Charles H. Morgan, Bellows sold three drawings for $500 (*George Bellows, Painter of America* [New York, 1965], p. 110).

66. Henri diary, April 27, 1910.

67. "Around the Galleries," New York *Sun*, April 7, 1910.

68. "The Independent Artists," *Nation*, XC (April 7, 1910), 360–61.

69. "With the Independent Artists," New York *Evening Mail*, April 4, 1910.

70. "The New York Exhibition of Independent Artists," *Craftsman*, XVIII (May, 1910), 160–161.

71. *Ibid.*, p. 161.

72. *Ibid.*, pp. 170–171.

73. As early as 1911, Henri's former pupil Rockwell Kent took the lead in organizing another independent show in New York, smaller than the first, which included the work of several of Henri's students and three members of the Eight, along with paintings by John Marin and Marsden Hartley. Henri was invited to participate, but declined because Kent insisted that the participants boycott the National Academy of Design by refusing to submit their work to the exhibition that year. "I have no thought of sending to the N.A.D.," Henri wrote, "but oppose anyone else dictating to me or to others about it" (letter to Helen Niles, April 6, 1911).

74. The Henris rented the studio until 1920, when they purchased it, along with the apartment on the floor below, on the cooperative plan.

Chapter 9. *Teachings and Philosophy of Art*

1. Robert Henri, "Progress in Our National Art . . . ," *Craftsman*, XV (Jan. 1909), 400, 392, 387.

2. Garnett McCoy, "Reaction and Revolution, 1900–1930," *Art in America*, LIII (Aug.–Sept., 1965), 70.

3. *Robert Henri and Five of His Pupils* (exhibition catalogue; The Century Association, New York, 1946), n.p.

4. *It's Me, O Lord: The Autobiography of Rockwell Kent* (New York, 1955), p. 82.

5. *Life*, XXVI (June 20, 1949), 66.

6. "Progress in Our National Art," p. 393.

7. Helen Appleton Read, *Robert Henri* (New York, 1931), p. 10.

8. "Progress in Our National Art," pp. 394, 398.

9. *Ibid.*, p. 393.

10. *Ibid.*

11. Henri letter to Joseph Edgar Chamberlin, May, 1908 (no day indicated).

12. Letter from Emil Holzhauer to the author, n.d. [July 6, 1964].

13. Letter to the author, June 7, 1964.

14. McCoy, "Reaction and Revolution," p. 69.

15. "Composition Talk," No. 4, Nov. 18, 1910, unpub. ms.

16. Henri letter to Dorothea Chase, Oct. 23, 1917.

17. "Composition Talk," No. 3, n.d. [1910], unpub. ms.

18. *Stuart Davis* (New York, 1945), n.p.

19. McCoy, "Reaction and Revolution," p. 70.

20. Henri diary, July 9–10, 1910.

21. Walter Pach, *Queer Thing, Painting; Forty Years in the World of Art* (New York and London, 1938), p. 47.

22. "Robert Henri," *Arts*, XVI (Sept. 1929), 3.

23. "Progress in Our National Art," p. 388.

Chapter 10. *Aspects of Henri's Career, 1910–1929*

1. Milton W. Brown, *The Story of the Armory Show* (Greenwich, Conn., 1963), p. 30; italics mine. It is significant that the first group application for a MacDowell Club show included three of the future founders of the A.P.S.—MacRae (the group's representative), Myers, and H. F. Taylor— and three who were to become members of the Association—Edward Kramer, Leon Dabo, and Allen Tucker. Theirs, however, was not the first exhibition to be hung, but the second; a group comprised of Bellows, Brinley, Dougherty, Haggin, Henri, Lie, Johansen, M. Jean, McLane, and Wiles

gained priority over the MacRae group.

2. Garnett McCoy, "The Walt Kuhn Papers," *Journal of the Archives of American Art*, V (Oct., 1965), 2.

3. Garnett McCoy, "Reaction and Revolution, 1900–1930," *Art in America*, LIII (Aug.–Sept., 1965), 70.

4. Sloan notes.

5. Henri diary, Jan. 2, 1912.

6. Draft of letter to Mrs. James Haggin, n.d. [Henri dated the letter 1912].

7. Jan. 2, 1912.

8. *Ibid.*, Jan. 23

9. *1913 Armory Show, 50th Anniversary Exhibition* (exhibition catalogue; Munson-Williams-Proctor Institute, Utica, Feb. 17–March 31, 1963; Armory of the Sixty-ninth Regiment, New York, April 6–28, 1963), p. 34.

10. Sloan notes.

11. *Catalogue of the First Annual Exhibition of the Society of Independent Artists* (Grand Central Palace, New York, April 10–May 6, 1917), n.p.

12. Sloan notes.

13. "The 'Big Exhibition,' the Artist and the Public," *Touchstone*, I (June, 1917), 174, 175.

14. Letter to Mrs. Alexander, April 14, 1917. Once the Independents became well established, he gave them his full support. Writing about the 1927 exhibition, he stated: "There is great life in the show and there are many things that are good to see. It is far more interesting than most exhibitions are" (Henri diary, March 11, 1927).

15. Letter from Emil Holzhauer to the author, n.d. [July 6, 1964].

16. Henri taught at the League almost every year from 1915 through 1928. He began by teaching painting classes, but was best known for his annual series, "Lectures on Painting," presented during the 1920's.

17. *Living My Life* (New York, 1931), p. 529.

18. Interview with Brackman, Oct. 21, 1964.

19. C. A. Z., "Henri and Manship," *Little Review*, II (Oct., 1915), 39.

20. *John Sloan, a Painter's Life* (New York, 1955), p. 18.

21. Violet Organ, "Art and Robert Henri" (unpub. MS in the possession of John C. Le Clair), pp. 132–133.

22. Letter from Dasburg to the author, July 6, 1964. We are fortunate in having a verbatim record of the opinions Henri expressed to his students about a Matisse exhibition held in New York during the winter of 1910 (undoubtedly it was at Alfred Stieglitz' gallery): "It will be interesting for you to visit the Matisse exhibition. . . . I am not prepared to tell my impression of it, but I do believe that these people have a thing—that there are those who are serious and have splendid intellects —those who are fakirs [Henri's spelling] consciously and those who are fakirs unconsciously—there is a manifestation and art made by men of unusual intelligence—I have seen some things which might be called Matisse art, which have had a remarkable dignity—The most ridiculous of drawings —a woman reclining—but it has a dignity enjoyed from another point of view—whether that drawing is a great work of art or not matters but little to me—I am not interested as to whether

Matisse is right—I am not interested in what those people think and what they are doing—but I am interested in the advance of art and I am not afraid of seeing it and I am not going to laugh and say, 'Nonsense, any child can do this.' . . . I think it is quite unimportant that Matisse be defended but the liberty of Matisse and the liberty of all people to go forward in the world" (transcript of Henri criticism delivered at the Henri School of Art, March 2, 1910).

23. Letter from Emil Holzhauer to the author, n.d. [July 6, 1964].

24. To Henri, Dec. 25, 1912.

25. To Marianna Sloan, May 29, 1911.

26. Henri diary, Aug. 25, 1926.

27. Meyer Schapiro, lecture, Warburg Institute, London, June 27, 1957.

28. It is interesting to note some of Henri's later remarks on Matisse and Picasso: "Matisse, evidently much influenced by Cézanne, perhaps Renoir, feeling kin to Manet, but possessed of a great love all his own, has persisted through the last twenty-five years of constant changes in fashion, painting the subjects, and in the manner, which best suits him. His work has the great stamp of individuality. They are lovely pictures, and they are not to be judged by other standards but by the law that lies within them" (Henri letter to Johnson [first name unknown], Dec. 5, 1925). On Picasso's Blue Period: "Picasso is certainly a great character in the art world. I would say that he is a great appreciator of [the] masters, and perhaps I am not doing him an

injustice in saying that he makes art out of art—makes very good art out of very good art" (Henri diary, Jan. 16, 1926).

29. "To the Students of the Art Students' League," Oct. 29, 1917 (mimeo.).

30. To Miss Crager-Smith, March 23, 1919.

31. Jan. 29, 1911.

32. *Ibid.*, Jan. 30.

33. Robert Henri, "An Appreciation by an Artist," *Mother Earth*, X (March, 1915), 415.

34. Precise clues to Henri's and his friends' interest in socialism can be gleaned from the sketchy notes he jotted down after a discussion with Sloan, Yeats, the Robertses, and others in 1910: "Sloan—socialist. . . . Yeats sympathetic socialistic because of breaking way for the desired condition. I sympathetic socialistic as intermediate for greater freedom of individual [*sic*]" (Henri diary, May 22, 1910). Thus, if Henri could confess an interest in socialism, it was only because it would serve distinctly individual rather than collective ends.

35. Sloan notes.

36. Brooks, *John Sloan*, p. 86.

37. This two-volume work, a record of Hunt's classroom remarks compiled by his pupil and assistant Helen M. Knowlton, was one of the most influential treatises on art in circulation during the late nineteenth century. Hunt had studied in Düsseldorf, worked under Couture in Paris, and cultivated the friendship of Jean-François Millet. Settling in Boston, he became one of America's leading painters and teachers.

His *Talks on Art*, Sloan recalled, "greatly influenced Henri's teaching and later my own" (Sloan notes).

38. Interview with Margery Ryerson, May 8, 1964.

39. *Ibid.*

40. Page 3.

41. Interview with Margery Ryerson, April 25, 1964.

42. Letter from Meredith Nugent to Henri, Dec. 27, 1928.

43. Sloan diary, Nov. 6, 1910.

44. July 3, 1911.

45. Maratta's ideas were also embodied in several small brochures designed to accompany his pigments: *The Maratta Scales of Artists' Oil Pigments* (H. G. Maratta, New York, 1916); and *Maratta Color Scales of Artists' Oil Pigments* (Fred Dusterdieck, Mariners Harbor, Staten Island, N.Y., 1921).

46. End paper.

47. Sloan notes. It is worth noting that the French Neoimpressionists Seurat and Signac, anticipating Maratta, realized that to paint according to a scientific technique, the intervals between their pigments, based on the band of the spectrum, should be equal. Earlier, Delacroix found that this was desirable in theory, but it is doubtful that he practiced it with any degree of precision. The Neoimpressionist belief in the equality of intervals was undoubtedly derived from the study of Ogden N. Rood's *Scientific Text-Book of Color (Modern Chromatics)* (New York, 1879). Although we have no specific information about the sources of Maratta's theories, much of his thinking about color is close to Rood's.

We know that Henri was acquainted with Rood's book as early as 1910.

48. While most of Henri's palettes were his own invention, he did derive some of his ideas from Charles Winter, who devised and promoted what he called a "universal palette." In addition, Henri was familiar with the teachings of Professor Denman W. Ross of the Department of Fine Arts, Harvard University, author of several pioneering books on color and tone in painting. Ross, like Maratta, advocated rationally determined harmonies based on the set palette and his work was studied by the Henri-Maratta group. Maratta and Ross influenced each other; Maratta visited Ross at Harvard and Ross cites Maratta's work in *The Painter's Palette* (Boston and New York, 1919). Henri also recommended that his students read Ross's books *A Theory of Pure Design: Harmony, Balance, Rhythm* (Boston, 1907) and *On Drawing and Painting* (Boston and New York, 1912).

49. Sloan notes. There are countless preparatory sketches and diagrams in Henri's notes and diaries showing how he planned the entire color composition of his later paintings in terms of broad interlocking areas of tone (see Figure 31). He also used the same technique to revise the color scheme of many of his earlier pictures, which he repainted according to this method.

50. Interview with Rudolph Dirks, July 5, 1964.

51. Letter from Bellows to Henri, Nov. 16, 1917.

52. That Henri greatly appreciated the value of Hambidge's teachings is

attested by the tribute the painter wrote when he heard of his friend's death: "What a loss! A friend who could be a friend because he knew so much. He gave us a lot, could have gone on giving and could always appreciate. My grief is mixed with anger. I can't help but think of those despicable dogs who went out of their way to bark their criticisms at him. . . . It was a great pleasure to know that Hambidge was in the world, working with a beautiful enthusiasm, that he might at any moment find new things to add to what he had already found and given out, and that there would be meetings with him such as we have had and so much enjoyed" (Henri letter to George Bellows, March 6, 1924).

53. Between 1918 and 1922, Henri wrote the draft of a book, "Artists' Pigments," which was destined for pub-

lication by the short-lived League of American Artists. It was to be, as the subtitle explained, "a summary of evidence gathered from authorities on the character, permanence, and mixability of pigments most generally used by painters in oil." The manuscript includes a great amount of information about the physical character of artists' oil pigments, their chemical composition, permanence, drying power, and effect on other colors. There are exemplary illustrations executed in oil, which demonstrate the effects of color mixture. In 1922, when the manuscript was almost ready for publication, the League of American Artists disbanded.

54. Unpub. MS draft of a book on social radicalism and the arts.

55. "My People," *Craftsman*, XXVII (Feb., 1915), 460.

56. Page 158.

Chapter 11. *Recollections of the Later Years*

1. Henri letter, April 26, 1919.

2. Violet Organ, "Art and Robert Henri" (unpub. MS in the possession of John C. Le Clair), p. 165.

3. Letter to Crowninshield, May 6, 1919.

4. The New Society of Artists was organized in 1918 for the purpose of holding annual exhibitions of members' work. Arthur Loring Paine, who reviewed the second annual exhibition and acquired some of his information from George Bellows, described its aims: "The forming of this notable group implies no revolt, no artistic pro-

paganda, no brief for this or that kind of art, as against any other kind of art. It is, frankly, a mutual admiration society of honest artistic craftsmen, organized as the result of spontaneous enthusiasm. . . . It starts with youth, the youth of vigorous artistic expression. Most of the men in it are young, but even among the members in it who might be called venerable, we find no man who has slipped into the senescent, repetitious workmanship of old age. . . . 'Pigeon-hole' critics will find the names in the catalogue of the artists to be those of the most diversified personalities, names they have been in the habit of identifying with all sorts of 'schools,' 'enemy camps,' 'movements,' and 'non-movements.' It is very satisfactory to find here a manifestation of the fact that the Society is neither conscious nor interested in these artificial and meaningless classifications. . . . Each and every man in this strong group reacts to beauty in his own individual way, each sees life through his own lens" (*Vanity Fair*, XV [Dec. 1920], 45). The society's commitment to the present rather than the future distinguished it from the Society of Independent Artists, which welcomed every school, including the "ultra modern." Although the New Society, as a "secession" group, claimed to be against academic ideas, many of their members were also members of the National Academy. In some respects the New Society of Artists was a haven for Henri's friends, former students, and associates. Six of the Eight were members (Davies and Shinn did not join), along with Bellows, A. Stirling Calder, Davey, du Bois, Charles Grafly, Kent,

Kroll, Myers, Perrine, Schofield, and Speicher.

5. Organ, "Art and Henri," p. 152.

6. "Robert Henri: The Man," *Arts and Decoration*, XIV (Nov., 1920), 36.

7. This story is recounted in Organ, "Art and Henri," p. 177.

8. Henri diary, March 28, 1928.

9. N.d.

10. Henri letter to Mr. Spaulding, Nov. 28, 1921.

11. Quoted by Mary L. Alexander, Cincinnati *Times-Star*, March 10, 1926.

12. Letter to Mr. C. C. Horn, June 7, 1927.

13. Letter, Aug. 18, 1913.

14. Letter to Arthur Cecil, Sept. 30, 1924.

15. Letter to Robert McIntyre, Jr., Oct. 20, 1926.

16. *William Glackens and the Ashcan Group: The Emergence of Realism in American Art* (New York, 1957), p. 227.

17. *Ibid.*, p. 229.

18. Letter to Marjorie Henri, Aug. 19, 1929.

Chapter 12. *The Art of Robert Henri, 1892–1928*

1. "The New York Realists" (unpub. Ph.D. diss., New York University, 1953), p. 75.

2. Illustrated in Nathaniel Pousette-Dart, *Robert Henri* (New York, 1922), n.p.

3. Letter to Mary Fanton Roberts, Aug. 24, 1911.

4. During his lifetime, Henri was given one-man exhibitions in the following museums and galleries (excluding commercial galleries): Syracuse Museum of Fine Arts (1911), Art Institute of Chicago (1915), Cincinnati Art Museum (1915), Toledo Museum of Art (1916), Milwaukee Art Institute (1916), Minneapolis Institute of Arts (1916), Syracuse Museum of Fine

Arts (1916), Albright Art Gallery, Buffalo (1919), Art Institute of Chicago (1919), Milwaukee Art Institute (1919), Detroit Institute of Arts (1919), Memorial Art Gallery, Rochester (1920), Kansas City Art Institute (1922), Brooks Memorial Art Gallery, Memphis (1924), Memorial Art Gallery, Rochester (1926).

5. To Margaret Eckerson, Jan. 26, 1920.

6. Letter, Aug. 16, 1913.

7. "My People," *Craftsman*, XCVII (Feb., 1915), 459.

8. *Ibid.*

9. When Henri was actively experimenting with the Maratta colors in collaboration with his friends from 1913 to 1920, he painted a number of small "compositions" (his term) on bristol board to illustrate the color relationships that could be obtained from a variety of "set palettes."

10. Walter Pach, *Queer Thing, Painting: Forty Years in the World of Art* (New York and London, 1938), pp. 47–48.

11. Letter to Henri, June 21, 1925.

12. At this time, he strongly recommended to his students Signac's *D'Eugène Delacroix au néo-impressionnisme* (Paris, 1899).

13. In a letter to Helen Niles, Feb. 13, 1915, he wrote about Bell's *Art:* "It comes nearer than anything to meeting my views and puts with wonderful clarity great ideas and great information."

14. Henri diary, Aug. 25, 1926.

15. *Art Spirit*, p. 166.

16. "Robert Henri," *Century*, CXX (spring, 1930), 271.

17. Henri, *The Art Spirit* (Philadelphia, 1923), p. 159.

18. *Ibid.*

19. Sloan notes.

20. *Ibid.*

21. Henri sketchbook, undated.

Chapter 13. *Epilogue*

1. In a sense, the project for a Robert Henri Memorial Gallery was the outgrowth of a plan proposed about 1922 by the League of American Artists, of which Henri, Sloan, and Bellows were prominent members. Their object had been to raise $4,000,000 to build a vast gallery in New York that would serve as a clearinghouse for contemporary American art. When philanthropists could not be persuaded to provide financial backing, the project was abandoned.

2. Letter to Emma Bellows, n.d. [July, 1929].

3. After the Metropolitan exhibition closed, fifty-three paintings from it were shown in a Henri memorial exhibition at the Baltimore Museum of Art.

Selected Bibliography

By Robert Henri

"A Practical Talk to Those Who Study Art," Philadelphia *Sunday Press*, May 12, 1901.

"Progress in Our National Art Must Spring from the Development of Individuality of Ideas and Freedom of Expression: A Suggestion for a New Art School," *Craftsman*, XV (Jan., 1909), 387–401.

"The New York Exhibition of Independent Artists," *Craftsman*, XVIII (May, 1910), 160–172.

"An Ideal Exhibition Scheme—the Official One a Failure," *Arts and Decoration*, V (Dec. 1914), 49–52, 76.

"My People," *Craftsman*, XXVII (Feb., 1915), 459–469.

"An Appreciation by an Artist," *Mother Earth*, X (March, 1915), 415.

Untitled article, *Conservator*, XXVI (May, 1915), 40–41.

"Like Pack-Rat on a Pile of Past Collected Art" (letter to the editor), Philadelphia *Public Ledger*, April 28, 1916.

"Robert Henri Calls Art the Manifestation of Race," Milwaukee Art Institute *Art Quarterly*, no. 5 (Oct., 1916), 7–8.

"The 'Big Exhibition,' the Artist and the Public," *Touchstone*, I (June, 1917), 174–177, 216.

"An Appreciation by Robert Henri" letter to the students of the Art Students League, Oct. 29, 1917), New York *Times Magazine*, Nov. 11, 1917.

"Thomas Eakins," *Conservator*, XXVIII (Feb. 1918), 184–185.

The Art Spirit. Philadelphia, 1923; paperback ed., Philadelphia and New York, 1960.

"What about Art in America?," *Arts and Decoration*, XXIV (Nov., 1925), 35–37, 75.

About Robert Henri

"The Artist's Partnership with His Public," *Literary Digest*, LXXX (Jan. 5, 1924), 27–28.

Barrell, Charles Wisner. "Robert Henri—'Revolutionary,'" *Independent*, LXIV (June 25, 1908), 1427–1432.

Burnside, Maud. "Robert Henri's Death Brings Sorrow to Students of Art," Buffalo *Evening News*, July 22, 1929.

Burrows, Carlyle. "Robert Henri and His Service to Painting," New York *Herald Tribune*, July 21, 1929.

Cary, Elisabeth Luther. "Robert Henri," *Bulletin of the Metropolitan Museum of Art*, XXVI (March, 1931), 58–62.

Cheyney, E. Ralph. "The Philosophy of a Portrait Painter: An Interview with Robert Henri," *Touchstone*, V (June, 1919), 212–219.

Cournos, John. "What Is Art? Answered by Henri, Art 'Insurgent,'" Philadelphia *Record*, Dec. 25, 1910.

Du Bois, Guy Pène. "Robert Henri: The Man," *Arts and Decoration*, XIV (Nov., 1920), 36, 76.

——. "Robert Henri," *Arts*, XVII (April, 1931), 495–499.

Grafly, Dorothy. "Events and Portents of Fifty Years," *Art and Archaeology*, XXI (April–May, 1926), 163–181.

——. "Robert Henri," *American Magazine of Art*, XXII (June, 1931), 435–445.

Henderson, Rose. "Robert Henri," *American Magazine of Art*, XXI (Jan., 1930), 3–12.

"Henri Estate to Widow," New York *Times*, Aug. 15, 1929.

"Henri Is Dead," *Art Digest*, III (July, 1929), 11.

"Henri Paintings To Be Exhibited at Metropolitan," New York *Herald Tribune*, March 8, 1931.

"Henri, Robert," *Dictionary of American Biography*, VIII (New York, 1932), 544–545.

"Henri, 'Typically American,' a 'Born Insurgent,'" *Literary Digest*, CII (Aug. 3, 1929), 19–20.

"In Defense of Henri" (letters to the editor by Marguerite Hanford Jordan and Violet Organ), *Art Digest*, XXIX (March 1, 1955), 6.

Kwiat, Joseph J. "Robert Henri and the Emerson-Whitman Tradition," *Publications of the Modern Language Association*, LXXI, Pt. I (Sept. 1956), 617–636.

Memorial Exhibition of the Work of Robert Henri (exhibition catalogue). Metropolitan Museum of Art, New York, March 9–April 19, 1931.

"Metropolitan Shows Art of Henri, Leader of Independents," *Art Digest*, V (March 15, 1931), 8, 22.

Pattison, James William. "Robert Henri—Painter," *House Beautiful*, XX (Aug., 1906), 18–19.

Perlman, Bennard B. "Robert Henri," *Arts Digest*, XXVIII (Aug. 1, 1954), 14–15.

——. "Robert Henri, Emancipator," *Art Voices*, V (winter, 1966), 42–47.

"Portrait Painters of Today: Robert Henri," *Vogue*, XXIX (Jan. 3, 1907), 3.

Pousette-Dart, Nathaniel. *Robert Henri*. New York, 1922.

Read, Helen Appleton. *Robert Henri*. New York, 1931.

"Robert Henri," *Art News*, XXVII (Aug. 17, 1929), 13.

"Robert Henri," *Broadway Magazine*, XIX (Feb., 1907), 589–590.

"Robert Henri," *Kennedy Quarterly*, IV (Dec., 1963), 73.

"Robert Henri," *The National Cyclopedia of American Biography*, XV (New York, 1916), 146–147.

"Robert Henri," New York *Times*, July 13, 1929.

Robert Henri, 1865–1929–1965 (exhibition catalogue). Sheldon Memorial Gallery, University of Nebraska, Lincoln, Oct. 12–Nov. 7, 1965.

"Robert Henri, an Apostle of Artistic Individuality," *Current Literature*, LII (April, 1912), 464–468.

Robert Henri and Five of his Pupils (exhibition catalogue). Intro. by Helen Appleton Read. Century Association, New York, April 5–June 1, 1946.

Robert Henri and His Circle (exhibition catalogue). American Academy of Arts and Letters, New York, Dec. 11, 1964–Jan. 10, 1965.

"Robert Henri Dies; Ill Eight Months," New York *Times*, July 13, 1929.

"Robert Henri, Head of Modern School, Dies," New York *Herald Tribune*, July 13, 1929.

"Robert Henri Left $122,009," New York *Times*, May 1, 1931.

"Robert Henri Memorial Exhibition," *Parnassus*, III (March, 1931), 27.

"Robert Henri, One of the Big Figures in American Painting," *Current Opinion*, LXXI (Dec. 1921), 793–796.

"Robert Henri—Painter," *Index of Twentieth Century Artists*, II (Jan., 1935), 49–60.

"Robert Henri, Some of His Ideas," *Art Center Bulletin*, IV (Jan., 1926), 144–147.

Roberts, Mary Fanton. "Visiting the Art Galleries" (Robert Henri obituary), *Arts and Decoration*, XXXII (Nov., 1929), 70–71.

——. "Robert Henri, Great American," *Century Magazine*, CXX (spring, 1930), 271–277.

——. "Speaking of Art" (on Robert Henri memorial exhibition), *Arts and Decoration*, XXXIV (March, 1931), 44–45.

Ruthrauff, Florence Barlow. "Robert Henri, Maker of Painters," *Fine Arts Journal*, XXVII (July, 1912), 463–466.

Sandoz, Mari. *Son of the Gamblin' Man: The Youth of an Artist.* New York, 1960.

St.-G., H. [Homer Saint-Gaudens?]. "Robert Henri," *Critic*, XLIX (Aug., 1906), 131.

Tonks, Oliver S. "Robert Henri—an Appreciation," *American Magazine of Art*, VII (Oct., 1916), 473–479.

Watson, Forbes. "Robert Henri," *Arts*, XVI (Sept., 1929), 3–6.

"Who's Who in American Art," *Arts and Decoration*, VI (Nov., 1915), 33.

Yarrow, William, and Louis Bouché. *Robert Henri: His Life and Works.* New York, 1921.

Z., C. A. [Carl Zigrosser?]. "Henri and Manship," *Little Review*, II (Oct., 1915), 38–39.

Zabel, Morton Dauwen. "Robert Henri," *New Republic*, LIX (July 31, 1929), 288–289.

BIBLIOGRAPHY

About the Period

Armstrong, Regina. "The New Leaders in American Illustration," *Bookman,* XI (May, 1900), 244–251.

Arthur B. Davies, 1862–1928 (exhibition catalogue). Intro. by Harris K. Prior. Munson-Williams-Proctor Institute, Utica, New York, July 8– Aug. 26, 1962.

"Art in New York This Season," *Craftsman,* XXIV (April, 1913), 134–136.

"An Artist of the New York Underworld," *Current Literature,* XLVIII (March, 1910), 326–330.

Artists of the Philadelphia Press (exhibition catalogue). Philadelphia Museum of Art, Philadelphia, Oct. 14– Nov. 18, 1945.

The Art of John Sloan, 1871–1951 (exhibition catalogue). Intro. by Philip C. Beam. Walker Art Museum, Bowdoin College, Brunswick, Maine, Jan. 20–Feb. 28, 1962.

Baur, John Ireland Howe. *Revolution and Tradition in Modern American Art.* Cambridge, Mass., 1951.

Baury, Louis. "The Message of Bohemia," *Bookman,* XXXIV (Nov., 1911), 256–266.

Beaux, Cecelia. *Background with Figures: Autobiography.* Boston and New York, 1930.

Bellows, George. "An Ideal Exhibition" (letter to the editor), *American Art News,* XII (Dec. 26, 1914), 2.

——. " 'The Art Spirit' by Robert Henri" (book review), *Arts and Decoration,* XX (Dec., 1923), 26, 87.

——. "What Dynamic Symmetry Means to Me," *American Art Student,* IX (Sept., 1925), 9–11.

Benton, Thomas Hart. *An Artist in America,* New York, 1939.

Berry-Hill, Henry and Sidney. *Ernest Lawson, N.A.: American Impressionist.* Leigh-on-Sea, Eng., 1968.

Blesh, Rudi. *Modern Art U.S.A.: Men, Rebellion, Conquest, 1900–1956.* New York, 1956.

——. *Stuart Davis.* New York and London, 1960.

Boswell, Peyton, Jr. *George Bellows.* New York, 1942.

Boyesen, Bayard. "The National Note in American Painting," *Putnam's Monthly,* IV (May, 1908), 131–140.

Bregler, Charles. "Thomas Eakins as a Teacher," *Arts,* XVII (March, 1931), 379–386; XVIII (Oct., 1931), 29–42.

Breuning, Margaret. *Maurice Prendergast.* New York, 1931.

——. "Realism at the Whitney," *Magazine of Art,* XXX (March, 1937), 174–175.

Brooks, Van Wyck. "The Eight's Battle for U.S. Art," *Art News,* LIII (Nov., 1954), 41–43, 69–70.

——. *John Sloan, a Painter's Life.* New York, 1955.

Brown, Milton Wolf. "Twentieth Century Nostrums: Pseudo-Scientific Theory in American Painting," *Magazine of Art,* XLI (March, 1948), 98–101.

——. "The Ash Can School," *American Quarterly,* I (summer, 1949), 127–134.

——. *American Painting from the Ar-*

mory Show to the Depression. Princeton, 1955.

——. *The Story of the Armory Show.* Greenwich, Conn., 1963.

Brownell, W. C. "The Art Schools of Philadelphia," *Scribner's Monthly,* XVIII (Sept., 1879), 737–750.

Buchheit, Christian. *Reminiscences.* As told to Lawrence Campbell. Privately printed, New York, Feb. 1956.

Caffin, Charles Henry. *American Masters of Painting.* New York, 1902.

——. "Some American Portrait Painters," *Critic,* XLIV (Jan., 1904), 31–48.

——. *The Story of American Painting.* New York, 1907.

Cahill, Holger. *Max Weber.* New York, 1930.

——. "Forty Years After: An Anniversary for the AFA," *Magazine of Art,* XLII (May, 1949), 169–178, 189.

——. and Alfred H. Barr. *Art in America: A Complete Survey.* New York, 1939.

Cary, Elisabeth Luther. *George Luks.* New York, 1931.

Catalog of an Exhibition of the Work of George Benjamin Luks (exhibition catalogue). Newark Museum, Newark, N.J., Oct. 30–Jan. 6, 1934.

Catalogue of a Memorial Exhibition of the Works of Arthur B. Davies (exhibition catalogue). Metropolitan Museum of Art, New York, Feb. 17–March 30, 1930.

Catalogue of the First Annual Exhibition of the Society of Independent Artists (exhibition catalogue). Grand Central Palace, New York, April 10–

May 6, 1917.

Christ-Janer, Albert. *Boardman Robinson.* Chicago, 1946.

Clark, Eliot Candee. *History of the National Academy of Design.* New York, 1954.

Coates, Robert M. "Profiles" (on John Sloan), *New Yorker,* XXV (May 7, 1949), 36–40, 42, 44–48, 51.

Cortissoz, Royal. *American Artists.* New York, 1923.

——. *Arthur B. Davies.* New York, 1931.

Cournos, John. "A Great Art Instructor: His Methods and Ideas," *Philadelphia Record,* May 29, 1910.

——. "Thomas P. Anshutz and His Service to American Art," *Boston Evening Transcript,* Feb. 10, 1912.

Craven, Thomas Jewell. "Realism and Robert Henri," *Dial,* LXXII (Jan., 1922), 84–86.

Davidson, Jo. *Between Sittings: An Informal Autobiography.* New York, 1951.

[Davis, Stuart.] *Stuart Davis.* New York, 1945.

Du Bois, Guy Pène. "Systems Are Crutches for the Lame in Art," *Arts and Decoration,* XIV (Nov., 1920), 11.

——. *John Sloan.* New York, 1931.

——. *William J. Glackens.* New York, 1931.

——. *Ernest Lawson.* New York, 1932.

——. *Artists Say the Silliest Things.* New York, 1940.

Eastman, Max. *The Enjoyment of Living.* New York, 1948.

Edgerton, Giles [Mary Fanton Roberts]. "Is America Selling Her Birthright in Art for a Mess of Pottage?" *Craftsman*, XI (March, 1907), 656–670.

——. "The Younger American Painters: Are They Creating a National Art?" *Craftsman*, XIII (Feb., 1908), 512–532.

——. "What Does the National Academy Stand For?" *Craftsman*, XV (Feb., 1909), 520–532.

Eggers, George W. *George Bellows*. New York, 1931.

The Eight (exhibition catalogue). Brooklyn Museum of Art, Brooklyn, Nov. 24, 1943–Jan. 16, 1944.

Ely, Catherine Beach. "The Modern Tendency in Henri, Sloan, and Bellows," *Art in America*, X (April, 1922), 132–143.

——. *The Modern Tendency in American Painting*. New York, 1925.

Exhibition of Independent Artists (exhibition catalogue). Galleries, 29–31 West 35th St., New York, April 1–27, 1910.

Exhibition of Paintings by Arthur B. Davies . . . (exhibition catalogue). Macbeth Galleries, New York, Feb. 3–15, 1908.

Fiftieth Anniversary of the Exhibition of Independent Artists in 1910 (exhibition catalogue). Delaware Art Center, Wilmington, Jan. 9–Feb. 21, 1960.

"Foremost American Illustrators: Vital Significance of Their Work," *Craftsman*, XVII (Dec., 1909), 266–280.

Frank, Waldo, Lewis Mumford, Dorothy Norman, Paul Rosenfeld, and Harold Rugg, eds. *America and Alfred Stieglitz: A Collective Portrait*. New York, 1934.

G., H. "The Hambidge Discovery," *American Art Student*, II (Dec., 1917), 3–4.

Gallatin, A. E. *John Sloan*. New York, 1925.

George Bellows (exhibition catalogue). Intro. by Eugene Speicher. Art Institute of Chicago, Chicago, Jan. 31–March 10, 1946.

George Luks, 1866–1933: Centennial Exhibition (exhibition catalogue). Intro. by Helen Farr Sloan. James V. Brown Library, Williamsport, Pa., and Annie Halenbake Ross Library, Lock Haven, Pa., Oct. 2–31, 1967.

Glackens, Ira. *William Glackens and the Ashcan Group: The Emergence of Realism in American Art*. New York, 1957.

Glackens, William J. "The American Section: The National Art," *Arts and Decoration*, III (March, 1913), 159–164.

——. "The Biggest Art Exhibition in America," *Touchstone*, I (June, 1917), 164–173, 210.

Goldman, Emma. *Living My Life*. 2 vols. New York, 1931.

Goodrich, Lloyd. *Thomas Eakins: His Life and Work*. New York, 1933.

——. *Max Weber*. New York, 1949.

——. *John Sloan, 1871–1951*. New York, 1952.

——. *Pioneers of Modern Art in America: The Decade of the Armory Show, 1910–1920*. New York, 1963.

Goossen, E. C. *Stuart Davis*. New York, 1959.

"Guy Pène du Bois," *Life*, XXVI (June 20, 1949), 66, 71.

H., S. [Sadakichi Hartmann?]. "Studio Talk," *International Studio*, XXX (Dec., 1906), 182–183.

Hambidge, Jay. *Elements of Dynamic Symmetry*. New Haven, 1948.

——. *Practical Applications of Dynamic Symmetry*. New Haven, 1932.

Hapgood, Hutchins. "Authority in Art," New York *Globe*, Jan. 23, 1912.

Hartmann, Sadakichi. *A History of American Art*. Rev. ed., 2 vols. Boston, 1932.

Henderson, Helen W. "Glimpses of the Studio Life in Philadelphia," Philadelphia *Public Ledger*, Oct. 4, 1903.

Hewett, Edgar L. "Recent Southwestern Art," *Art and Archaeology*, IX (Jan., 1920), 31–48.

Hirschfield, Charles. " 'Ash Can' vs. 'Modern' Art in America," *Western Humanities Review*, X (autumn, 1956), 353–373.

Homer, William Innes. "Stuart Davis, 1894–1965: Last Interview," *Art News*, LXIII (Sept., 1964), 43, 56.

Hopper, Edward. "John Sloan and the Philadelphians," *Arts*, XI (April, 1927), 169–178.

Hunter, Sam. " 'The Eight'—Insurgent Realists," *Art in America*, XLIV (fall, 1956), 20–22, 56–58.

"Ideal Art Exhibitions; George Bellows, N.A., Discusses the Plan as Put Forward by Robert Henri, N.A., and Later Discussed by Mr. Hoeber," New York *Commercial Advertiser*, Sept. 18, 1914.

" 'Insurgency' in Art," *American Review of Reviews*, XLI (May, 1910), 611–612.

Isham, Samuel. *The History of American Painting*. With supplemental chapters by Royal Cortissoz. New York, 1927.

Jerome Myers: An Artist in Manhattan, 1867–1967 (exhibition catalogue). Intros. by Harry Wickey and Bruce St. John. Delaware Art Center, Wilmington, Jan. 13–Feb. 19, 1967.

Jerome Myers Memorial Exhibition (exhibition catalogue). Intro. by Harry Wickey. Whitney Museum of American Art, New York, April 22–May 29, 1941.

Juliana Force and American Art: A Memorial Exhibition (exhibition catalogue). Whitney Museum of American Art, New York, Sept. 24–Oct. 30, 1949.

Katz, Leslie. "The Breakthrough of Anshutz," *Arts Magazine*, XXXVII March, 1963), 26–29.

Kent, Rockwell. *It's Me, O Lord: The Autobiography of Rockwell Kent*. New York, 1955.

Kuhn, Walt. *The Story of the Armory Show*. New York, 1938.

——. "The Story of the Armory Show," *Art News Annual*, XXXVII (1939), 63–64, 168–174.

Kwiat, Joseph J. "John Sloan: An American Artist as a Social Critic, 1900–1917," *Arizona Quarterly*, X (spring, 1954), 52–64.

La Follette, Suzanne. *Art in America, from Colonial Times to the Present Day*. New York, 1929.

Landgren, Marchal E. *Years of Art: The Story of the Art Students League of New York.* New York, 1940.

The Life and Times of John Sloan (exhibition catalogue). Intros. by Helen Farr Sloan and Bruce St. John. Delaware Art Center, Wilmington, Sept. 22–Oct. 29, 1961.

Luhan, Mabel D. *Intimate Memories: Movers and Shakers,* 3 vols. New York, 1936.

Maratta, H. G. "A Rediscovery of the Principles of Form Measurement," *Arts and Decoration,* IV (April, 1914), 230–232.

——. *The Web of Equilateral Triangles.* New York, 1915.

——. "Colors and Paints," *Touchstone,* VII (June, 1920), 249–250.

"The Maratta System of Color," *Scientific American Supplement,* LXVIII (Nov. 13, 1909), 311.

McBride, Henry. "The Discovery of Louis Eilshemius," *Arts,* X (Dec., 1926), 316–320.

McCausland, Elizabeth. *A. H. Maurer.* New York, 1951.

McCoy, Garnett. "Reaction and Revolution, 1900–1930," *Art in America,* LIII (Aug.–Sept., 1965), 68–71.

McHenry, Margaret. *Thomas Eakins Who Painted.* Oreland, Pa., 1946.

Mellquist, Jerome. *The Emergence of an American Art.* New York, 1942.

——. "The Armory Show 30 Years Later," *Magazine of Art,* XXXVI (Dec., 1943), 298–301.

Memorial Exhibition of the Work of George Bellows (exhibition catalogue). Metropolitan Museum of Art, New York, Oct. 12–Nov. 22, 1925.

Memorial Exhibition of the Work of Thomas Anshutz (exhibition catalogue). Intro. by Helen W. Henderson. Philadelphia Art Alliance, Philadelphia, Oct. 6–Nov. 1, 1942.

Morgan, Charles Hill. *George Bellows, Painter of America.* New York, 1965.

Morris, Harrison. *Confessions in Art.* New York, 1930.

Mumford, Lewis. *The Brown Decades: A Study of the Arts in America, 1865–1895.* New York, 1931.

Myers, Jerome. *Artist in Manhattan.* New York, 1940.

New York Realists, 1900–1914 (exhibition catalogue). Whitney Museum of American Art, New York, Feb. 9–Mar. 5, 1937.

"Notes and Reviews" (review of the exhibition of the Eight), *Craftsman,* XIV (April, 1908), 120.

One Hundred and Fiftieth Anniversary Exhibition (exhibition catalogue). Pennsylvania Academy of the Fine Arts, Philadelphia, Jan. 15–Mar. 13, 1955.

"Only Out of Home's Narrow Confines Is Full Growth Possible for Children, Says Robert Henri," New York *Tribune,* Jan. 25, 1915.

Pach, Walter. "Quelques notes sur les peintres americains," *Gazette des beaux-arts,* 4th per., II (Oct., 1909), 324–335.

——. *Queer Thing, Painting: Forty Years in the World of Art.* New York and London, 1938.

——. "The Eight Then and Now," *Art News,* XLII (Jan. 1, 1944), 25, 31.

———. "John Sloan," *Atlantic Monthly*, CXCIV (Aug., 1954), 68–72.

The Paintings of George Bellows. [Ed. Emma S. Bellows.] Intro. by George Bellows. New York, 1929.

Perlman, Bennard B. *The Immortal Eight.* New York, 1962.

———. "The Years Before," *Art in America*, LI (Feb., 1963), 38–43.

Phillips, Duncan, *et al. Arthur B. Davies: Essays on the Man and His Art.* Cambridge, Mass., 1924.

Pioneers of Modern Art in America (exhibition catalogue). New York: Whitney Museum of American Art, April 9–May 19, 1946.

Pope, Arthur. *Tone Relations in Painting.* Cambridge, Mass., 1922.

———. *An Introduction to the Language of Drawing and Painting.* 2 vols. Cambridge, Mass., 1929–1931.

———. *The Language of Drawing and Painting.* Cambridge, Mass., 1949.

Price, Frederic Newlin. *Ernest Lawson, Canadian-American.* New York, 1930.

Price, William L. "Is American Art Captive to the Dead Past?" *Craftsman*, XV (Feb., 1909), 515–519.

Ray, Man. *Self Portrait.* Boston and Toronto, 1963.

Read, Helen Appleton. "Artist and Critic Writes Important Book on American Art," Brooklyn *Eagle*, Dec. 30, 1923.

Rhys, Hedley Howell. *Maurice Prendergast.* Cambridge, Mass., 1960.

Roberts, Mary Fanton. "John Sloan: His Art and Its Inspiration," *Touchstone*, IV (Feb., 1919), 362–370.

———. "Art Reviews: A Point of View," *Arts and Decoration*, XXVIII (March, 1928), 69.

Rogers, Fairman. "The Schools of the Pennsylvania Academy of the Fine Arts," *Penn Monthly*, XII (June, 1881), 453–462.

The Role of the Macbeth Gallery (exhibition catalogue). Intros. by E. P. Richardson and R. G. McIntyre. American Federation of Arts, New York, Oct. 1962–May 1963.

Rosenfeld, Paul. *Port of New York.* New York, 1925.

Ross, Denman W. *A Theory of Pure Design: Harmony, Balance, Rhythm.* Boston and New York, 1907.

———. *On Drawing and Painting.* Boston and New York, 1912.

———. *The Painter's Palette.* Boston and New York, 1919.

Saarinen, Aline B. *The Proud Possessors.* New York, 1958.

Saint-Gaudens, Homer. *The American Artist and His Times.* New York, 1941.

St. John, Bruce, ed. *John Sloan's New York Scene.* New York, 1965.

Sartain, John. *The Reminiscences of a Very Old Man, 1808–1897.* New York, 1899.

Schack, William. *And He Sat among the Ashes: A Biography of Louis M. Eilshemius.* New York, 1939.

Schendler, Sylvan. *Eakins.* Boston, 1967.

Schwab, Arnold T. *James Gibbons Huneker: Critic of the Seven Arts.* Stanford, 1963.

Seckler, Dorothy Gees. "50th Anniversary for the 8," *Art in America*, XLV (winter, 1957–1958), 61–64.

"Seeing the Shows," review of reconstructed exhibition of the Eight, *Magazine of Art*, XXXI (Feb., 1938), 101.

Seton, Ernest Thompson. *Trail of an Artist-Naturalist*. New York, 1940.

Sloan, Helen Farr, ed. *American Art Nouveau: The Poster Period of John Sloan*. Lock Haven, Pa., 1967.

Sloan, John. *Gist of Art*. Recorded with the assistance of Helen Farr. New York, 1939.

Smith, Anita M. *Woodstock: History and Hearsay*. Saugerties, N. Y., 1959.

"The Soul of the Sitter," *Literary Digest*, XXXIX (Aug. 21, 1909), 276–277.

Sweeney, James Johnson. *Stuart Davis*. New York, 1945.

Swift, Samuel. "Revolutionary Figures in American Art," *Harper's Weekly*, LI (April 13, 1907), 534–536.

"To Free Art from Prizes and Juries," *Literary Digest*, XLII (Jan. 21, 1911), 114.

Walker, Don D. "American Art on the Left, 1911–1950," *Western Humanities Review*, VIII (autumn, 1954), 323–346.

Walter, Paul A. F. "The Santa Fe–Taos Art Movement," *Art and Archaeology*, IV (Dec., 1916), 330–338.

Watson, Forbes. "Realism Undefeated," *Parnassus*, IX (March, 1937), 11–14.

West, Herbert Faulkner. *John Sloan's Last Summer*. Iowa City, 1952.

Wickey, Harry. *Thus Far—the Growth of an American Artist*. New York, 1941.

William Glackens in Retrospect (exhibition catalogue). City Art Museum, St. Louis, Nov. 19–Dec. 31, 1966.

William Glackens Memorial Exhibition (exhibition catalogue). Whitney Museum of American Art, New York, Dec. 14, 1938–Jan. 15, 1939.

Woods, Alice. *Edges*. Indianapolis, 1902.

Wright, Willard Huntington. "The Aesthetic Struggle in America," *Forum*, LV (Feb., 1916), 201–220.

——. "The Forum Exhibition," *Forum*, LV (April, 1916), 457–471.

——. *Modern Painting*, New York, 1930.

Yeats, John Butler. *J. B. Yeats' Letters to His Son W. B. Yeats and Others, 1869–1922*. Ed. Joseph Hone. London, 1946.

Young, Art. *On My Way*. New York, 1928.

Ziegler, Francis J. "An Unassuming Painter—Thomas P. Anshutz," *Brush and Pencil*, IV (Sept., 1899), 277–284.

Index

Page references to illustrations are indicated by italic numerals.

Abbey, Edwin A., 32
Abstract-Expressionism, 266
Académie Julian, 36, 40–44, 47, 49, 55, 60, 66, 71, 162, 164
Academy, *see* National Academy of Design
Achill Island, 202, 206, 207
Action painting, 266
Allan Gallery (New York), 106
Allen, William, 8
American Impressionism, *see* Impressionism, American
American Painters and Sculptors, 155, 166-168, 170
Anarchism, 78, 173, 180, 181, 193, 197
Anshutz, Thomas Pollock, 25, 27, 28, 30, 34, 36, 38, 43, 68-69, 80, 81, 119, 120, 161; methods of teaching, 25, 27-28, 161
   Iron Workers' Noon-Day Rest (Steelworkers—Noontime), 25, *26*
Armory Show (International Exhibition of Modern Art), 100, 131, 157, 163, 166, 168-170, 172, 173, 174, 175, 197, 205, 247, 257, 260, 262, 263
Art Spirit, The, 60, 179, 182-184, 194, 266
Art Students League (New York), 21, 133, 150, 157-158, 173, 176, 177, 182, 183, 192, 195, 202, 266
Ashcan school, 25, 81
Asiego, Felix, 123
Association of American Painters and Sculptors, 155, 166-168, 170
Atherton, Gertrude, 197
Automatism, 266
Avalon Summer Assembly, 72

Baciccio, 57
Bakunin, Mikhail, 78

Balzac, Honoré de, 84
Barbizon school, 2, 51, 65, 107, 154, 213, 214, 216, 235
Barnes, Dr. Albert C., 175
Barrell, Charles Wisner, 181
Barry, Edith C., 154
Bastien-Lepage, Jules, 45, 65
Baylinson, A. S., 150, 173
Beal, Gifford, 197
Beaux, Cecilia, 32
Becker, Maurice, 161, 181, 182
Bell, Clive, 263
Bellamy, Edward, 61, 63, 78
Bellows, Emma, 195
Bellows, George, 101, 113, 129, 130, 154, 167, 169, 170, 173, 174, 182, 184, 186, 187, 189, 192, 193, 194, 195, 197, 199, 203, 205, 269
   Kids, 199, *200*
Benson, Frank W., 4, 69
Benton, Thomas Hart, 141
Berkman, Alexander, 173
Bernhardt, Sarah, 50
Besnard, Albert, 62, 65
Billings, Josh, 15
Blakelock, Albert, 106
Blashfield, Edwin, 82
Bonnard, Pierre, 40, 220
   Moulin Rouge (Place Blanche), Le, 220, *222*
Borglum, Gutzon, 167, 168
Boss, Homer, 161, 172-173
Botticelli, Sandro, 100
Bouché, Louis, 48
Boudin, Eugène, 211
Bouguereau, Adolphe William, 32, 36, 42, 43, 47, 49, 52, 60, 71
Boycott, Capt. Charles Cunningham, 206

Brackman, Robert, 174
Bragdon, Claude, 193
Braque, Georges, 174
Breckenridge, Hugh, 35, 76
Bronzino, 57
Brooks, Van Wyck, 7, 174
Brown, J. G., 252
Brown, Milton, 169
Browning, Robert, 205
Bruce, Patrick Henry, 149, 262
Bryant, William Cullen, 15
Bulletin (Philadelphia), 81
Bunce, William Gedney, 63
Burchfield, Charles, 229
Burns, Robert, 50
Burroughs, Bryson, 118, 268
Bustamente, Anna Maria, 118, 241
Byron, George, 50

Cabanel, Alexandre, 62
Calder, A. Stirling, 35, 59, 76, 197
Calder, Alexander, 35
Camoin, Charles, 149
Carlyle, Thomas, 46
Carolus-Duran, 52, 62
Carpaccio, Vittore, 102
Cathgart, James Albert, 19
Catlin, George, 254
Central High School (Philadelphia), 22, 80
Cézanne, Paul, 83, 102, 163, 164, 169, 174, 224, 263
Chamberlin, Joseph E., 154
Charcoal Club, 72-73
Charpentier, Mme, 51
Chase, William Merritt, 4, 82, 89, 106, 110, 111, 113, 122, 131, 132, 149, 228, 238, 241, 267
Chase School, *see* New York School of Art
Chekhov, Anton Pavlovich, 196
Chickering Classical and Scientific Institute (Cincinnati), 10, 16
Christ, 56, 58, 66
Church of the Evangelists (Philadelphia), 70
Cimino, Emilia, 87, 90, 92, 96, 97
Clark, F. Ambrose, 116
Cobb, Sylvanus, Jr., 15
Cogniet, Léon, 42
Coleman, Edward R., 35, 68
Coleman, Glenn O., 154, 182
Connah, Douglas John, 110, 111, 113, 146, 149
Constable, John, 232, 249
Constant, Benjamin, 102
Cooper, Colin Campbell, 85
Corot, Jean Baptiste Camille, 213, 216, 235
"Corrymore," 206, 207
Cortissoz, Royal, 139
Cosimo, Piero di, 100
Cot, Pierre, 119

Courbet, Gustave, 5, 39, 44, 163, 164, 214, 216, 224, 267
Max Buchon, Portrait of, 224, 227
Couture, Thomas, 45
Cox, Kenyon, 82, 120
Cozad (Nebraska), 12, 15, 16, 17; founding of, 10-13
Cozad, Henry, 8
Cozad, John A., see Southrn, Frank L.
Cozad, John Jackson, see Lee, Richard H.
Cozad, Margaret Clark, 8
Cozad, Robert Henry, see Henri, Robert
Cozad, Theresa Gatewood, see Lee, Mrs. Richard H.
Cozaddale (Ohio), 10
Craddock, Olive (Roshanara), 196, 257
Craige, Linda, see Henri, Linda Craige
Craige, T. Huston, 90
Crane, Stephen, 84
Crane, Walter, 19
Cross, Henri-Edmond, 102, 262
Crowninshield, Frank, 196
Cubism, 155, 169, 170, 173, 247
Cummings, Johnny, 249
Curry, John Steuart, 141
Custer, General George Armstrong, 65

Dabo, Leon, 168
Dagnan-Bouveret, Pascal Adolphe Jean, 62, 87
Dante, 50
Darwin, Charles, 78
Dasburg, Andrew, 150, 174
Daudet, Alphonse, 35, 50, 54
Daumier, Honoré, 83, 163, 174
Dauphin, Eugène-Baptiste-Emile, 54
Davey, Randall, 170, 186, 205
David, Jacques Louis, 42
Davidson, Jo, 168
Davies, Arthur B., 74, 90, 100, 102, 106, 107, 115, 118, 121, 128, 129, 130, 136, 138, 146, 152, 153, 154, 155, 167, 168-169, 170, 182, 257
Unicorns, 101
Davis, Edward Wyatt, 35, 100, 237
Davis, Stuart, 158, 159, 162, 182
Debs, Eugene V., 181
Degas, Edgar, 87, 106, 141, 163, 164, 174, 214
De Kock, Paul, 51
Delacroix, Eugène, 169, 194, 262
Delaroche, Paul, 42
Delaunay, Robert, 193, 260
De Neuville, Alphonse Marie, 32
Denis, Maurice, 40, 160
Derain, André, 149
De Staël, Nicolas, 260
Detaille, Jean Baptiste Edouard, 32
Dickens, Charles, 15, 35, 39, 50
Diegito Roybal, 205

Dimock, Edith, 111
Dirks, Rudolph, 119, 148, 151
Dixey, Harry E., 32
Dostoievsky, Feodor, 159
Dougherty, Paul, 197
Dove, Arthur, 175, 197
Dreiser, Theodore, 159
Du Bois, Guy Pène, 150, 153, 158, 160, 167, 170, 201
Duchamp, Marcel, 170, 171, 257
Dudeen, 189
Du Maurier, George, 79
Du Mond, Frank Vincent, 86, 100
Dumont, Augustin-Alexandre, 23
Duncan, Isadora, 151, 159, 196, 197, 257
Duncan Girls, 196
Dupré, Jules, 35
Duveneck, Frank, 228, 238, 267
Dynamic symmetry, 189

Eakins, Thomas, 4, 21, 25, 27, 30, 32, 34, 39, 43, 45, 65, 70, 83, 106, 107, 120, 161, 163, 176, 177, 179, 184, 268; methods of teaching, 21-22; life and work, 22-24; resignation from the Pennsylvania Academy, 24; memorial exhibition, Metropolitan Museum of Art, 177
   Gross Clinic, The, 32, *33*, 34, 177
   Professor Leslie W. Miller, Portrait of, 177, *178*
Eastman, Max, 181
Ecole des Beaux-Arts (Paris), 2, 23, 40, 47, 51, 61, 164
Egbert, Donald D., 193
Eight, the, 35, 79, 100, 106, 107, 122, 129-130, 131, 149, 151, 152, 154, 157, 165, 169, 197, 228; exhibition of, 136-146
El Greco, 8, 122, 163, 176
Emerson, Ralph Waldo, 46, 57, 66, 76, 84, 158, 159, 160, 181, 244
Exhibition of Independent Artists, 1910, 53, 131, 152-156, 157, 165, 168, 228
Expressionism, 155, 235, 264

Fauvism, 155, 169, 247
Ferrer Center (New York), 158, 173-174, 180, 194
Ferrer Guardia, Francisco, 173
Ferrer School, *see* Modern School of the Ferrer Center
Finney, Harry, 35, 36, 40, 53
Fisher, James, 35, 36, 40, 47, 49, 50, 53, 68
Fitz Gerald, Charles, 100, 108-109, 110, 115, 138, 151
Flaubert, Gustave, 86
Forquereau, Segus, 7
Fox, Benjamin, 35
Frazer, James E., 153
Frieseke, Frederick, 4

Friesz, Othon, 149
Frost, Arthur B., 262
Fuhr, Ernest, 97, 100, 106, 119
Futurism, 173

Garfield, President James, 15
Garland, Hamlin, 84
Gatewood, Julia Ann, 8
Gatewood, Robert Burke, 8
Gauguin, Paul, 49, 52, 75, 160, 163, 164, 169, 174, 262
George, Henry, 78
Gérôme, Jean-Léon, 23, 45, 71, 87
Gilbert and Sullivan, 79
Gillam, Bernhard, 19
Giorgione, 100
Girardot, Louis-Auguste, 87
Glackens, Edith, 209
Glackens, Ira, 138, 209
Glackens, William, 25, 35, 76, 77, 79, 80, 81, 85, 86, 90, 99, 100, 102, 106, 107, 115, 116, 119, 121, 127, 129, 141, 145, 146, 153, 154, 168, 171, 182, 197, 237, 239
   Shoppers, The, 139, *140*
Gleizes, Albert, 193
Glintenkamp, Henry J., 150, 182
Gogh, Vincent van, 52, 53, 163, 169, 174, 229, 235, 264
Goldman, Emma, 173, 180, 181, 197
Gorky, Maxim, 105
Gottlieb, Adolph, 266
Goya y Lucientes, Francisco de, 83, 84, 97, 122, 141, 145, 163, 169, 176
Gozzoli, Benozzo, 70
Grafly, Charles, 35, 36, 40, 50, 53, 59, 68, 76, 77, 85, 86
Greenaway, Kate, 19
Gregg, Frederick James, 119, 130, 138, 151
Gregorita, 254
Gris, Juan, 193
Gruger, F. R., 76, 77
Guardia, Francisco Ferrer, 173
Guillaumin, Armand, 102

Haefcker, William, 35, 36, 40, 50, 53
Haggin, Mrs. Ben Ali, 196
Haggin, Mrs. James, 165
Hals, Frans, 2, 74, 83, 84, 85, 86, 87, 88, 94, 116, 141, 145, 163, 237, 238, 241, 249
Hambidge, Jay, 184, 189-192, 199
Hamerton, Philip Gilbert, 46, 65
Hamsun, Knut, 196
Hanlon Brothers, 32
Harrison, Alexander, 47, 88
Harte, Bret, 51
Hartley, Marsden, 169
Hartmann, Sadakichi, 74, 100, 237
Hassam, Childe, 4, 82, 118, 121
Haworth, Edith, 154

Hawthorne, Charles W., 149

Henri, John and Theresa (pseud.), 7

Henri, Linda Craige, 90-94, *91*, 98, 99, 105, 109, 112, 119

Henri, Marjorie Organ, 146-148, 151, 195-196, 199-201, 202, 206, 207, 208, 209, 210, 268

Henri, Robert (Robert Henry Cozad), *frontis., 14, 29, 41, 77, 132;* childhood, 7, 10-20; formal education, 10, 13, 16, 17, 19, 21-67, 68-69; style and technique, 27-28, 48, 51-52, 54-55, 84, 184-194, 211-267; religious views, 36, 66, 78; philosophy of art, 38, 59-60, 74-75, 82-84, 158-160, 184-194; views on European art, 39, 44-45, 52, 55-59, 62, 64-65, 83, 87-88, 144-145, 163-164, 174-175; *The Art Spirit,* 60, 179, 182-184, 194, 266; political views, 65, 78, 179-182; methods of teaching, 71-73, 150, 158-164; views on American art, 74, 106-107, 144-145, 159, 164, 176-179; and the Eight, 76-84, 100-105, 128-131, 136-145; marriages, *see* Henri, Linda Craige, *and* Henri, Marjorie Organ

Ancient Dress (The Masquerade Dress), The, 146, *147*

Antonio Banos (Calero), Picador, 148, 241, 244, *246*

Asiego, 127

Bishop Henry C. Potter, Portrait of, 116, *117*

Blonde Bridget Lavelle, 252, *facing 252*

Boulevard, Paris, A, 216, *218*

Calero, 148, 241, 244, *246*

Chow Choy, 254, *255*

Cinco Centimo, 148

Clinic, The, 34

Coal Breaker, The, 229

Colonel David Perry, 127

Color Chart, 188

Color Notations for Portrait of Helen Geary, Diagram of, 191

Color Notes, 260, *facing 260*

Cori Looking over Back of Chair, 133, *134,* 241

Cumulus Clouds—East River, 229, *230*

Dame en brun, La, 88

Derricks on the North River, 229, *231*

Diegito Roybal (Po-Tse-Nu-Tsa), 203, *204,* 254

Dutch Soldier, 139

Echarpe Rouge, L', 94

Edna Smith, 260, *261*

Eva Green, 136, *137,* 241

Figure in Motion, 257, *259*

Figures on Boardwalk, 211, *212*

Fish Market Man, The, 244

Flight into Egypt, The, 70

Fourteenth of July—Boulevard Saint-Michel, 219, 220

Fourteenth of July, "La Place," 220, *221*

Francis Vaux-Wilson, Portrait de M., 88

George Luks, Portrait of, 113, *114,* 237

Girl in White Waist, 113

Girl Seated by the Sea, 213, *facing 214*

Gitano (Gypsy with Guitar), 123, 241

Gypsy Mother, 124, *125*

Gypsy of Madrid (La Trinidad), 123

Herself, 249, *251*

Hill-Top, The, 108

Himself, 249, *250*

John Jackson Cozad, 8, *9*

Josephine Nivison (The Art Student), Portrait of Miss, 119

Julianita, 254, *256,* 263

Lady in Black, 90, *91,* 113, 119, 237

Landscape at Black Walnut, Pa., 232, *233,* 235

Laughing Child, 139

Maine Coast, 234, *235*

Man Who Posed as Richelieu, The, 225, *227*

Martsche in White Apron, 133, *135,* 241

Menaune Cliffs, 247, *248,* 249

Neige, La, 94, *95,* 96, 98, 108, 224

Normandie Fireplace, A, 214, *215*

Old Brittany Farmhouses, 235, *236*

Patrick, 252, *253*

Picador, 148, 241, 244, *246*

Profile, A, 216, *217*

P'tit, Un, 94

Rain Storm—Wyoming Valley, The, 232, *facing 232*

Reina Mora, La, 123

Ruth St. Denis in the Peacock Dance, 257, *258*

Segovia Girl, Half-Length, 241, *243,* 244

Spanish Dancer—Sevillana, 118

Spanish Dancing Girl, 118

Spanish Gypsy and Child, 127

Sudden Shower, A, 108

Summer Storm, 264, *265*

Suzanne, 88

Triangle Palette (Charles Winter "Universal" Palette), 190

Venetian Canal, 69

Venetian Girl, 69

W. J. Glackens, Portrait of, 238, *239*

Willie Gee, 113

Woman in Manteau, 93, *94,* 224

Working Man, The, 241, *242,* 244

Young Woman in Black, Portrait of a, 115, *238*

Young Woman in White, 238, *240*

Henri School of Art, 150, 172, 185

Hewett, Dr. Edgar L., 202, 203, 205

Holmes, Mary J., 15

Homer, Winslow, 4, 25, 121, 163, 235

Hovenden, Thomas, 27, 28, 30, 34, 35, 38, 43

Hudson River school, 1, 118

Hugo, Victor, 50
Huneker, James Gibbons, 138
Hunt, William Morris, 2, 106, 182

Ibsen, Henrik, 84, 159
Impressionism, 4, 44, 51-53, 54, 62, 64, 68, 69, 72, 73, 82, 83, 102, 105, 107, 164, 169, 174, 211, 213, 214, 216, 232; American, 4, 74, 102, 213
Independent School (New York), 172-173
Ingersoll, Robert, 78-79
Ingres, Jean Auguste Dominique, 2, 42, 169
Inquirer (Philadelphia), 80, 81
International Exhibition of Modern Art, *see* Armory Show
Isham, Samuel, 120

Japanese art, 52, 75
Jefferson Medical College (Philadelphia), 20, 23, 30, 32, 176
Johnson, Eastman, 25
Jones, John, 7
Julian, Rodolphe, 40, 42

Kahn, Otto, 196
Kandinsky, Wassily, 169
Karfiol, Bernard, 150, 169
Karl, Adolph, 227
Keen, Dr. William, 22, 28
Keene, Charles, 81
Kelly, James P., 27, 28, 30, 68, 69
Kemble, Marion, 19
Kent, Rockwell, 112-113, 127, 158, 159
Kimura, 197
Kipling, Rudyard, 92
Klee, Paul, 260
Kokoschka, Oskar, 235
Komroff, Manuel, 194
Koopman, Augustus, 35, 85, 86, 97, 100
Kreymborg, Alfred, 151, 196
Kroll, Leon, 170, 192, 197, 205
Kubota, Beisen, 75
Kuhn, Walt, 148, 151, 152, 153, 155, 157, 166, 167, 168, 169, 257
Kwiat, Joseph J., 76

La Farge, John, 2, 100, 118
Lahey, Richard, 197
Laub, Joseph, 73, 100
Laurent, Jean Paul, 102
Lavery, Sir John, 89
Lawson, Ernest, 102, 119, 121, 128, 129, 138, 146, 168, 197
    Harbor in Winter, 104
Le Corbusier, 193
Lee, Jim, 254
Lee, Richard H. (John Jackson Cozad), 7, 8-12, *9*, 16-17, 18-19, 126

Lee, Mrs. Richard H. (Theresa Gatewood Cozad), 7-8, 10, *11*, 17, 126, 205
Leech, John, 81
Leonardo da Vinci, 58
Lever, Hayley, 197
Levinson, A. F., 186
Lewisohn, Adolph, 196
Lichtenstein, J. B., 152
Lie, Jonas, 168
Linares, Don Federico Nieto, 123
Lindsay, Vachel, 151
Luks, George, 25, 76, 79, 80-81, 101, 106, 107, *114*, 115, 116, 119, 121, 127, 129, 138, 141, 145, 146, 169, 182, 237, 267, 269
    East Side Docks, 141, *143*

Macbeth, William, 89, 107, 108, 136, 138
Macbeth Galleries, 90, 100, 129, 146, 151
McCarter, Henry, 35, 68, 69, 70
McCarthy, Dan, 146
Macdonald-Wright, Stanton, 262
MacDowell, Edward, 165
MacDowell Club (New York), 165, 166, 167, 172
McElroy, John, 15
McFee, Henry L., 197
McIntyre, Robert, 151
MacRae, Elmer, 166, 167, 168
Manet, Edouard, 5, 39, 44, 74, 83, 84, 86, 87, 88, 89, 106, 141, 145, 163, 164, 174, 214, 216, 224, 232, 244, 257, 267
    Roudier, Portrait of, 224, *226*
    Torero Saluting, 244, *245*
Mangasarian, Mangasar, 36
Manguin, Henri Charles, 149
Manolete, 123
Manship, Paul, 150
Manuel of Tesuque, 205
Maraquis, Manaleta, 148
Maratta, Hardesty Gillmore, 172, 176, 184-189, 192, 193, 260, 262
Maria of Tesuque, 203
Marin, John, 169
Marquet, Albert, 149
Martin, Bradley, 196
Martin, Homer, 106
Marx, Karl, 78
Masses, 159, 181-182
Matisse, Henri, 149, 163, 169, 174, 175
Maupassant, Guy de, 71, 159
Maurer, Alfred, 97, 100, 106, 169, 192
Meissonier, Jean Louis, 52
Metcalf, Willard L., 4, 121
Michelangelo, 55, 56, 57, 58, 65
Millet, Jean François, 32, 35, 52, 65, 106, 107, 214, 235
Milton, John, 50
Modern School of the Ferrer Center (New York), 158, 173-174, 180, 194

Monet, Claude, 54, 62, 65, 69, 72, 87, 106, 164, 211, 235
Montenard, Frédéric, 54
Moore, George, 42, 195, 199
Moore, James B., 119
Mora, F. Luis, 113
Moreno, Milagros, 123
Morrice, James Wilson, 86, 97, 100, 119, 149
Morris, William, 19
Motherwell, Robert, 260
Mowbray-Clark, John, 167
Munkácsy, Michael, 32
Murillo, Bartolomé Estéban, 39, 44
Murray, Samuel, 70
Museum of New Mexico (Santa Fe), 205
Muybridge, Eadweard, 22
Myers, Jerome, 128, 129, 153, 154, 155, 166, 170

Nabis, 86, 220
National Academy of Design (New York), 2, 3, 21, 74, 90, 106, 113, 116, 118, 119, 120, 122, 126, 127, 128, 145, 146, 153, 154, 155, 167, 241, 267
National Arts Club (New York), 115, 195
National Institute of Arts and Letters, 146
Neoimpressionism, 52, 102, 229
New York School of Art (Chase School), 4, 110, 111, 113, 116, 120, 122, 126, 131, 133, 136, 149, 157, 176, 199
Nijinsky, Vaslav, 199
Norris, Frank, 84
Noyes, Carleton, 100, 105

O'Donnell, Mary, 206, 208
O'Donnell, Pat, 206, 208
O'Neill, Eugene, 196
Opper, Frederick Burr, 19
Organ, Mr. and Mrs. John, 146
Organ, Marjorie, see Henri, Marjorie Organ
Organ, Violet, 148, 174, 268
Orphists, 193

Pach, Walter, 151, 155, 157, 158, 168, 171
Paine, Thomas, 51
Pancoast, Dr. Joseph, 23
Parker, William E., 35, 68
Pearson, Alfred, 16
Penn, Jesseca, 111, 126, 136, 238
Pennsylvania Academy of the Fine Arts (Philadelphia), 19, 21-22, 32, 35, 43, 53, 68, 69, 70, 71, 72, 75, 79, 80, 83, 88, 110, 111, 118, 120; system of art education, 21-22
Perrine, Van Dearing, 100, 105, 106
Picabia, Francis, 171
Picasso, Pablo, 174, 175, 262
Picot, François Edouard, 42
Pissarro, Camille, 54, 87, 211, 216
Players' Club (New York), 121

Poe, Edgar Allan, 71
Possades, 123
Postimpressionism, 5, 53, 164, 169, 173, 247
Potter, Bishop Henry C., 116
Pratt Institute (Brooklyn), 110, 111
Prendergast, Maurice, 100-102, 106, 115, 121, 129, 138, 146, 149, 167, 168, 171
    Flying Horses, The, 102, 103
Pre-Raphaelites, 2
Press (Philadelphia), 80, 81, 105, 116
Preston, James, 76, 97, 100, 119
Price, Willard, 106
Public Ledger (Philadelphia), 80, 81
Puvis de Chavannes, Pierre Cécile, 52, 62, 65, 100, 106, 107
Puy, Jean, 149

Raffaelli, Jean François, 89
Raphael, 39, 44, 55, 56, 57, 58, 65
Ray, Man, 174
Read, Helen Appleton, 150, 158, 159
Realism, 5, 22, 64, 164, 169, 260
Record (Philadelphia), 80
Redfield, Edward, 35, 50, 53, 54, 59, 61, 63, 68, 76, 88, 92, 97, 105, 106, 107, 112
Redon, Odilon, 169
Regnault, Alexandre Georges Henri, 45
Reid, Robert, 121
Rembrandt, 24, 39, 40, 44, 57, 65, 74, 83, 86, 87, 141, 145, 163, 176, 224, 237, 238, 244, 249, 267
Renoir, Auguste, 51, 106, 141, 163, 174, 262
Renouf, Emile, 32
Reynolds, Edith, 136
Ribera, José, 23, 39, 44, 87, 97
Robert-Fleury, Tony, 36, 42, 49, 60
Roberts, Mary Fanton, 130, 136, 139, 151, 197, 199, 203, 264
Roberts, William Carman, 151, 197, 199, 203
Robinson, Theodore, 4, 74, 169, 213
Rodin, Auguste, 87, 92, 174
Rohland, Paul, 150, 174
Roshanara (Olive Craddock), 196, 257
Rothko, Mark, 260
Rouault, Georges, 174
Rousseau, Henri, 52
Rousseau, Jean-Jacques, 63, 159, 244
Roussel, Ker-Xavier, 40
Royal Academy (London), 2
Royal Academy of Painting and Sculpture (France), 3
Rubens, Peter Paul, 39, 44, 65, 227
Rubino, Betalo, 257
Rudy, J. Horace, 78
Ruskin, John, 38, 39, 40, 65, 82
Russell, Morgan, 150, 262
Ryder, Albert Pinkham, 100, 106, 107, 129, 130, 163
Ryerson, Margery, 182, 183, 210

St. Denis, Ruth, 196, 257
Salon d'Automne, 149, 175
Salon des Indépendants (Paris), 52, 53
Sargent, John Singer, 2, 52, 82, 111, 113, 116, 228, 238, 241
Sartain, Emily, 70
Sartain, John, 32, 70
Sarto, Andrea del, 58
Schapiro, Meyer, 176
Schofield, Elmer, 76, 85
School of Design for Women (Philadelphia), 70-71, 72, 85, 107
Schussele, Christian, 21
Science and art, 194
Sérusier, Paul, 160, 193
Set palette, 187
Seton, Ernest Thompson, see Thompson, Ernest Seton
Seurat, Georges, 193, 194
Severini, Gino, 169
Shakespeare, William, 32, 50
Sheeler, Charles, 169
Sheffield, Mrs. George, 122
Sheridan, Richard Brinsley, 32
Shinn, Everett, 76, 77, 79, 80, 81, 116, 119, 121, 127, 129, 138, 139, 141, 145, 146, 154, 167, 169, 267
    Sixth Avenue Elevated After Midnight, 141, 144
Shinnecock School of Drawing and Painting (Bayport, Long Island), 113
Signac, Paul, 102, 193, 262
Sisley, Alfred, 87, 106, 211
Sloan, Dolly, 119, 181, 199
Sloan, John, 8, 25, 40, 72, 73, 75, 76, 77, 78, 79-80, 81-83, 84, 88, 89, 92, 105, 106, 115, 116, 120, 121, 126, 128, 129, 130, 136, 138, 139, 141, 146, 152, 153, 154, 166, 167, 169, 170, 171, 172, 181, 182, 184, 185, 186, 187, 189, 197, 199, 205, 237, 263, 266, 268, 269
    Election Night, 141, 142
    Studio of Robert Henri, A.D. 1950, 197, 198
Smedley, William T., 121
Smith, Mr. and Mrs. George Cotton, 136
Socialism, 65-66, 78, 159, 181, 182, 197
Société des Artistes-Indépendants (Paris), 170; see also Salon des Indépendants
Society of American Artists, New York, 90, 111, 113, 115, 116, 118, 120, 122
Society of Independent Artists (New York), 53, 155, 170-172, 262
Sorolla, Joaquín, 82
Southrn, Frank L. (John A. Cozad), 7, 10, 12, 17, 20, 68
Soutine, Chaim, 235
Soyer, Moses, 174
Speicher, Elsie, 199
Speicher, Eugene, 170, 184, 197, 199, 268, 269
Sprinchorn, Carl, 127, 150

Spring Garden Institute (Philadelphia), 80
Stein, Eugenie (Zenka of Bohemia), 113, 238
Stein, Gertrude and Leo, 175
Stein, Sarah and Michael, 175
Stella, Joseph, 169
Stephenson, Byron, 100, 109, 119, 138, 151, 237
Sterner, Albert, 121, 197
Stevenson, Robert Louis, 86
Stieglitz, Alfred, 157, 164
Sullivan, Louis, 158, 244
Surrealism, 266
Swedenborg, Emanuel, 36
Swedenborgian Church, 36
Sylvester, 254
Symbolism, 5, 52, 86
Symbolist-Nabi idiom, 220
Symbolist-Synthetists, 52, 53, 160, 193
Synchromism, 193, 262
Synge, J. M., 206
Synthetist-Nabi style, 86

Taine, Hippolyte, 141
Talmadge, DeWitt, 15
Tarbell, Edmund C., 69
Taylor, Henry Fitch, 166
Ten American Painters, 118, 121, 122, 145, 167
Thackeray, William Makepeace, 35
Theosophy, 193, 194
Thompson, Ernest Seton, 59, 61
Thoreau, Henry David, 76, 78
Thouron, Henry, 80
Tice, Clara, 154
Tintoretto, 56, 57, 87
Titian, 24, 56, 57, 58, 65, 87, 94
Tolstoi, Leo, 54, 66, 159, 197
Trotsky, Leon, 174
Troyon, Constant, 45
Tucker, Allen, 169
Turner, Frederick Jackson, 18
Turner, James M. W., 262, 264
Twachtman, John H., 4, 74, 102, 121, 163, 169
Twain, Mark, 15

Ullman, Eugene Paul, 149, 152

Van Dongen, Kees, 149
Van Dyck, Anthony, 39, 74
Vedder, Elihu, 100
Velázquez, Diego de, 2, 23, 39, 44, 56, 57, 65, 83, 84, 87, 89, 94, 97, 111, 122, 141, 145, 163, 214, 224, 237, 238, 267
Veltin School (New York), 99, 157
Verdi, Giuseppe, 63
Verestchagin, Vasili, 45
Verne, Jules, 15
Veronese, Paolo, 56, 58
Villon, Jacques, 171
Vlaminck, Maurice, 149

Vonnoh, Robert, 68, 88, 213
Vuillard, Edouard, 40, 220
   At the Pastry Cook's, 220, *223*

Wagner, Richard, 159
Wallace, Lew, 63
Walters, Carl, 150
Watson, Forbes, 164, 209
Weber, Max, 175, 196, 197
Weir, J. Alden, 82, 102, 121, 167, 213
Whirling square rectangle, 192
Whistler, James McNeill, 5, 44, 82, 83, 86, 87,
   89, 92, 105, 106, 107, 111, 118, 163, 211,
   214, 216, 220, 228, 238
Whitman, Walt, 76, 78, 84, 145, 158, 159, 160,
   181
Whitney, Gertrude Vanderbilt, 122, 138

Wickey, Harry, 174
Wilde, Oscar, 86
Williams, Mary A., 179
Williamson,——[in Paris], 61
Williamson, Charles S., 79
Winter, Charles, 181, 186, 187
Wood, Grant, 141

Yarrow, William, 48
Yeats, John Butler, 151, 199, 205
Yeats, William Butler, 205-206
Young, Art, 181
Young, Mahonri, 170

Zenka of Bohemia (Eugenie Stein), 113, 238
Zola, Emile, 50, 51, 84, 159
Zorn, Anders, 82